New ENTERPRISE

A1

Teacher's Book

Jenny Dooley

Express Publishing

Published by Express Publishing

Liberty House, Greenham Business Park, Newbury,
Berkshire RG19 6HW, United Kingdom
Tel.: (0044) 1635 817 363
Fax: (0044) 1635 817 463
email: inquiries@expresspublishing.co.uk
www.expresspublishing.co.uk

© Jenny Dooley, 2018

Design and Illustration © Express Publishing, 2018

First published 2018
Third impression 2020

Made in EU

ISBN978-4-7647-4135-5

(4)

X / T 14

3/5

Contents

Introduction to the Teacher

New Enterprise A1 is a modular course for young adults and adults studying British English at CEFR Level A1. It allows flexibility of approach, which makes it suitable for classes of all kinds, including large or mixed ability classes.

New Enterprise A1 consists of twelve units. Each unit consists of three lessons plus Culture sections, Reviews & Competences. The corresponding unit in the Workbook provides the option of additional practice.

COURSE COMPONENTS

Student's Book

The **Student's Book** is the main component of the course. Each unit is based on specific themes and the topics covered are of general interest. All units follow the same basic structure (see **Elements of the Coursebook**).

Workbook

The **Workbook** is in full colour and contains units corresponding to those in the Student's Book, with practice in Vocabulary, Grammar, Everyday English & Reading. There is a Revision Section every three units for students to revise the vocabulary and grammar taught. There is also a Skills Practice section for students to get more practice in Listening, Everyday English, Reading and Writing. All the exercises in the Workbook are marked with graded level of difficulty (*, **, ***).

Teacher's Book

The **Teacher's Book** contains step-by-step lesson plans and suggestions on how to present the material. It also includes answers to the exercises in the Student's Book, the audioscripts of all the listening material, suggested speaking and writing models, and evaluation sheets as well as the answers to the exercises in the Workbook and Grammar book.

Class Audio CDs

The Class Audio CDs contain all the recorded material which accompanies the course. This includes the monologues/dialogues and texts in the Listening and Reading sections as well as the Pronunciation/Intonation sections in the Student's Book, and the material for all listening tasks in the Workbook.

IWB

The IWB contains all the material in the Student's Book, Teacher's Book, Workbook, Grammar Book and Audio CDs and aims to facilitate lessons in the classroom. It also contains grammar presentations of all the grammar structures in the Student's Book as well as **videos** closely linked to the texts in the course and activities for Ss to further practise their English and expand their knowledge, as well as **games** for students to revise the vocabulary and grammar taught.

Digibook applications

The **Digi apps** contain all the material in the Student's Book, Workbook and Grammar Book and help students monitor their progress and improve their stats which are stored so that they can be accessed at any time.

Grammar Book

The Grammar Book contains clear, simple presentations of all grammar structures that appear in the course with a variety of graded exercises.

ELEMENTS OF THE COURSEBOOK

Each unit begins with a brief overview of what will be covered in the unit.

Each unit contains the following sections:

Vocabulary

Vocabulary is introduced in a functional and meaningful context. It is practised through a variety of exercises such as picture-word association and completing set phrases in order to help students use everyday English correctly.

Reading

Each unit contains reading texts, such as: articles, blog entries, postcards, emails, etc. These allow skills such as reading for gist and reading for specific information to be systematically practised.

Grammar

The grammar items taught in each unit are first presented in context, then highlighted and clarified by means of clear, concise theory boxes. Specific exercises and activities methodically reinforce learners' understanding and mastery of each item. The Workbook contains practice on each grammar structure presented within each unit. Detailed explanations of all grammar points and exercises are in the Grammar Bank.

Listening

Learners develop their listening skills through a variety of tasks which employ the vocabulary and grammar practised in the unit in realistic contexts. This reinforces learners' understanding of the language taught in the unit.

Speaking

Controlled speaking activities have been carefully designed to allow learners' guided practice before leading them to less structured speaking activities.

Everyday English

Functional dialogues set in everyday contexts familiarise students with natural language. The dialogues are followed by language boxes to help learners practise.

Pronunciation/Intonation

Pronunciation/Intonation activities help learners to recognise the various sounds of the English language, distinguish between them and reproduce them correctly.

Writing

There are writing activities throughout the units, based on realistic types and styles of writing, such as emails, letters, blogs, postcards, stories, articles, etc. These progress from short sentences to paragraphs and finally to full texts, allowing learners to gradually build up their writing skills.

Culture

Each unit is accompanied by a *Culture* section.

In each *Culture* section, learners are provided with cultural information about aspects of English speaking countries that are thematically linked to the unit. Learners are given the chance to process the information they have learnt and compare it to the culture of their own country.

Study Skills

Brief tips, explanations and reminders, at various points throughout each unit, help learners to develop strategies which improve holistic learning skills and enable them to become autonomous learners of the English language.

Review

This section appears at the end of each unit, and reinforces students' understanding of the topics, vocabulary and structures that have been presented in the unit. A *Competences* marking scheme at the end of every Review section allows learners to evaluate their own progress and identify their strengths and weaknesses.

Values

This section aims to develop moral values learners need to have in our globalised world.

Public Speaking Skills

This section aims to help learners develop their public speaking skills, giving them guidance on how to become competent public speakers.

CLIL

The *CLIL* sections enable learners to link the themes of the units to an academic subject, thus helping them contextualise the language they have learnt by relating it to their own personal frame of reference. Lively and creative tasks stimulate learners and allow them to consolidate the language they have learnt throughout the units.

Each *CLIL* section is aimed to be taught after the corresponding Values & Public Speaking Skills sections.

Irregular Verbs

This provides students with a quick reference list for verb forms they might be unsure of at times.

SUGGESTED TEACHING TECHNIQUES

A Presenting new vocabulary

Much of the new vocabulary in *New Enterprise A1* is presented through pictures *(see Student's Book, Unit 1, p. 8, Ex. 1)*.

Further techniques that you may use to introduce new vocabulary include:

- **Miming.** Mime the word you want to introduce. For instance, to present the verb sing, pretend you are singing and ask learners to guess the meaning of the word.
- **Synonyms, opposites, paraphrasing, and giving definitions.** Examples:
  - present the word **strong** by giving a synonym: 'powerful'.
  - present the word **strong** by giving its opposite: 'weak'.
  - present the word **weekend** by paraphrasing it: 'Saturday and Sunday'.
  - present the word **famous** by giving its definition: 'very well-known (person or thing)'.
- **Example.** Use of examples places vocabulary into context and consequently makes understanding easier. For instance, introduce the words **city** and **town** by referring to a city and a town in the learners' country: 'Rome is a city, but Parma is a town.'
- **Sketching.** Draw a simple sketch of the word or words you want to explain on the board. For instance:

tall

short

- **Use of L1.** In a monolingual class, you may explain vocabulary in the learners' native language. This method, though, should be employed in moderation.
- **Use of a dictionary.** In a multilingual class, learners may occasionally refer to a bilingual dictionary.

The choice of technique depends on the type of word or

expression. For example, you may find it easier to describe an action verb through miming than through a synonym or a definition.

> **Note:** ✅ sections can be treated as follows: Go through the list of words after Ss have read the text and ask Ss to explain the words using the context they appear in. Ss can give examples, mime/draw the meaning, or look up the meaning in their dictionaries.

B Choral & individual repetition

Repetition will ensure that learners are thoroughly familiar with the sound and pronunciation of the lexical items and structures being taught and confident in their ability to reproduce them.

Always ask learners to repeat chorally before you ask them to repeat individually. Repeating chorally will help learners feel confident enough to then perform the task on their own.

C Reading & Listening

You may ask learners to read and listen for a variety of purposes:

- **Reading for detail.** Ask learners to read for specific information. *(See Student's Book, Unit 1, p. 9, Ex. 6. Ss will have to read the text in order to do the task. They are looking for specific details in the text and not for general information.)*
- **Listening for detail.** Learners listen for specific information. *(See Student's Book, Unit 1, p. 8, Ex. 2b)*
- **Listening and reading for gist.** Ask learners to read and/or listen to get the gist of the dialogue or text being dealt with. *(See Student's Book, Unit 1, p. 4, Ex. 1. Tell Ss that in order to complete this task successfully, they do not need to understand every single detail in the text.)*

> **Note:** ▶ VIDEO
>
> Main texts in the Student's Book are accompanied by videos that are included in the digi applications and the IWB. The videos can be watched after learners have read the texts. Activities that accompany the videos can be done in class or assigned as HW.

D Speaking

- Speaking activities are initially controlled, allowing for guided practice *(see Student's Book, Unit 1, p. 7, Ex. 10 where Ss use the same structures to act out a dialogue.)*
- Ss are led to free speaking activities. *(See Student's Book, Unit 1, p. 8, Ex. 4 where Ss are provided with the necessary lexical items and structures and are asked to act out their dialogue.)*

E Writing

All writing tasks in *New Enterprise A1* have been carefully designed to closely guide learners to produce a successful piece of writing. They are fully analysed in the *Skills in Action* sections in the Student's Book with model texts and exercises that aim to help learners improve their writing skills.

- Make sure that Ss understand that they are writing for a purpose. Go through the writing task so that Ss are fully aware of why they are writing and who they are writing to *(see Student's Book, Unit 3, p. 25, Ex. 9. Ss are asked to write an email.)*.
- It would be well-advised to actually complete the task orally in class before assigning it as written homework. Ss will then feel more confident with producing a complete piece of writing on their own.

F Assigning homework

When assigning homework, prepare learners as well as possible in advance. This will help them avoid errors and get maximum benefit from the task.

Commonly assigned tasks include:

Copy – learners copy an assigned extract;

Dictation – learners learn the spelling of particular words without memorising the text in which they appear;

Vocabulary – learners memorise the meaning of words and phrases or use the new words in sentences of their own;

Reading Aloud – assisted by the digi apps, learners practise at home in preparation for reading aloud in class;

Writing – after thorough preparation in class, learners are asked to produce a complete piece of writing.

G Correcting learners' work

All learners make errors – it is part of the learning process. The way you deal with errors depends on what the learners are doing.

- **Oral accuracy work:**
  Correct learners on the spot, either by providing the correct answer and allowing them to repeat, or by indicating the error but allowing learners to correct it. Alternatively, indicate the error and ask other Ss to provide the answer.

- **Oral fluency work:**
  Allow learners to finish the task without interrupting, but make a note of the errors made and correct them afterwards.

Written work:

Do not over-correct; focus on errors that are directly relevant to the point of the exercise. When giving feedback, you may write the most common errors on the board and get the class to attempt to correct them.

Remember that rewarding work and praising learners is of great importance. Praise effort as well as success.

H   Class organisation

• Open pairs

The class focuses its attention on two learners doing the set task together. Use this technique when you want your learners to offer an example of how a task is done *(see Student's Book, Unit 3, p. 22, Ex. 3a)*.

• Closed pairs

Pairs of learners work together on a task or activity while you move around offering assistance and suggestions. Explain the task clearly before beginning closed pairwork. *(See Student's Book, Unit 3, p. 24, Ex. 4)*

• Stages of pairwork
- Put Ss in pairs.
- Explain the task and set a time limit.
- Rehearse the task in open pairs.
- In closed pairs, get Ss to do the task.
- Go around the class and help Ss.
- Open pairs report back to the class.

• Group work

Groups of three or more Ss work together on a task or activity. Class projects or role play are most easily done in groups. Again, give Ss a solid understanding of the task in advance.

• Rolling questions

Ask Ss one after the other to ask and answer questions based on the texts.

I   Using L1 in class

Use L1 in moderation and only when necessary.

ABBREVIATIONS

Abbreviations used in the Student's and Teacher's Books.

T	Teacher	p(p).	Page(s)
S(s)	Student(s)	e.g.	For example
HW	Homework	i.e.	That is
L1	Students' native language	etc	Et cetera
		sb	Somebody
Ex(s).	Exercise(s)	sth	Something

Key to symbols used in the Student's/Teacher's Books

 audio

 pairwork

 groupwork

✓ words to be explained using the context each appears in

ICT research

Study Skills suggestions to help learners become autonomous

Writing Tip suggestions to help learners develop their writing skills

THINK sections to develop Ss' critical thinking skills

Culture texts to familiarise Ss with the culture of the English-speaking countries, and develop cross-cultural awareness

VALUES sections to help Ss develop critical thinking skills & values

CLIL Sections that link the themes of the units to a subject from the core curriculum

Hi!

<table>
<tr><td colspan="2">Topic</td></tr>
<tr><td colspan="2">In this unit, Ss will explore the topics of countries, nationalities, jobs, abilities and colours.</td></tr>
</table>

1a   Reading & Vocabulary   4-5

Lesson objectives: To listen and read for specific information; to ask and answer questions; to learn cardinal numbers; to learn countries/nationalities; to write a short text about a friend

Vocabulary: Cardinal numbers *(1-1,000)*; Countries & Nationalities *(Brazil, Spain, Canada, Japan, Argentina, the USA, Greece, Finland, Mexico, Turkey, Brazilian, Spanish, Canadian, Japanese, Argentinian, American, Greek, Finnish, Mexican, Turkish)*; Nouns *(outfit, snapshot)*; Verbs *(become, draw, design)*; Adjectives *(amazing, interested in)*; Phrases *(good at, crazy about, mad about)*

1b   Grammar in Use   6-7

Lesson objectives: To learn the verb *to be*; to learn subject pronouns; to learn *a/an*; to learn the verb *can*; to talk about abilities

Vocabulary: Jobs *(waiter, waitress, pilot, secretary, police officer, doctor, astronaut, vet, artist, architect, actress/actor)*

1c   Skills in Action   8-9

Lesson objectives: To learn school/college subjects; to listen for specific information (multiple choice); to act out a dialogue and practise everyday English for greetings, introductions and personal questions; to learn intonation in *wh*-questions; to read for specific information; to write a social media profile

Vocabulary: School/College subjects *(Maths, Computer Science, Physics, Geography, English Language, Music, History, Art, Biology, Chemistry, Literature, Drama)*

Culture 1   10

Lesson objectives: To listen and read for specific information; to talk about colours; to write a fact file

Vocabulary: Continents *(North America, Europe, Oceania)*; Nouns *(continent, capital, population, currency)*; Phrases *(official language, native speaker)*

Review 1   11

Lesson objectives: To test/consolidate vocabulary and grammar learnt throughout the unit; to practise everyday English

---

Go through the objectives box and tell Ss that these are the topics, skills and activities this unit will cover.

1a

Reading

1 **Aim** To listen and read for specific information

- Ask Ss to look at the social media profiles.
- Play the recording.
- Elicit the people's ages and dream jobs.
- Check Ss' answers.

Answer Key

Peter is 16. His dream job is to become a singer.
Maria is 18. Her dream job is to become a fashion designer.
Ju is 19. Her dream job is to become a writer.
Janusz is 20. His dream job is to become a photographer.

- Play the video for Ss and elicit their comments.

Background Information

The UK is a country in Europe made up of England, Scotland, Wales and Northern Ireland. The capital city is London and the population is around 66 million people.

Argentina is a country in South America. The capital city is Buenos Aires and the people speak Spanish. The population is around 44 million people.

Thailand is a country in Southeast Asia. The capital city is Bangkok. The population is around 69 million people.

Poland is a country is Eastern Europe. The capital city is Warsaw. The population is around 38 million people.

2 **Aim** To identify reference in a text

- Give Ss time to read the texts again and then read the sentences and replace the words in bold with words from the text.
- Check Ss' answers.

Answer Key

1 *singing*	3 *Ju*
2 *Art and ICT*	4 *snapshots*

- Give Ss time to look up the meanings of the words in the **Check these words** box in the Word List.

Speaking

3 a) **Aim** To consolidate information in a text by asking and answering questions

- Read the example aloud.
- Ask Ss to ask and answer questions in pairs using the information in the texts.
- Monitor the activity around the class and then ask some pairs to ask and answer in front of the class.

Suggested Answer Key

A: What is Maria's surname?
B: Álvarez.
A: How old is she?
B: She's 18 years old.
A: Where is she from?
B: She's from Argentina.
A: What is her dream job?
B: Her dream job is to become a fashion designer.

A: What is Ju's surname?
B: Luó.
A: How old is she?
B: She's 19 years old.
A: Where is she from?
B: She's from Thailand.
A: What is her dream job?
B: Her dream job is to become a writer.

A: What is Janusz's surname?
B: Florek.
A: How old is he?
B: He's 20 years old.
A: Where is he from?
B: He's from Poland.
A: What is his dream job?
B: His dream job is to become a photographer.

b) **Aim** To consolidate information from a text, to complete a table

- Ask Ss to copy the table into their notebooks and then refer back to the texts and complete it.
- Then ask Ss to use the completed table to make sentences about the people in the texts following the example.
- Check Ss' answers.

Answer Key

First name	Surname	Age	Country	Dream Job
Peter	*Smith*	*16*	*the UK*	*singer*
Maria	*Álvarez*	18	Argentina	*fashion designer*
Ju	*Luó*	19	Thailand	*writer*
Janusz	*Florek*	20	Poland	*photographer*

Peter Smith is 16 years old. He is from the UK. His dream job is to become a singer.
Maria Álvarez is 18 years old. She is from Argentina. Her dream job is to become a fashion designer.
Ju Luó is 19 years old. She is from Thailand. Her dream job is to become a writer.
Janusz Florek is 20 years old. He is from Poland. His dream job is to become a photographer.

Vocabulary

4 a) **Aim** To present cardinal numbers

Play the recording with pauses for Ss to listen and repeat chorally and/or individually.

b) **Aim** To listen and identify cardinal numbers

- Play the recording. Ss listen and circle the numbers they hear.
- Check Ss' answers.

Answer Key

13 – thirteen   100 – a hundred
28 – twenty-eight   64 – sixty-four

5 **Aim** To present and practise countries and nationalities

- Explain the task.
- Ask Ss to copy and complete the gaps in their notebooks and then make sentences, as in the example.
- Check Ss' answers around the class.

Suggested Answer Key

2 Spain   5 Argentina   8 Finland
3 Canada   6 American   9 Mexican
4 Japanese   7 Greek   10 Turkey

Pablo is Spanish. He's from Madrid, Spain.
Jason is Canadian. He's from Ottawa, Canada.
Ito is Japanese. He's from Tokyo, Japan.
Tomás is Argentinian. He's from Buenos Aires, Argentina.

Mike is American. He's from Washington DC, the USA.
Costas is Greek. He's from Athens, Greece.
Hans is Finnish. He's from Helsinki, Finland.
Rico is Mexican. He's from Mexico City, Mexico.
Ali is Turkish. He's from Ankara, Turkey.

Pronunciation key for names, nationalities, capitals and countries in Ex. 5

Paolo /ˈpaʊləʊ/
Brazilian /brəˈzɪliən/
Brasilia /brəˈzɪliə/
Brazil /brəˈzɪl/
Pablo /ˈpɒbləʊ/
Spanish /ˈspænɪʃ/
Madrid /məˈdrɪd/
Spain /speɪn/
Jason /ˈdʒeɪsən/
Canadian /kəˈneɪdiən/
Ottawa /ˈɒtəwə/
Canada /ˈkænədə/
Ito /ˈiːtəʊ/
Japanese /ˌdʒæpəˈniːz/
Tokyo /ˈtəʊkjəʊ/
Japan /dʒəˈpæn/
Tomás /ˈtɒməs/
Argentinian /ˌɑːdʒənˈtɪniən/
Buenos Aires /ˌbwɛnəs ˈɛriːz/
Argentina /ˌɑːdʒənˈtiːnə/

Mike /maɪk/
American /əˈmerɪkən/
Washington DC /ˈwɒʃɪŋtən diː siː/
the USA /ðə ˈjuːweseɪ/
Costas /ˈkɒstas/
Greek /griːk/
Athens /ˈæθənz/
Greece /griːs/
Hans /hæns/
Finnish /ˈfɪnɪʃ/
Helsinki /hɛlˈsɪŋkiː/
Finland /ˈfɪnlənd/
Rico /ˈriːkəʊ/
Mexican /ˈmeksɪkən/
Mexico City /ˈmeksɪkəʊ ˈsɪtiː/
Mexico /ˈmeksɪkəʊ/
Ali /alɪ/
Turkish /ˈtɜːkɪʃ/
Ankara /ˈæŋkərə/
Turkey /ˈtɜːkiː/

Optional game

Choose a S to be the leader. The leader chooses a country and writes its name on a piece of paper. The rest of the class try to guess which country by asking questions. The S who guesses correctly becomes the leader and Ss play the game again.

Suggested Answer Key

S1:   Are you from Poland?
L: No, I'm not.
S2:   Are you from Spain?
L: No, I'm not.
S3:   Are you from the USA?
L: Yes, I am.

S3 becomes the leader and the game continues.

Writing

6   **Aim** To write a paragraph about a friend
   • Ask Ss to copy and complete the table from Ex. 3b in their notebooks with information about a friend of theirs.

   • Then give Ss time to use their notes to write a paragraph about their friend and include a photo if possible.
   • Ask various Ss to present their work to the class.

Suggested Answer Key

First name	Surname	Age	Country	Dream Job
Sandrine	Dubois	16	France	chef

My friend Sandrine Dubois is 16 years old. She's from France. She is interested in cooking with different foods. She can make lots of amazing meals. Her dream job is to become a chef.

1b Grammar in Use

1   **Aim** To present/practise the verb *to be*
   • Present the verb **to be**. Write on the board: *I am Ingrid. I'm Ingrid.* Present the full and contracted forms of the present simple affirmative of the verb **to be**.
   • Point to a S. Say: *You're Mario.* Then write it on the board.
   • Point to a male S in the class and say: *He's Tony.* Then write it on the board.
   • Point to a female S in the class and say: *She's Maria.* Then write it on the board. Continue with the rest.
   • Then present the present simple negative of the verb **to be**. Say, then write on the board: *I'm English. I'm not French.* Underline the words: *I'm not.* Elicit how the negative of the verb **to be** is formed (by adding **not** after **am**, **is**, **are**). Do the same to present all persons, singular and plural in both full and contracted forms.
   • Present the interrogative form and short answers. Say, then write on the board: *Am I a teacher?* Underline: *Am I.* Explain that we form the interrogative of the verb **to be** by putting the verb **to be** before the subject pronoun.
   • Answer the question on the board: *Yes, I am.* Explain that this is a positive short answer. Explain that we form positive short answers with **yes**, the appropriate personal pronoun and the verb in the affirmative.
   • Write on the board: *Am I a doctor? No, I'm not.* Explain that we form a negative short answer with **no**, the appropriate personal pronoun and the verb in the negative.
   • Ask Ss to read the table and then ask Ss to read the profile and find examples.
   • Check Ss' answers.

Answer Key

Affirmative long form: *Tony is from London, the UK. Tony is good at drawing. His dream job is to become an architect.*
Affirmative short form: *He's 18 years old.*
Negative short form: *..., but he isn't good at singing.*

2 **Aim** To practise the verb *to be*

- Explain the task and give Ss time to complete it.
- Check Ss' answers.

Answer Key

1 isn't, is/'s
2 Are, aren't, are/'re
3 is/'s, is/'s
4 Is, is, is/'s
5 are, am/'m
6 Is, is, is/'s

3 a) **Aim** To practise the verb *to be*

- Explain the task and give Ss time to complete it.
- Check Ss' answers.

Answer Key

2 am/'m
3 am/'m
4 is
5 is/'s
6 is/'s
7 are/'re
8 am/'m
9 is/'s
10 are/'re

b) **Aim** To practise the verb *to be*

- Explain the task and read out the example.
- Give Ss time to complete the task.
- Check Ss' answers.

Answer Key

2 Monica isn't 25 years old. She's 28 years old. / Andrea is 25 years old.
3 Andrea and Monica aren't American. Andrea is British and Monica is Polish.
4 Andrea isn't a good singer. Monica is a good singer. / Andrea is good at drawing.

4 **Aim** To practise the verb *to be* and ask and answer about countries

- Ask Ss to ask and answer in pairs using the countries in the list and the verb **to be** following the example.
- Monitor the activity around the class and then ask some pairs to ask and answer in front of the class.

Suggested Answer Key

A: *Are you from Australia?*
B: *No, I'm not. / Yes, I am. Are you from Bahrain?*
A: *No, I'm not. / Yes, I am. Are you from India?*
B: *No, I'm not. / Yes, I am. Are you from Portugal?*
A: *No, I'm not. / Yes, I am. Are you from Peru?*
B: *No, I'm not. / Yes, I am. Are you from Brazil?*

A: *No, I'm not. / Yes, I am. Are you from Germany?*
B: *No, I'm not. / Yes, I am. Are you from Egypt?*
A: *No, I'm not. / Yes, I am.*

5 **Aim** To present subject pronouns

- Read out the theory box.
- Present the subject pronouns.
- Point to yourself and say: *I*, then write it on the board. Point to a S and say: *you*, then write it on the board. Point to a male S and say: *he*. Then write it on the board. Explain that we use **he** for a boy or a man. Continue for the rest of the subject pronouns.
- Explain the task. Allow Ss some time to complete the gaps.
- Check Ss' answers.

Answer Key

1 She
2 We
3 They
4 It
5 He
6 You

6 **Aim** To present *a/an*

- Read out the theory box.
- Present *a/an*.
- Refer Ss to the profile on p. 6 and elicit an example.

Answer Key

an architect

7 a) **Aim** To practise *a/an*; to present vocabulary for jobs

- Ask Ss to look at the pictures. Present the jobs in the list and give Ss time to match them to the pictures and use **a/an**.
- Check Ss' answers.

Answer Key

2 a waitress
3 a pilot
4 a secretary
5 a police officer
6 a doctor
7 an astronaut
8 a vet
9 an artist
10 an engineer
11 an actress/actor

b) **Aim** To practise asking questions, talking about jobs and using *a/an*

- Explain the task and read out the example.
- Ask Ss to talk in pairs and ask and answer questions about the people and their jobs in Ex. 7a following the example.
- Monitor the activity around the class and then ask some pairs to ask and answer in front of the class.

Suggested Answer Key

A: *What's her name?* | B: *Twenty-six.*
B: *Kathy.* | A: *What's her job?*
A: *How old is she?* | B: *She's a waitress.*

A: *What's her name?* | B: *Thirty.*
B: *Mary.* | A: *What's her job?*
A: *How old is she?* | B: *She's a pilot.*

A: *What's her name?* | B: *Twenty-nine.*
B: *Laura.* | A: *What's her job?*
A: *How old is she?* | B: *She's a secretary.*

A: *What's his name?* | B: *Thirty-five.*
B: *Bob.* | A: *What's his job?*
A: *How old is he?* | B: *He's a police officer.*

A: *What's her name?* | B: *Thirty-four.*
B: *Helen.* | A: *What's her job?*
A: *How old is she?* | B: *She's a doctor.*

A: *What's his name?* | B: *Forty-two.*
B: *Steve.* | A: *What's his job?*
A: *How old is he?* | B: *He's an astronaut.*

A: *What's his name?* | B: *Thirty-six.*
B: *Paul.* | A: *What's his job?*
A: *How old is he?* | B: *He's a vet.*

A: *What's her name?* | B: *Twenty-eight.*
B: *Stella.* | A: *What's her job?*
A: *How old is she?* | B: *She's an artist.*

A: *What's his name?* | B: *Thirty-eight.*
B: *Tom.* | A: *What's his job?*
A: *How old is he?* | B: *He's an engineer.*

A: *What are their names?* | B: *Pam is twenty-eight and Peter is thirty.*
B: *Pam and Peter.* | A: *What are their jobs?*
A: *How old are they?* | B: *Pam is an actress and Peter is an actor.*

8 (Aim) To present *can*

- Present *can*. Say, then write on the board: *I can sing*. Underline the word *can* and explain that it shows that we are able to do sth. Say, then write on the board: *I can't sing*. Underline the word *can't* and explain that this word shows that we are unable to do sth. Say, then write on the board: *Can you sing?* Underline the word *can* and explain that this is how we ask if someone is able to do sth.

- Ask Ss to provide examples from Tony's profile on p. 6.

Answer Key

He **can** play football well, but he **can't** play tennis.

9 (Aim) To practise *can*

Ask various Ss to tell the class what each of the people in the pictures can and can't do.

Answer Key

2   *Mary can type.*
3   *Lora can't dance.*
4   *Steve can swim.*
5   *Sam can't play the guitar.*
6   *Kate can run.*

10 (Aim) To talk about abilities

- Ask Ss to work in small groups and ask and answer questions using *can* and the phrases in the table while following the example.
- Monitor the activity around the class and then ask various Ss to tell the class what their friends can/can't do.

Suggested Answer Key

A: *Can you dance?*
B: *Yes, I can dance very well. Can you swim?*
A: *No, I can't swim very well. Can you swim?*
C: *Yes, I can swim very fast. Can you play the guitar?*
B: *Yes, I can play the guitar quite well. Can you run?*
A: *Yes, I can run quite fast. Can you run?*
C: *No, I can't run very fast.*

1c Skills in Action

Vocabulary

1 a) (Aim) To present vocabulary for school/college subjects

- Play the recording. Ss listen and repeat chorally and/or individually.
- Check Ss' pronunciation and intonation.

b) (Aim) To practise vocabulary for school/college subjects

- Read out the example and then ask Ss to talk in pairs about which subjects they are/aren't good at.
- Monitor the activity around the class and then ask some Ss to tell the class.

13

Suggested Answer Key

I'm good at Biology. I'm not very good at Geography. My best friend is good at Art. She isn't very good at Chemistry.

Listening

2 a) **Aim** **To prepare for a listening task**

- Read out the **Study Skills** box and tell Ss this tip will help them complete the listening task successfully.
- Ask Ss to read the questions and answers and then elicit what the dialogue is about.

Answer Key

The dialogue is about three students and their subjects at college.

b) **Aim** **To listen for specific information (multiple choice)**

- Play the recording. Ss listen and choose the correct answers for the questions.
- Check Ss' answers.

Answer Key

1 A   2 B   3 B   4 C   5 A

Everyday English

3 a) **Aim** **To complete a dialogue**

Give Ss time to read the dialogue and then to think of appropriate words to complete the gaps in the dialogue.

b) **Aim** **To listen for confirmation**

Play the recording for Ss to check their answers in Ex. 3a.

Answer Key

1 What   2 Where   3 What   4 How

4 **Aim** **To practise everyday English expressions for greeting people, introducing yourself and others and asking personal questions**

- Explain the task and give Ss time to read through the useful language box. Then ask Ss to act out similar dialogues to the one in Ex. 3a in pairs.
- Write this diagram on the board for Ss to follow.

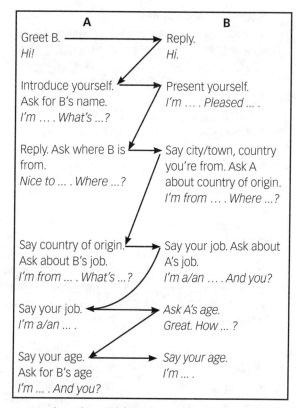

A	B
Greet B. *Hi!*	Reply. *Hi.*
Introduce yourself. Ask for B's name. *I'm … . What's …?*	Present yourself. *I'm … . Pleased … .*
Reply. Ask where B is from. *Nice to … . Where …?*	Say city/town, country you're from. Ask A about country of origin. *I'm from … . Where …?*
Say country of origin. Ask about B's job. *I'm from … . What's …?*	Say your job. Ask about A's job. *I'm a/an … . And you?*
Say your job. *I'm a/an … .*	Ask A's age. *Great. How … ?*
Say your age. Ask for B's age *I'm … . And you?*	Say your age. *I'm … .*

- Monitor the activity around the class and offer assistance as necessary.
- Then ask some pairs to act out their dialogues in front of the rest of the class.

Suggested Answer Key

A: Hi.
B: Hi.
A: I'm Lucy. What is your name?
B: I'm Thomas, Thomas Smith. Pleased to meet you.
A: Nice to meet you! Where are you from?
B: I'm from Paris, France. What about you?
A: I'm from London, England. What's your job?
B: I'm a pilot. And you?
A: I'm an artist.
B: Great. How old are you?
A: I'm twenty-seven. And you?
B: I'm thirty-two.

Intonation in *wh*-questions

5 **Aim** **To learn intonation in *wh*-questions**

- Ask Ss to read out the theory box.
- Play the recording. Ss listen and repeat chorally and/or individually.

Reading & Writing

6 **Aim** To read for specific information; to complete a table

- Direct Ss to the texts and give them time to read them.
- Then ask Ss to copy and complete the table in their notebooks; one for each person.
- Check Ss' answers on the board.

Answer Key

Name	Michael Stephenson
Age	18
Where from	Los Angeles, the USA
Favourite subjects	Maths and Physics
Abilities	can swim and run very fast
Favourite singer	Eminem

Name	Mumba Akua
Age	22
Where from	Nairobi, Kenya
Favourite subjects	Drama and Literature
Abilities	can write really good stories, can cook very well
Favourite singer	Sia

Background Information

Los Angeles is a large city in the state of California in the USA. It is also called LA and 'The City of Angels'. It is also the home of Hollywood, a major centre for the entertainment industry.

Nairobi is the capital city of Kenya in Africa. It is also called 'The Green City in the Sun' and is famous for its national park. It is home to the United Nations Environment Programme.

7 **Aim** To present and practise punctuation (capital letters)

- Read out the **Writing Tip** box and make sure Ss understand when we use capital letters (when we start a sentence, with proper nouns, with the subject personal pronoun **I**, with months/days of the week).
- Then give Ss time to rewrite the sentences using the correct punctuation.
- Check Ss' answers by asking various Ss to write on the board.

Answer Key

1. I am from France.
2. You are interested in Maths.
3. Jenny can dance very well.
4. They are British.
5. My favourite sportsman is Michael Phelps. He's American.

8 **Aim** To present and practise linkers

- Read out the **Writing Tip** box and make sure Ss understand when we use **and** and **but**.
- Then give Ss time to join the sentences using the correct linker.
- Check Ss' answers.

Suggested Answer key

1. Dan is 16 years old and he is good at Maths.
2. Mary can draw, but she can't sing.
3. I am good at Music and I can play the piano very well.
4. I am interested in Drama and I can sing well.
5. Jenny can swim really fast, but she can't cook very well.

Writing

9 **Aim** To prepare for a writing task

- Ask S to copy and complete the table from Ex. 6 about themselves.
- Ask various Ss to read out their completed table to the class.

Suggested Answer Key

Name	Isabella Romano
Age	18
Where from	Rome, Italy
Favourite subjects	Art and Music
Abilities	can play the guitar, can dance very well
Favourite singer	Beyoncé

10 **Aim** To write a social media profile

- Explain the task and give Ss time to write their profiles using the information from Ex. 9.
- Check Ss' answers.
- Alternatively, assign the task as HW and check Ss' answers in the next lesson.

Suggested Answer Key

About me:

I'm Isabella Romano and I'm 18 years old. I'm from Rome in Italy. My favourite subjects in school are Art and Music. My favourite artists are Pablo Picasso and Vincent van Gogh. I can play the guitar and I can dance very well. I'm crazy about Beyoncé. She's a great singer.

Values

Ss try to explain the quotation in their mother tongue. If Ss have difficulty, explain the quotation. Ask Ss to memorise this quotation and check in the next lesson.
The quotation means we should all be united and care for each other the way we care for ourselves.

Culture 1
Listening & Reading

1 **Aim** **To listen and read for specific information**

- Ask Ss to look at the map and the fact files and read out the question.
- Play the recording. Ss listen and read to find out.

Answer Key

English is the official language in these countries.

- Play the video for Ss and elicit their comments.

2 **Aim** **To read for specific information**

- Ask Ss to read the fact files again and then correct the sentences.
- Check Ss' answers.

Answer Key

1 *Australia and New Zealand are in Oceania.*
2 *Wellington is in New Zealand.*
3 *Ireland's currency is euros.*
4 *Canada and the UK are not the same size.*
5 *The population of New Zealand is not the same as the UK/is the same as Ireland.*

Speaking & Writing

3 **Aim** **To present and practise colours**

Explain the task and elicit answers from Ss around the class.

Answer Key

Canada's flag is red and white.
The USA's flag is red, white and blue.
Ireland's flag is green, white and orange.
The UK's flag is red, white and blue.
Australia's flag is red, white and blue.
New Zealand's flag is red, white and blue.

4 **Aim** **To write a fact file about your country**

- Explain the task and give Ss time to write a short fact file following the examples in Ex. 1.
- Ask various Ss to read out their fact files to the class.

Suggested Answer Key

Argentina	
Continent	South America
Population	44,461,058
Capital	Buenos Aires
Area	2,736,690 km²
Currency	Peso ($)

Review 1
Vocabulary

1 **Aim** **To practise numbers**

- Explain the task.
- Give Ss time to complete it.
- Check Ss' answers.

Answer Key

1	five	7	thirty-eight
2	fifteen	8	a/one hundred and
3	twelve		five
4	twenty	9	sixteen
5	seventy-three	10	eighty-two
6	three		

2 **Aim** **To practise nationalities**

- Explain the task.
- Give Ss time to complete it.
- Check Ss' answers.

Answer Key

1	British	3	Canadian	5	Spanish
2	Japanese	4	Turkish		

3 **Aim** **To practise jobs**

- Explain the task.
- Give Ss time to complete it.
- Check Ss' answers.

Answer Key

1	photographer	4	artist
2	writer	5	singer
3	fashion designer		

Grammar

4 **Aim** **To practise the verb *to be***

- Explain the task.
- Give Ss time to complete it.
- Check Ss' answers.

Answer Key

1 Are, am/'m not, am/'m
2 Is, is, is/'s
3 Are, are not/aren't, are/'re
4 Are, are, are/'re
5 Is, is not/isn't, is/'s

5 **Aim** To practise *a/an*

- Explain the task.
- Give Ss time to complete it.
- Check Ss' answers.

Answer Key

1 a   2 an   3 an   4 a   5 an

6 **Aim** To practise *can/can't*

- Explain the task.
- Give Ss time to complete it.
- Check Ss' answers.

Answer Key

1 Can, I can   4 Can, they can
2 Can, we can't   5 Can, he can't
3 Can, she can

7 **Aim** To practise the verb *to be* and *can*

- Explain the task.
- Give Ss time to complete it.
- Check Ss' answers.

Answer Key

1	am/'m	5	is	9	can
2	is	6	can	10	can
3	are/'re	7	can't		
4	are	8	is		

Everyday English

8 **Aim** To match questions and answers

- Explain the task.
- Give Ss time to complete it.
- Check Ss' answers.

Answer Key

1 D   2 A   3 E   4 B   5 C

Competences

Ask Ss to assess their own performance in the unit by ticking the items according to how competent they feel for each of the listed activities.

2 Families

Topic
In this unit, Ss will explore the topics of family members, appearance and character.

2a Reading & Vocabulary	12-13
Lesson objectives: To listen and read for specific information, to learn family members, to learn about appearance, to describe appearance, to present TV/film characters **Vocabulary:** Family *(brother, father, daughter, sister, aunt, granddaughter, son, nephew, cousin, son, husband, uncle, parents, grandparents)*; Nouns *(billionaire, moustache, gardening, spider, octopus)*; Verbs *(laugh, cry, juggle, look after)*; Adjective *(naughty)*	

2b Grammar in Use	14-15
Lesson objectives: To learn the verb *have got*, to learn object pronouns – possessive adjectives/pronouns, to learn the possessive case ('/'s), to learn question words *Who/Whose*, to learn plurals	

2c Skills in Action	16-17
Lesson objectives: To learn character adjectives, to listen for specific information (multiple matching), to act out a dialogue and practise everyday English for identifying and describing people, to pronounce /iː/, /ɪ/, to read for specific information, to write a blog entry about a famous person **Vocabulary:** Character adjectives *(outgoing, shy, clever, silly, hard-working, lazy, quiet, noisy, funny, serious, kind, impolite)*	

Culture 2	18
Lesson objectives: To listen and read for specific information, to read for detailed understanding, to ask and answer questions about famous siblings, to write short descriptions of famous siblings **Vocabulary:** Nouns *(sibling, ex-coach, fashion, company)*, Adjectives *(famous, proud, talented)*	

Review 2	19
Lesson objectives: To test/consolidate vocabulary and grammar learnt throughout the unit; to practise everyday English	

Go through the objectives box and tell Ss that these are the topics, skills and activities this unit will cover.

2a

Reading

1 **Aim** To listen and read for specific information
   - Ask Ss to look at the family tree.
   - Play the recording.
   - Elicit the answers to the questions.

   Answer Key

   These characters are from the Addams family.

   Wednesday has got a pet spider.

   - Play the video for Ss and elicit their comments.

> ## Background Information
>
> **The Addams Family** was originally a fictional family from a cartoon created by Charles Addams that appeared in the New Yorker magazine. In 1964 it became a popular TV series. Then a feature film series appeared in the 1990s. There have also been animated films, TV series and a live musical. It is a huge part of American popular culture.

2 **Aim** To read for specific information (answer questions)
   - Give Ss time to read the text again and answer the questions.
   - Check Ss' answers around the class.

   Answer Key

   1 Gomez's favourite hobby is playing with his toy trains.
   2 Morticia can speak French, play music and do gardening.
   3 Wednesday is very serious.
   4 Pugsley has got a pet octopus.

   - Give Ss time to look up the meanings of the words in the ***Check these words*** box in the Word List.

Vocabulary

3 **Aim** To learn/consolidate family members
   - Explain the task.
   - Ask Ss to read the sentences and choose the correct word referring to the text and family tree as necessary.
   - Check Ss' answers.

Answer Key

1	brother	5	son
2	sister	6	husband
3	granddaughter	7	brother
4	nephew	8	grandparents

4 **Aim** **To consolidate information from a text**

- Ask Ss to work in pairs. One says a sentence about a person in the family tree and their partner says who the person is, as in the example.
- Monitor the activity around the class.

Suggested Answer Key

A: It's Morticia's sister.
B: Ophelia.

A: It's Wednesday's uncle.
B: Fester.

A: It's Pugsley's brother.
B: Pubert. etc

5 **Aim** **To present vocabulary for appearance**

- Ask Ss to look at the family tree again. Then read out the sentences and explain/elicit the meanings of the words in bold.
- Then give Ss time to answer the questions.
- Check Ss' answers.

Answer Key

1	Morticia	4	Pugsley
2	Grandmama	5	Fester
3	Gomez		

6 **Aim** **To learn and practise vocabulary for parts of the face**

- Ask Ss to work in pairs.
- Explain/Elicit the meanings of the words in the list. Then give Ss time to use them to label the parts of the face.
- Check Ss' answers by asking them to point to them on their face and name them.

Answer Key

2	eye	5	chin	8	ear
3	cheek	6	teeth	9	mouth
4	lips	7	nose		

7 **Aim** **To present and practise vocabulary for appearance through antonyms**

- Explain the task.
- Explain/Elicit the meanings of the words in the list. Then give Ss time to use them to write the opposite phrases.
- Check Ss' answers around the class by asking them to find images on their smartphones and show them to the class.

Answer Key

2	plump girl	6	thin lips
3	short hair	7	small nose
4	curly hair	8	small eyes
5	fair hair		

Speaking & Writing

8 **Aim** **To talk about appearance**

- Ask Ss to work in pairs and choose a person from the Addams family and ask and answer questions about their appearance following the example.
- Monitor the activity around the class and then ask some pairs to ask and answer in front of the class.

Suggested Answer Key

A: What does Gomez look like?
B: He's well-built with short straight black hair and a moustache.

A: What does Wednesday look like?
B: She's young and thin. She's got short straight black hair.

A: What does Pugsley look like?
B: He's young, short and plump. He's got short fair hair.

Optional game

As an extension, play a game with Ss. Divide the class into two teams and choose a leader. The leader chooses a person from the class and describes him/her without saying his/her name. Teams take turns and try to guess who this person is. The team which guesses correctly gets one point. Choose another leader from the winning team and play the game again. The team with the most points is the winner.

2

9 **Aim** **To describe people from a famous TV/film family**

- Explain the task and give Ss time to find pictures of a famous TV/film family and then label them.
- Ask various Ss to present them to the class.

Suggested Answer Key

The Griffins

Peter Griffin: *He is tall and plump with short brown hair.*

Lois Griffin: *She is Peter's wife. She is tall and slim with red hair.*

Meg Griffin: *She is Peter and Lois's daughter. She is short and slim with straight brown hair.*

Chris Griffin: *He is Peter and Lois's son. He is tall and plump with long fair hair.*

Stewie Griffin: *He is Peter and Lois's son. He is short and small with short fair hair.*

2b Grammar in Use

1 **Aim** **To present/practise the verb** *have got*

- Present the verb *have got*. Write on the board: *I have got blue eyes. I've got blue eyes.* Present the full and contracted forms of the present simple affirmative of the verb *have got*.
- Point to a S. Say: *You have got brown eyes.* Then write it on the board.
- Point to a male S in the class and say: *He's got brown hair.* Then write it on the board.
- Point to a female S in the class and say: *She's got fair hair.* Then write it on the board. Continue with the rest.
- Then present the present simple negative of the verb *have got*. Say, then write on the board: *I haven't got fair hair.* Underline the words *haven't got*. Elicit how the negative of the verb *have got* is formed (by adding *not* after *have/has*). Do the same to present all persons singular and plural in both full and contracted forms.

- Present the interrogative form and short answers. Say, then write on the board: *Have I got dark hair?* Underline: *Have I got.* Explain that we form the interrogative of the verb *have got* by putting the verb *have* before the subject pronoun.
- Answer the question on the board: *Yes, I have.* Explain that this is a positive short answer. Explain that we form positive short answers with *yes*, the appropriate personal pronoun and *have* in the affirmative.
- Write on the board: *Have I got fair hair? No, I haven't.* Explain that we form a negative short answer with *no*, the appropriate personal pronoun and *have* in the negative.
- Ask Ss to read the table and then ask Ss to read the dialogue and find examples.
- Check Ss' answers.

Answer Key

Yes, she's got long dark hair now.
Have you got her phone number?
My dog's got a bad tooth.
No, sorry, I haven't.
She's got it.

2 **a)** **Aim** **To practise the verb** *have got*

- Explain the task and give Ss time to complete it.
- Check Ss' answers.

Answer Key

1 *has got, hasn't got*
2 *has got, hasn't got*
3 *haven't got, have got*
4 *hasn't got, has got*
5 *haven't got, have got*
6 *has got*
7 *hasn't got, has got*
8 *has got, has got*
9 *hasn't got, has got*
10 *have got, has got*

b) **Aim** **To practise the verb** *have got*

- Ask Ss to work in pairs and form questions and then answer them following the example.
- Monitor the activity around the class and check Ss' answers.

Answer Key

2 A: *Has Ben got a moustache?*
    B: *Yes, he has.*
3 A: *Has Mary got brown eyes?*
    B: *No, she hasn't. She's got blue eyes.*
4 A: *Has John got short hair?*
    B: *Yes, he has.*

5 A: *Has Charlotte got blue eyes?*
   B: *No, she hasn't. She's got green eyes.*
6 A: *Has John got a beard?*
   B: *No, he hasn't.*
7 A: *Has Daniel got fair hair?*
   B: *Yes, he has.*
8 A: *Has Jessica got red hair?*
   B: *No, she hasn't. She's got dark hair.*
9 A: *Has Andrea got straight hair?*
   B: *No, she hasn't. She's got curly hair.*
10 A: *Has Jessica got wavy hair?*
   B: *No, she hasn't. She's got straight hair.*

3 (Aim) To practise the verb *have got*

- Ask Ss to work in pairs.
- Explain the task and read out the example.
- Give Ss time to complete the task.
- Check Ss' answers.

Suggested Answer Key

A: *Is it a woman?*
B: *Yes, it is.*
A: *Has she got brown hair?*
B: *Yes, she has.*
A: *Has she got curly hair?*
B: *Yes, she has.*
A: *Is it Andrea?*
B: *Yes, it is. etc*

4 (Aim) To present object pronouns and possessive adjectives/pronouns

- Read out the theory box.
- Present the object pronouns.
- Point to yourself and say: *me*, then write it on the board. Point to a S and say: *you*, then write it on the board. Point to a male S and say: *him*. Then write it on the board. Explain that we use **him** for a boy or a man. Continue for the rest of the object pronouns.
- Present the possessive adjectives/pronouns. Hold up a pen. Say, then write on the board: *This is my pen. It's mine.* Underline the words *my/mine*. Explain that **my** is a possessive adjective and **mine** is a possessive pronoun. Present the other possessive adjectives/pronouns in the same way: *This is his pen. It's his. This is her pen. It's hers.*, etc.
- Ask Ss to read the theory and then elicit examples from the dialogue on p. 14.
- Give Ss time to complete the task and then check Ss' answers.

Answer Key

*They're **my** friends, Danny and **his** sister Jane.*
*The new place on Cook Street is **hers**.*

*Have you got **her** phone number? **My** dog's got a bad tooth.*
*She's got **it**.*

5 (Aim) To practise object pronouns and possessive adjectives/pronouns

- Give Ss time to read the short text and choose the correct items.
- Check Ss' answers.

Answer Key

1	My	5	our	9	Our
2	I	6	We	10	She
3	my	7	us	11	her
4	my	8	He	12	us

6 (Aim) To present the possessive case ('/s')

- Present the possessive case. Point to a student's book and say: *Whose book is this? (It's [Paula's].)* Write it on the board. Point to some desks in the classroom and say: *Whose desks are these? (They are the [students'] desks.)*
- Ask Ss to read the table and then elicit examples from the dialogue on p. 14.

Answer Key

*That's **Danny's** cousin, Lynn.*

7 (Aim) To practise the possessive case ('/'s) and *who's/whose*

- Explain the task and give Ss time to complete it.
- Check Ss' answers.

Answer Key

1	Whose, Kelly's	4	John's and Ann's
2	Who, boy's	5	girls'
3	Who, Sam and Mary's		

8 (Aim) To present plurals

- Explain that when we talk about more than one thing, we usually add **-s** to the noun.
  e.g. *desk – desks*
- Read the examples in the table aloud and focus Ss' attention on the different plural endings.
- Ss close their books. Drill Ss. Read nouns in the singular aloud. Ss say the relevant plural form. Then Ss open their books and elicit an example from the dialogue on p. 14.

Answer Key

friends

9 **Aim** To practise plurals

- Give Ss time to complete the gaps with the plural of the words in brackets.
- Check Ss' answers around the class.

Answer Key

1 brothers
2 personalities
3 hobbies
4 goldfish
5 universities
6 paintings, brushes
7 leaves

10 **Aim** To talk about friends

- Ask Ss to work in pairs and act out a dialogue similar to the one on p.14 using pictures of their friends from their smartphones.
- Monitor the activity around the class.

Suggested Answer Key

A: This photo is great. Who are they?
B: My brother Joe and his friend David.
A: Yes, I can see your brother. He's the one with the short fair hair. So, who's the girl with the long black hair?
B: That's David's sister, Daphne. She's got two cats.
A: Really? Have you got any pictures of her cats?
B: Yes, I have. Here they are.

2c Skills in Action

Vocabulary

1 **a)** **Aim** To present character adjectives

- Play the recording. Ss listen and repeat chorally and/or individually.
- Check Ss' pronunciation and intonation.

b) **Aim** To practise character adjectives

Read out the example and then ask Ss to tell the class which adjectives best describe them.

Suggested Answer Key

I'm outgoing and funny. I can be lazy at times.
I'm serious and hard-working. I can be noisy at times.
I'm quiet and hard-working. I can be silly at times.

Listening

2 **a)** **Aim** To listen for specific information (multiple matching)

- Read out the **Study Skills** box and tell Ss this tip will help them to complete the listening task successfully.

- Ask Ss to read the lists and then play the recording. Ss listen and match the people to their relationship with Tom.
- Check Ss' answers.

Answer Key

1 C   2 A   3 G   4 H   5 F

b) **Aim** To listen for specific information

- Play the recording again. Ss listen and make notes about each person's character.
- Then ask various Ss to tell the class what each person is like.

Answer Key

1 Alex is clever.
2 Margaret is funny.
3 Martha is silly.
4 David is kind.
5 Claire is shy.
6 Michelle is friendly.

Everyday English

3 **Aim** To complete a dialogue

- Give Ss time to read the dialogue and then use the sentences to complete the gaps in the dialogue.
- Play the recording for Ss to check their answers. Then, elicit which person in the picture is Mr Jones.

Answer Key

1 A   2 C   3 D

Mr Jones is the man on the left in the photo.

4 **Aim** To practise everyday English expressions for identifying & describing people

- Explain the task and give Ss time to read through the useful language box. Then ask Ss to act out a similar dialogue to the one in Ex. 3 in pairs.
- Write this diagram on the board for Ss to follow.

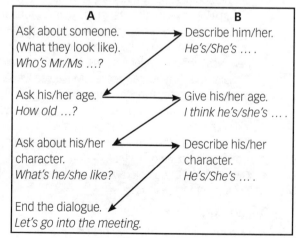

- Monitor the activity around the class and offer assistance as necessary.
- Then ask some pairs to act out their dialogues in front of the class.

Suggested Answer Key

Martha: Who's Ms Brown?
David: She's the one with the long dark hair.
Martha: How old is she?
David: I think she's 30.
Martha: What's she like?
David: She's friendly and very clever.
Martha: Let's go into the meeting.

Pronunciation

5 Aim To pronounce /iː/, /ɪ/

- Play the recording. Ss listen and tick the correct boxes.
- Play the recording again with pauses for Ss to repeat chorally and/or individually.

Answer Key

	/iː/	/ɪ/		/iː/	/ɪ/		/iː/	/ɪ/
six		✓	three	✓		teacher	✓	
read	✓		slim		✓	singer		✓

Reading & Writing

6 Aim To read for gist

- Direct Ss to the text.
- Ss read to find out what the text is about.

Suggested Answer Key

The text is Jamie's blog. He is telling us about his favourite actor Kit Harington.

Background Information

Game of Thrones is an American fantasy drama TV series based on the series of novels by George R.R. Martin called *A Song of Ice and Fire*. It is set in the fictional lands of Westeros and Essos with their seven kingdoms and the story revolves around the battles for the Iron Throne that rules over them. The series has won many awards and is very popular all around the world.

7 Aim To read for specific information (answer questions)

- Give Ss time to read the text again and answer the questions.
- Check Ss' answers.

Answer Key

1 Kit Harington is from the UK.
2 His mum's a playwright.
3 He is in 'Game of Thrones'.
4 Jon Snow's dad is Lord Ned Stark.
5 Jon Snow is brave.

8 Aim To present and practise punctuation

- Read out the **Writing Tip** box and make sure Ss understand when we use full stops, question marks, commas and exclamation marks (at the end of sentences, at the end of questions, to separate a list of items at the end of an exclamation or to express strong feelings).
- Then give Ss time to rewrite the sentences using the correct punctuation.
- Check Ss' answers by asking various Ss to write on the board.

Answer Key

1 His real name is Christopher.
2 His hair isn't black.
3 Who's your favourite actor?
4 He's an actor, a writer and a poet.
5 He is amazing!

9 Aim ICT To present and write about your favourite actor/actress

- Give Ss time to research online and find out information about their favourite actor/actress and answer the questions.
- Ask various Ss to share their answers with the class.

Suggested Answer Key

1 Kaley Cuoco
2 She's from the USA.
3 She's got one sister.
4 She's in the TV series 'The Big Bang Theory'.
5 She's very funny and a very good friend.

Writing

10 Aim To write a blog entry about a famous person

- Explain the task and give Ss time to write their blog entry using the information from Ex. 9.
- Check Ss' answers.
- Alternatively, assign the task as HW and check Ss' answers in the next lesson.

Suggested Answer Key

Mary's Blog

My favourite actress is Kaley Cuoco. She is from the USA with short blonde hair, green eyes and a big smile. Her mum's a housewife and her dad's a realtor. She's got a sister, Briana.
Kaley is very famous for her role as Penny in the 'Big Bang Theory'. Penny works as a waitress, but she wants to be an actress. She is good friends with a group of scientists. They're like her family. She's very funny as Penny.

Values

Ss try to explain the quotation in their mother tongue. If Ss have difficulty, explain the quotation. Ask Ss to memorise this quotation and check in the next lesson.
The quotation means that family is the most important thing in our lives.

Culture 2

Listening & Reading

1 Aim To listen and read for specific information

- Ask Ss to look at the pictures and read out the question.
- Play the recording. Ss listen and read the texts to find out.

Answer Key

The pictures show Venus and Serena Williams and James, Dave and Tom Franco.
The Franco brothers' dad is a businessman.

- Play the video for Ss and elicit their comments.

2 Aim To read for specific information

- Ask Ss to read the text again and then replace the words in bold with the correct words from the text.
- Check Ss' answers.

Answer Key

1	tennis	4	California
2	Serena's	5	Dave
3	in Florida	6	Tom

- Refer Ss to the Word List to look up the meanings of the words in the **Check these words** box.

Speaking & Writing

3 Aim To talk about celebrity siblings

- Ask Ss to talk in pairs about the celebrity siblings in the texts using the question words provided.
- Monitor the activity around the class.

Suggested Answer Key

A: *Who's Serena's big sister?*
B: *Venus is Serena's big sister.*
A: *Who's their ex-coach?*
B: *Their dad Richard is their ex-coach.*
A: *What is Dave Franco like?*
B: *Dave Franco is quite shy. etc*

4 Aim ICT To write descriptions of famous siblings

- Explain the task and give Ss time to research online and find out information about other famous siblings and write short descriptions.
- Ask various Ss to read out their descriptions to the class.
- Alternatively, assign the task as HW and ask Ss to read out their descriptions in the next lesson.

Suggested Answer Key

The Cruz sisters

These two sisters from Spain are great actresses. Mónica is an actress and a dancer. Penélope is Mónica's big sister and she is also an actress and a model. Their dad is a retailer and their mum is a hairdresser. Both sisters love fashion and they are both very hard-working.

Review 2

Vocabulary

1 Aim To practise vocabulary for family members

- Explain the task.
- Give Ss time to complete it.
- Check Ss' answers.

Answer Key

1	mother	3	cousin	5	aunt
2	father	4	nephew		

2 **Aim** To practise collocations

- Explain the task.
- Give Ss time to complete it.
- Check Ss' answers.

Answer Key

1 B   2 D   3 A   4 C

3 **Aim** To practise antonyms

- Explain the task.
- Give Ss time to complete it.
- Check Ss' answers.

Answer Key

1 short hair   4 quiet boy
2 short boy   5 curly hair
3 plump girl   6 serious boy

Grammar

4 **Aim** To practise the verb *have got*

- Explain the task.
- Give Ss time to complete it.
- Check Ss' answers.

Answer Key

1 Have, haven't   4 Have, have
2 Has, has   5 Has, hasn't
3 Have, haven't

5 **Aim** To practise object pronouns and possessive pronouns/adjectives

- Explain the task.
- Give Ss time to complete it.
- Check Ss' answers.

Answer Key

1 us, We   3 your, mine
2 My, him   4 their, theirs

6 **Aim** To practise plurals

- Explain the task.
- Give Ss time to complete it.
- Check Ss' answers.

Answer Key

1 hobbies   3 men   5 feet
2 brothers   4 children   6 fish

7 **Aim** To practise the possessive case and *who's/whose*

- Explain the task.
- Give Ss time to complete it.
- Check Ss' answers.

Answer Key

1 Whose, Vicky's   4 Who, George's
2 Who's, Tom and   5 Whose, Mary and
   Anna's   Ann's
3 Whose, girl's

Everyday English

8 **Aim** To match questions and answers

- Explain the task.
- Give Ss time to complete it.
- Check Ss' answers.

Answer Key

1 E   2 C   3 A   4 D   5 B

Competences

Ask Ss to assess their own performance in the unit by ticking the items according to how competent they feel for each of the listed activities.

3 Home sweet home!

Topic
In this unit, Ss will explore the topics of rooms, furniture, appliances, and types of houses.

3a Reading & Vocabulary	20-21
Lesson objectives: To listen and read for gist, to read for specific information, to learn about rooms, furniture & appliances, to compare houses, to describe your favourite room **Vocabulary:** Furniture & Appliances (*bookcase, chair, bedside cabinet, cupboards, washbasin, desk, armchair, wardrobe, towel, toilet, cooker, sofa, bath, sink, fridge, single bed, double bed, coffee table, table and chairs, chimney, roof, light, window, curtains, floor, mirror, rug, garden, picture, carpet, door, wall, stairs*); Rooms (*study, main bedroom, bathroom, child's room, kitchen, dining room, living room*); Nouns (*ground, neighbourhood, hill, environment*); Verb (*save*); Adjectives (*wooden, cool, warm*)	

3b Grammar in Use	22-23
Lesson objectives: To learn *there is/there are*, *a/an*, *some/any*, to learn *this/these, that/those*, to learn ordinal numbers, to learn prepositions of place, to write an advert for a house	

3c Skills in Action	24-25
Lesson objectives: To learn about types of houses, to listen for specific information (gap fill), to act out a dialogue and practise everyday English and situational language for renting a flat, to ask for and give information, to pronounce /ɑː/, /æ/, to read for gist, to write an email describing your new flat **Vocabulary:** Types of houses (*block of flats, terraced, detached, semi-detached*)	

Culture 3	26
Lesson objectives: To listen and read for specific information, to read for detailed understanding, to talk about royal buildings, to write about a special building **Vocabulary:** Nouns (*head of state, county, gatehouse, office*), Adjective (*powerful*)	

Review 3	27
Lesson objectives: To test/consolidate vocabulary and grammar learnt throughout the unit; to practise everyday English	

Go through the objectives box and tell Ss that these are the topics, skills and activities this unit will cover.

3a

Vocabulary

1 **Aim** **To present vocabulary for rooms in a house**

- Ask Ss to look at the picture of the house and then give them time to answer the questions.
- Explain/Elicit the meanings of any unknown words and then elicit the answers to the questions.

Answer Key

The dining room is on the ground floor downstairs.
The living room is on the ground floor downstairs.
The main bedroom is on the first floor upstairs.
The bathroom is on the first floor upstairs.
The child's room is on the first floor upstairs.
The study is in the attic.
The garage is outside the house.

2 **Aim** **To present vocabulary for furniture and appliances**

- Ask Ss to look at the pictures and say which items belong in which rooms.
- Give Ss time to complete the task.
- Play the recording for Ss to check their answers.

Answer Key

A STUDY
| 2 desk | 3 chair |

B MAIN BEDROOM
| 4 double bed | 5 bedside cabinet |

C BATHROOM
| 6 bath | 8 towel |
| 7 washbasin | 9 toilet |

D CHILD'S ROOM
| 11 single bed | |

E KITCHEN
| 12 cooker | 14 cupboards |
| 13 fridge | 15 sink |

F DINING ROOM
| 16 table and chairs | |

G LIVING ROOM
| 17 sofa | 19 coffee table |
| 18 armchair | |

Reading

3 **Aim** To listen and read for gist

- Ask Ss to look at the pictures.
- Elicit what is special about these houses.
- Play the recording. Ss listen and read to find out.
- Check Ss' answers.

Answer Key

What makes these houses special is that they are under the ground.

- Play the video for Ss and elicit their comments.

Background Information

Guadix is a small city in Southern Spain in the northern foothills of the Sierra Nevada. Around 18,000 people live there.

4 **Aim** To read for specific information (T/F statements)

- Ask Ss to read statements 1-5 and then give them time to read the text again and mark them according to what they read.
- Check Ss' answers around the class.

Answer Key

| 1 F | 2 F | 3 T | 4 F | 5 T |

- Refer Ss to the Word List to look up the meanings of the words in the **Check these words** box.

5 **Aim** To match adjectives to nouns; to consolidate collocations from a text

- Ask Ss to look at the adjectives in bold in the text and complete the collocations with the correct nouns.
- Check Ss' answers.

Answer Key

2	unique cave houses	6	beautiful garden
3	modern furniture and appliances	7	huge bathroom
4	cosy kitchen	8	large bedroom
5	wonderful view	9	spacious living room
		10	pretty homes

6 **Aim** To consolidate new vocabulary through synonyms

- Explain the task and read out the example.
- Give Ss time to complete the task.
- Check Ss' answers.

Answer Key

1 beautiful, pretty   *2 huge, large, spacious*

Speaking & Writing

7 **Aim** THINK To compare your house to a typical cave house

- Explain the task.
- Give Ss time to consider their answers and then write a few sentences comparing their house with a typical cave house.
- Check Ss' answers around the class.

Suggested Answer Key

My house is not like a typical cave house. My house is above ground. My house is only ten years old. It has got a small kitchen, a bathroom and a large dining room. It hasn't got a view of a beautiful garden. My house has got a view of a busy street.

8 **Aim** To group words

- Read out the **Study Skills** box and ask Ss to write the headings into their notebooks.
- Then give Ss time to work in pairs and write the words from Exs. 1 & 2 under the headings.
- Check Ss' answers on the board.

Suggested Answer Key

ROOMS
living room, dining room, kitchen, main bedroom, bathroom, child's room, study, garage

FURNITURE
bookcase, desk, chair, double bed, bedside cabinet, wardrobe, single bed, cupboards, table and chairs, sofa, armchair, coffee table

APPLIANCES
cooker, fridge

OTHER/DECORATION
washbasin, towel, toilet, sink, cushion, bath, pillow, chimney, roof, light, window, curtains, floor, mirror, rug, picture, carpet, door, stairs, wall, garden

9 **Aim** THINK To describe your favourite room

- Explain the task and give Ss time to consider their answers and describe their favourite room.
- Ask various Ss to present their answers to the class including reasons.

Suggested Answer Key

My favourite room is the living room. It is very spacious and the whole family spends a lot of time there together. It has got a big sofa and coffee table. It also has a very comfortable armchair. There are two colourful rugs on the floor and my brother and I usually sit on these and play board games. There are also many family photos

around the room. This is my favourite room because it is very cosy.

3b Grammar in Use

1 a) **Aim** To present/practise *there is/there are – a/an – some/any*

- Ss close their books. Present **there is/there are**. Point to the board and say: *There is a board in the classroom.* Write it on the board. Underline *There is.* Say: *There isn't a computer in the classroom.* Write it on the board. Underline *There isn't.* Ask Ss: *Is there a window in the classroom?* Write it on the board. Say: *There are eight desks in the classroom. There aren't any flowers in the classroom. Are there computers in the classroom?* Then write the sentences on the board. Underline *there are, there aren't* and *Are there.* Say that *there are* is the plural form of *there is.*

- Present **a/an – some/any.** Write on the board: *I have an apple. I have some bread.* Underline *an apple* and *some bread.* Elicit/Explain that nouns like **apple** can be counted, so we call them countable nouns *(e.g. one apple, two apples, three apples, etc).* Ask Ss to look at the second example. Point out that we cannot use **a/an** before the word **bread.** Explain that nouns like **bread** cannot be counted, so we call them uncountable nouns.

- Elicit/Explain the use of **some/any.** Ask Ss to give you examples. Point out that we use **any** in the negative and interrogative and **some** in the affirmative.

- Ss open their books. Read the theory box and then elicit examples from the advert.

Answer Key

Outside there is a garage.
Upstairs there are the bedrooms and the bathrooms.

Background Information

Edgbaston is a suburb in the city of **Birmingham** in the UK. It is famous for being the home of Edgbaston Cricket Ground where Test matches are played. **Birmingham** is a large city in the West Midlands of England. It is the largest city outside London with 1.1 million people living there.

b) **Aim** To practise *there is/there – some/any*

- Explain the task and give Ss time to complete it.
- Check Ss' answers

Answer Key

1 *Are there, there aren't*
2 *Is there, there is*
3 *Is there, there isn't*
4 *Are there, there are*

2 **Aim** To practise *a/an – some/any*

- Give Ss time to complete the sentences referring to the theory box if necessary.
- Check Ss' answers.

Answer Key

1 *a*	5 *an*	9 *a*
2 *some*	6 *any*	10 *an*
3 *any*	7 *some*	
4 *a*	8 *a*	

3 a) **Aim** To practise *there is/there are – a/an – some/any*

- Ask Ss to work in pairs.
- Explain the task and give Ss time to mark the items with a tick or a cross.
- Ss work in pairs and ask and answer following the example.
- Monitor the activity around the class and then ask some pairs to ask and answer in front of the class.

Answer Key

3 *cushions* ✓	10 *single bed* ✗
4 *pillows* ✓	11 *light* ✓
5 *posters* ✗	12 *desk* ✗
6 *lamps* ✓	13 *rug* ✓
7 *sofa* ✗	14 *bookcase* ✗
8 *armchair* ✓	15 *curtains* ✓
9 *double bed* ✓	16 *fireplace* ✗

Answer Key

A: *Are there any cushions?*
B: *Yes, there are. Are there any pillows?*
A: *Yes, there are. Are there any posters?*
B: *No, there aren't. Are there any lamps?*
A: *Yes, there are. Is there a sofa?*
B: *No, there isn't. Is there an armchair?*
A: *Yes, there is. Is there a double bed?*
B: *Yes, there is. Is there a single bed?*
A: *No, there isn't. Is there a light?*
B: *Yes, there is. Is there a desk?*
A: *No, there isn't. Is there a rug?*
B: *Yes, there is. Is there a bookcase?*

A: *No, there isn't. Are there curtains?*
B: *Yes, there are. Is there a fireplace?*
A: *No, there isn't.*

b) **Aim** To practise *there is/there are – a/an – some/any*

- Explain the task and give Ss time to complete it in pairs.
- Monitor the activity around the class.

Suggested Answer Key

A: *The room in the picture has got two bedside cabinets with lamps on them. There are posters on the wall.*
B: *No! There aren't any posters on the wall.*
A: *No, there aren't. There is a big double bed and there aren't any pillows on it.*
B: *No! There are some pillows on it.*
A: *Yes, there are. There are some curtains and a sofa.*
B: *No, there isn't a sofa. There's an armchair.*
A: *Yes, there is.*

Optional Game

Ask Ss to look at their answers to Ex. 1b again. Ss are expected to use *there is/there are* to play this memory game.
e.g. *Team A S1: There is a bed in the bedroom.*
    Teacher: Correct! Team A wins one point.
        T: Very good. Team A gets one point.
Team B S1: There is a desk in the bedroom.
    Teacher: Wrong! Team B doesn't win a point. etc.)

4 **Aim** To present *this/these – that/those*

- Read out the theory box and explain that we use **this/these** for items near us (singular/plural) and **that/those** for items far away from us (singular/plural).
- Demonstrate using items in the classroom.
  e.g. (hold up a pen) This is a pen.
  (Point to something at the back of the classroom.) *That is a picture. etc*

5 **Aim** To practise *this/these – that/those*

- Explain the task and read out the example.
- Give Ss time to complete the task.
- Check Ss' answers.

Answer Key

2 *This is a desk and those are chairs.*
3 *Those are armchairs and this is a single bed.*
4 *These are bookcases and that is a fireplace.*
5 *That is a cooker and this is a bath.*

6 **Aim** To present ordinal numbers

- Play the recording. Ss listen and repeat chorally and/or individually.
- Then elicit which floor each person's flat is on from Ss around the class.

Answer Key

Steve's and Paul's flats are on the 9th floor.
Mary's flat is on the third floor.
Jane's flat is on the first floor.
Tony's and Larry's flats are on the eighth floor.
Sue's and Ann's flats are on the twelfth floor.

Optional Game

Divide the class into two teams. Team A says cardinal numbers [1-12] then team B says the relevant ordinal numbers [first – twelfth], and vice versa.
Each correct match gets one point. The team with the most points is the winner.
e.g. *Team A S1: three.*
    Team B S1: third.
        Teacher: Correct! Team B gets one point.
    Team B S2: ten.
    Team A S2: tenth. etc

7 **Aim** To present and practise prepositions of place

- Ask Ss to study the sketches with the prepositions of place and explain any that Ss are unclear about.
- Then ask Ss to look at the picture and read the text and choose the correct prepositions.
- Check Ss' answers.

Answer Key

1 on	4 on	7 Next to
2 on	5 under	8 in front of
3 in	6 between	9 next to

8 **Aim** To practise prepositions of place

- Explain the task and read out the example.
- Ss work in pairs and ask and answer about items in the picture of the bedroom using the prompts and the correct prepositions of place.
- Monitor the activity around the class and then ask some pairs to ask and answer in front of the class.

Suggested Answer Key

B: *Where's the bed?*
A: *It's in front of the window. Where's the ball?*
B: *It's on the wardrobe. Where's the rug?*
A: *It's on the floor. Where's the wardrobe?*
B: *It's near the window. Where's the pillow?*
A: *It's on the bed. Where's the bedside cabinet?*

B: *It's next to the bed. Where's the window?*
A: *It's behind the bed. Where's the chair?*
B: *It's in front of the desk. Where's the lamp?*
A: *It's on the bedside cabinet.*

9 **Aim** THINK **To design an ideal house**

• Divide the class into small groups and have Ss work together to come up with a design for an ideal house.
• Remind Ss to answer all the questions in the rubric and then ask various groups to present their house to the class.

Suggested Answer Key

Our ideal house has got two floors. On the first floor, there is the main bedroom and two children's bedrooms. There is also a study and a bathroom. The bedrooms are spacious. The main bedroom has got a double bed, a big wardrobe and an armchair. The walls are a grey colour. The children's bedrooms have got single beds, a wardrobe and colourful curtains. In the study, there are two desks, two chairs and carpets on the floor. There are also two bookcases. There are many pictures on the walls.

On the ground floor, there is the kitchen, the living room and the dining room. The kitchen has got a modern cooker, fridge and some cupboards. The dining room has got a big table and eight chairs. The living room has got a brown sofa and an armchair. There is a coffee table and a television. The curtains are yellow and the walls are white.

10 **Aim** **To write an advert**

• Give Ss time to write an advert for their house.
• Refer Ss to the advert on p. 22 to help them.
• Give Ss time to complete the task and then ask various Ss to read their advert to the class.
• Alternatively, assign the task as HW and have Ss read out their adverts in the next lesson.

Suggested Answer Key

This unique house has got three bedrooms, a kitchen, a bathroom, a living room, a dining room and a study. There is a large garden in front of the house. The kitchen, the living room and the dining room are on the ground floor. Upstairs are the bedrooms, the study and the bathroom. This is a great home for all the family.

3c Skills in Action

Vocabulary

1 **Aim** **To present vocabulary for types of houses**

• Play the recording. Ss listen and repeat chorally and/or individually.
• Check Ss' pronunciation and intonation.
• Elicit which types of houses there are in Ss' city/village.

Suggested Answer Key

In my city, there are blocks of flats and detached houses.

Listening

2 **Aim** **To listen for specific information (gap fill)**

• Read out the **Study Skills** box and tell Ss this tip will help them to complete the listening task successfully.
• Ask Ss to read the gapped text and decide which type of word is missing from each gap.
• Then play the recording.
• Ss listen and complete the gaps.
• Check Ss' answers.

Answer Key

1 *12 (a number)*   3 *large (an adjective)*
2 *spacious (an*   4 *garage (a noun)*
   adjective)   5 *month (a noun)*

Everyday English

3 a) **Aim** **To complete a dialogue**

Give Ss time to read the dialogue and then use the sentences to complete the gaps in the dialogue.

Answer Key

1 D   2 E   3 A   4 B   5 C

b) **Aim** **To listen for confirmation**

Play the recording for Ss to check their answers to Ex. 3a.

4 **Aim** **To practise everyday English expressions for renting a flat**

• Explain the task and give Ss time to read through the language box. Then ask Ss to act out a similar dialogue to the one in Ex. 3a in pairs.
• Write this diagram on the board for Ss to follow.

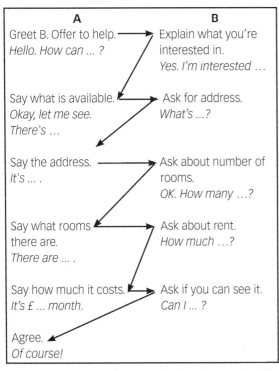

	A	B
	Greet B. Offer to help. *Hello. How can ... ?*	Explain what you're interested in. *Yes. I'm interested ...*
	Say what is available. *Okay, let me see. There's ...*	Ask for address. *What's ...?*
	Say the address. *It's ... .*	Ask about number of rooms. *OK. How many ...?*
	Say what rooms there are. *There are ... .*	Ask about rent. *How much ...?*
	Say how much it costs. *It's £ ... month.*	Ask if you can see it. *Can I ... ?*
	Agree. *Of course!*	

- Monitor the activity around the class and offer assistance as necessary.
- Then ask some pairs to act out their dialogues in front of the class.

Suggested Answer Key

A: *Hello. How can I help you?*
B: *Yes. I'm interested in a flat near the city centre.*
A: *Okay, let me see. There is a nice flat for rent very close to the city centre.*
B: *What's the address?*
A: *It's 12 Greenbank Park.*
B: *OK. How many rooms has it got?*
A: *There are five rooms: two bedrooms, one kitchen, one bathroom and a living room.*
B: *How much is the rent?*
A: *It's £800 per month.*
B: *Can I see it?*
A: *Of course!*

Pronunciation

5 Aim To pronounce /ɑː/, /æ/

- Play the recording. Ss listen and tick the correct boxes.
- Play the recording again with pauses for Ss to repeat chorally and/or individually.

Answer Key

	/ɑː/	/æ/		/ɑː/	/æ/
attic		✓	lamp		✓
garden	✓		armchair	✓	
carpet	✓		flat		✓

Reading & Writing

6 Aim To read for gist

- Direct Ss to the email and read out the rubric.
- Ask Ss to read the text and find out.
- Check Ss' answers.

Answer Key

The email is from Gina. It's for her dad. It's about her new flat.

7 Aim To read for content and structure

- Read out the **Study Skills** box and ask Ss to read the email again.
- Elicit which paragraphs contain which information.

Answer Key

Paragraph one is a description of the flat.
Paragraph two is a description of Gina's room.

8 Aim To present informal language

- Read out the **Writing Tip** box and make sure Ss understand when we use informal language (when we write to someone we know well).
- Then give Ss time to find examples of informal language in the email.
- Check Ss' answers around the class.

Answer Key

Thanks for the... / I'm in my new... / It's on the seventh... / It's got a wonderful... / It's got a large... / ... that's OK. / Can't wait... / Bye for now!

Writing

9 Aim To analyse a rubric

- Ask Ss to read the rubric and then answer the questions.
- Check Ss' answers.

Answer Key

1 *an email*
2 *my Australian friend*
3 *about life in London, my flat and my bedroom*
4 *80 words*

3

10 a) **Aim** **To prepare for a writing task**

- Read out the **Study Skills** box and ask Ss to copy the spidergram into their notebooks.
- Then give them time to complete it with information about their flat/house.
- Check Ss' answers by writing a spidergram on the board and complete it with answers from Ss around the class.

Suggested Answer Key

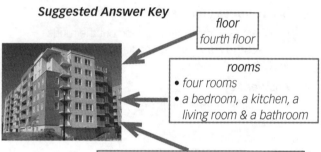

floor
fourth floor

rooms
- *four rooms*
- *a bedroom, a kitchen, a living room & a bathroom*

bedroom/description
- *a double bed, a bedside cabinet, a mirror, a wardrobe, paintings*
- *a green wall, a yellow and green carpet*

b) **Aim** **To write an email describing your new flat**

- Give Ss time to write their email using their answers to Ex. 10a and following the plan.
- Ask various Ss to share their answers with the class.
- Alternatively, assign the task as HW and check Ss' answers in the next lesson.

Suggested Answer key

Hi Krista,

Thanks for your email! London's great! My new flat is on the fourth floor of a big block of flats near a beautiful park. It's got four rooms: a large living room and kitchen, a bathroom and a spacious bedroom.

My bedroom's great. The walls are green. It's got a double bed, a bedside cabinet, a small wardrobe, a mirror, paintings on the walls and a yellow and green carpet on the floor.

How are you? Drop me a line soon.

Bye for now,

Jennifer

Values

Ss try to explain the quotation in their mother tongue. If Ss have difficulty, explain the quotation. Ask Ss to memorise this quotation and check in the next lesson.

The quotation means that a house is just a building, but a home is a place where people who love one another live together.

Culture 3

Listening & Reading

1 **Aim** **To listen and read for specific information**

- Ask Ss to look at the pictures and read out the question.
- Play the recording. Ss listen and read the texts to find out.

Answer Key

Windsor Castle is in (the county of) Berkshire, England.
Buckingham Palace is in London (next to Hyde Park).
St James's Palace is in London (next to St James's Park).

- Play the video for Ss and elicit their comments.

2 **Aim** **To read for specific information**

- Ask Ss to read the texts again and then match the buildings to the questions.
- Check Ss' answers.

Answer Key

1 C	3 A	5 C
2 B, C	4 B, C	

- Refer Ss to the Word List to look up the meanings of the words in the **Check these words** box.

Speaking & Writing

3 **Aim** **THINK** **To talk about royal buildings**

Ask various Ss around the class to say which of the buildings they think is the most impressive and why.

Suggested Answer Key

Buckingham Palace is the most impressive because it is in the centre of London and it has got 775 rooms with 52 royal bedrooms, 188 staff bedrooms and 78 bathrooms.

4 **Aim** **ICT** **To write about a special building**

- Explain the task and give Ss time to work in pairs and research online and find out information about a special building for the head of state in their country to live in. Collect information under the headings.
- Ask various Ss to present their information to the class.
- Alternatively, assign the task as HW and ask Ss to present their information in the next lesson.

Suggested Answer Key

Location: *The White House, Washington D.C., USA*
Age: *over 200 years old*
Size: *6 floors*

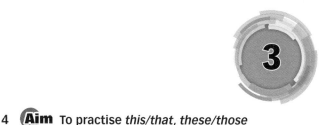

Rooms: 132 rooms, 15 bedrooms, 35 bathrooms,
3 kitchcns

The White House is the home of the President of the United States of America and it's in Washington, D.C. It is over 200 years old and has got 6 floors. It has got 132 rooms, with 15 bedrooms, 35 bathrooms and 3 kitchens.

Review 3

Vocabulary

1 **Aim** **To practise vocabulary for rooms, furniture & appliances**

- Explain the task.
- Give Ss time to complete it.
- Check Ss' answers.

Answer Key

1 pillow	4 bathroom	7 sofa
2 garden	5 cushion	8 window
3 garage	6 stairs	9 cooker

2 **Aim** **To practise vocabulary from the unit**

- Explain the task.
- Give Ss time to complete it.
- Check Ss' answers.

Answer Key

1 towels, mirror	3 armchairs, cushions
2 wardrobe, rug	4 pillows, curtains

Grammar

3 **Aim** **To practise grammar from the unit**

- Explain the task.
- Give Ss time to complete it.
- Check Ss' answers.

Answer Key

1 is a, isn't a	4 isn't a, are
2 is a, aren't any	5 is a, isn't a
3 isn't an, is a	6 are some, isn't a

4 **Aim** **To practise *this/that, these/those***

- Explain the task.
- Give Ss time to complete it.
- Check Ss' answers.

Answer Key

1 This, those   2 These, that   3 Those, this

5 **Aim** **To practise prepositions of place**

- Explain the task.
- Give Ss time to complete it.
- Check Ss' answers.

Answer Key

1 behind		6 in
2 on		7 opposite
3 on		8 between
4 next to		9 under
5 in front of		10 above

Everyday English

6 **Aim** **To match questions and answers**

- Explain the task.
- Give Ss time to complete it.
- Check Ss' answers.

Answer Key

1 B   2 C   3 A   4 E   5 D

Competences

Ask Ss to assess their own performance in the unit by ticking the items according to how competent they feel for each of the listed activities.

A Values: National pride

1 **Aim** **To listen and read for specific information**
- Ask Ss to look at the flags in the pictures.
- Elicit why the colours and symbols are important.
- Play the recording. Ss listen and read the text to find out.

Answer Key

The different colours and symbols on flags are important because they are the values the people in each country have got. They are also national symbols.

- Play the video for Ss and elicit their comments.

2 **Aim** **To read for detailed understanding**
- Ask Ss to copy the table into their notebooks.
- Give Ss time to read the text again and then ask them to complete the table.
- Ask Ss to then choose two flags and explain to the class what the colours and symbols mean.

Answer Key

colours	meaning	symbols	meaning
red	life, courage, strength	the Sun	energy
blue	water, sky, wisdom, honesty	stars	power
green	nature, peace, harmony	stripes	freedom

Suggested Answer Key

The flag of Nigeria has got green and white stripes. The green is for nature, peace and harmony. The stripes are a symbol of freedom.

The flag of Myanmar has got yellow, green and red stripes and it has got a white star. The green is for nature, peace and harmony. The red is for life, courage and strength. The stripes are a symbol of freedom and the star is a symbol of power.

3 **Aim** **ICT** **To prepare a poster**
- Ask Ss to work in small groups. They research online and collect information about other colours and symbols on flags and their meanings.
- Then give Ss time to use this information to prepare a poster.
- Ask various groups of Ss to present their posters to the class.
- Alternatively, assign the task as HW and ask Ss to present their posters in the next lesson.

Answer Key

colours	meaning	symbols	meaning
white	peace	dragon	monarchy
yellow	the Sun, wealth	circle	the Sun
orange	joy, strength	eagle	courage, strength

The flag of Kazakhstan is blue. It has got a yellow sun and a yellow eagle. Yellow means the Sun and wealth. The eagle is a symbol of courage and strength.

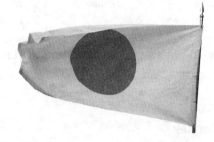

The flag of Japan is white and red. It has got a red circle. White means peace and the circle is a symbol of the Sun.

The flag of Bhutan is yellow and orange. It has got a white dragon. Yellow means the Sun and wealth and orange means joy and strength. The dragon is a symbol for the monarchy.

4 **Aim** **THINK** **To design a flag**
- Ask Ss to work in small groups and come up with a flag for their sports team.
- Give Ss time to consider their answers and decide on the colours, symbols and meanings.

Suggested Answer Key

5 **Aim** To present a flag

- Ask each group to choose a representative who then presents the flag to the class.
- After all the flags have been presented, have the class vote for the one with the best idea

Suggested Answer Key

Hello. I'm Diana Abdulov.

Look at the flag. Do you know what this animal is? … That's right, it's an eagle! This is our team's flag. Let me tell you all about it!

The flag of our team is orange and it has got an eagle. The colour and the symbol show our team's values. Our team is very happy so our flag is orange because orange means joy.

The eagle is a symbol of strength and courage. Our team wants to be strong and have courage, so we have got an eagle on our flag.

The flag is our team's symbol and it has got a special meaning for us. Thank you for listening.

Public Speaking Skills A

1 a) **Aim** To present a public speaking task

Ask Ss to read the task.

b) **Aim** To analyse a model public speaking task

- Play the recording. Ss listen and read the model.
- Ask Ss to copy the spidergram into their notebooks and complete it.
- Play the recording again if necessary.

Suggested Answer Key

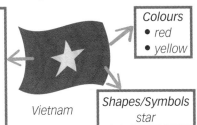

Meaning
• red: life
• yellow: people of Vietnam
• five points of star: soldiers, traders, students, farmers & workers

Colours
• red
• yellow

Vietnam

Shapes/Symbols
star

2 **Aim** To present opening techniques

Ask Ss to read the theory and then elicit which opening technique is used in the model.

Answer Key

Opening technique: using humour/a riddle (You can see it on public buildings during national celebrations in Vietnam. What is it? … That's right! It's the flag of Vietnam.)

3 **Aim** To give a presentation

- Ask Ss to copy the spidergram from Ex. 1b into their notebooks and give them time to complete it with information about the flag of their country.
- Then ask Ss to use their notes and the model to help them prepare a presentation on their country's flag.
- Ask various Ss to give their presentation to the class.
- Alternatively, assign the task as HW and have Ss give their presentations in the next lesson

Suggested Answer Key

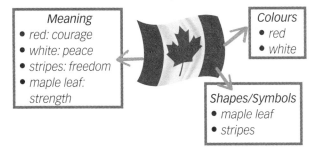

Meaning
• red: courage
• white: peace
• stripes: freedom
• maple leaf: strength

Colours
• red
• white

Shapes/Symbols
• maple leaf
• stripes

Hello. I'm Lisa Smith.

Aren't we all proud of our country's flag? Well, I am! This is the flag of my country, Canada.

The colours and symbols on the flag of Canada show the country's values. Canada is peaceful, so the flag is white because white means peace. Also, the people of Canada have got courage, so our flag is red because red means courage. The people of Canada are free, so the flag has got two stripes on the outside. Finally, the red maple leaf is a symbol for strength. So, Canada is a very strong country!

The flag is my country's national symbol and it has got a special meaning to me. I'm proud of my country's flag. I think the flags of your country have got a special meaning to you, too. Thank you for listening.

4 Busy days

Topic
In this unit, Ss will explore the topics of daily routines, free-time activities, days of the week, telling the time and sports

4a Reading & Vocabulary	30-31
Lesson objectives: To listen and read for gist, to read for specific information (matching headings to paragraphs and T/F statements), to learn vocabulary for daily routines, to learn the days of the week, to practise telling the time, to listen for specific information, to write an email **Vocabulary:** Daily routines *(wake up early, have a shower, get dressed, have breakfast, catch the bus to college, have a break for lunch, finish college, go jogging, do homework, work part-time, go back home, chat with friends online, have dinner, go to bed);* Times of the day *(in the morning, at midday, in the afternoon, in the evening);* The days of the week *(Monday, Tuesday, Wednesday, Thursday, Friday, Saturday, Sunday);* Telling the time *(o'clock, [a] quarter to, half past, [a] quarter past, twenty to, twenty past);* Nouns *(animal shelter, break, walk, countryside);* Phrasal verb *(care for);* Adjectives *(tiring, satisfied);* Phrase *(catch the bus)*	

4b Grammar in Use	32-33
Lesson objectives: To learn the present simple, to learn adverbs of frequency, to learn *love/like/hate + -ing*, to learn prepositions of time	

4c Skills in Action	34-35
Lesson objectives: To learn vocabulary for free-time activities, to listen for specific information (T/F statements), to act out a dialogue and practise everyday English for making arrangements, to pronounce /s/, /z/, /ɪz/, to read for cohesion and coherence, to write a blog entry about your typical Sunday **Vocabulary:** Free-time activities *(listen to music, read a book, go dancing, go on a picnic, go to the mall, go to the cinema, visit museums, meet friends, watch a film, do yoga, play football, go to the library)*	

Culture 4	36
Lesson objectives: To listen and read for specific information, to compare and contrast sports, to write about popular sports in your country **Vocabulary:** Sports *(baseball, cricket, lacrosse, rugby, curling, ice hockey, surfing, skiing, snowboarding);* Noun *(competition),* Verb *(take part);* Adjectives *(annual, official)*	

Review 4	45
Lesson objectives: To test/consolidate vocabulary and grammar learnt throughout the unit; to practise everyday English	

Go through the objectives box and tell Ss that these are the topics, skills and activities this unit will cover.

4a

Vocabulary

1 **Aim** **To present vocabulary for daily routines**
- Ask Ss to look at the pictures.
- Play the recording.
- Ss listen and repeat chorally and/or individually.
- Check Ss' intonation and pronunciation.

Reading

2 a) **Aim** **To listen and read for specific information**
- Read out the question and play the recording.
- Ss listen and read to find out.
- Check Ss' answers.

Answer Key

Valeria doesn't go to work every morning. She goes to work every Monday, Wednesday and Friday and works from 5:00 pm to 9:00 pm.

- Play the video for Ss and elicit their comments.

b) **Aim** **To suggest a title for the text**

Give Ss a minute to come up with a title for the text and elicit suggestions from Ss around the class.

Suggested Answer Key

A Day in the Life of Valeria López

3 a) **Aim** **To identify the main idea of a paragraph (matching headings to paragraphs)**
- Ask Ss to read headings A-E and then give them time to read the text again and match the headings to the paragraphs (1-4).
- Check Ss' answers around the class.

Answer Key

1 D	2 B	3 E	4 A

- Refer Ss to the Word List to look up the meanings of the words in the **Check these words** box.

b) **Aim** To read for specific information (T/F statements)

- Give Ss time to look through the text again and mark the statements according to what they read.
- Check Ss' answers and then elicit explanations for the words in bold.

Answer Key

1 T 2 F 3 F 4 T

Suggested Answer Key

part-time – for less than 8 hours a day
break – a time to rest
care for – take care of
satisfied – content; happy enough

Speaking

4 **Aim** To present and practise telling the time

- Go through the table and explain how we tell the time using the clock faces.
- Read out the *Note* and explain *am* and *pm*.
- Ask Ss to work in pairs and look at the clock faces a-e and the digital clocks f-i and ask and answer questions to practise telling the time following the example.
- Monitor the activity around the class and assist as necessary.

Answer Key

b A: What's the time?
  B: It's (a) quarter past seven./It's seven fifteen.

c A: What time is it?
  B: It's half past nine./It's nine thirty.

d A: What's the time?
  B: It's half past two./It's two thirty.

e A: What time is it?
  B: It's nine o'clock./It's nine.

f A: What's the time?
  B: It's half past four./It's four thirty.

g A: What time is it?
  B: It's ten to three./It's two fifty.

h A: What's the time?
  B: It's (a) quarter past ten./It's ten fifteen.

i A: What time is it?
  B: It's twenty past nine./It's nine twenty.

Optional Game

Play a game with Ss. Divide the class into two teams. Write a time on the board. In teams, Ss tell the time in both ways. Each correct answer gets one point. The team with the most points is the winner.

e.g. Teacher: [T writes 7:30 on the board].
  Team A S1: Half past seven or seven thirty.
  Teacher: Very good. One point for Team A. Team B now. etc

5 **Aim** To present and practise the days of the week

- Play the recording with pauses for Ss to listen and repeat chorally and/or individually.
- Check Ss' intonation and pronunciation.
- Elicit answers to the questions.

Answer Key

Weekdays = Monday, Tuesday, Wednesday, Thursday, Friday
(Weekend = Saturday, Sunday)

Listening

6 **Aim** To listen for specific information and present a daily routine

- Ask Ss to copy the headings into their notebooks and then play the recording.
- Ss listen and make notes under the headings.
- Then ask various Ss to present Tony's daily routine to the class.

Suggested Answer Key

In the morning: wakes up at 7:30; has a shower; gets dressed; has breakfast; catches bus to college at 8:15
At noon: has a break for lunch
In the afternoon: finishes college at 4 pm; works at a café 5-8
In the evening: does homework at 9 pm; watches TV; goes to bed at 11 pm

Tony has a really busy daily schedule on weekdays. He wakes up quite early in the morning, at 7:30, and then he has a shower and gets dressed. Then, he eats his breakfast and catches the bus to college at 8:15. At noon, he has a break for lunch and he finishes college at 4 pm in the afternoon. Then, Tony works at a café from 5 to 8. At 9 pm, he goes home and does his homework and then he watches some TV. Then, he goes to bed at about 11 pm.

37

7 **Aim** **To talk about your daily routine**

Ask various Ss to tell the class about their daily routine using the headings in Ex. 6 to help them.

Suggested Answer Key

In the morning, I wake up at 7:15 and have a shower. Then, I eat my breakfast before I go to school. At noon, we have a break and I eat my lunch. In the afternoon, I do my homework or play football with my friends. In the evening, I usually watch TV. I go to bed at 10 pm.

Writing

8 **Aim** **To write an email**

- Explain the task and give Ss time to write their email following the directions and using the email skeleton to help them.
- Ask various Ss to read their email to the class.

Suggested Answer Key

Hi Alan!

Hope you're well. Life here is great. In the morning, I wake up at 6:30. I have a shower, get dressed and I catch the bus to school at 7:00. School starts really early here! In the afternoon, I play rugby in a club. In the evenings, I usually watch TV with my family. What do you usually do every day?

Write back,

Greg

4b Grammar in Use

1 **Aim** **To present the present simple (affirmative)**

- Present the present simple. Say: *I go to school.* Write it on the board.
- Underline *go* and explain that this verb is in the present simple. Point to a S, say: *You go to school.* Then write it on the board. Underline *go*. Gesture to yourself and the class, say: *We go to school.* Then write it on the board. Underline *go*. Point to a group of Ss, say: *They go to school.* Then write it on the board. Underline *go*.
- Explain that we use the present simple for habits & routines (actions we do every day) and permanent states (something that is true all the time). Explain that we form the present simple in the affirmative with personal pronoun + bare infinitive.
- Direct Ss' attention to the table and ask various Ss to read the examples aloud.
- Then elicit examples from the dialogue.

Answer Key

permanent states: *She lives at number 14, Elm Park. It's never open after 2:30*

repeated actions: *On Thursdays, she has football practice ..., so she always leaves quite early, at four o'clock.*

daily routines: *She usually eats in the cafeteria at noon.*

2 **Aim** **To practise the present simple affirmative (third-person singular)**

- Point to a S. Say: *He/She likes Maths.* Then write it on the board. Underline *likes*. Explain that the 3rd person singular usually takes ***-s***.
- Explain the task and give Ss time to complete it.
- Check Ss' answers.

Answer Key

1	goes	3	loves	5	flies
2	works	4	washes	6	enjoys

3 **Aim** **To practise the present simple**

- Explain the task and read out the example.
- Give Ss time to complete the sentences referring to the theory box if necessary.
- Check Ss' answers.

Answer Key

2	catches	5	goes	8	has
3	works	6	tidies	9	meets
4	finishes	7	watches	10	likes

Optional Game

Play a game to drill Ss. Say various verbs in the first person singular. Ss, in teams, say the third-person singular. Check spelling on the board. Each correct sentence gets 1 point. The team with the most points is the winner.

e.g.   Teacher: I brush.

   Team A S1: He brushes (B-R-U-S-H-E-S).

   Teacher: Correct! Team A wins a point. I fix.

   Team B S1: He fixes (F-I-X-E-S). etc

4 **Aim** **To present the present simple (negative, interrogative & short answers)**

- Present the present simple negative. Write on the board: *I do not/don't drive.* and *She does not/doesn't drive.* Underline *I do not/don't* in the first sentence and *She does not/doesn't* in the second sentence. Explain that we use **I/you/we/they do not/don't** and **he/she/it does not/doesn't** to form the present simple negative.
- Present the present simple interrogative and short answers. Say then write on the board: *Do I work in a school? – Yes, I do.* and *Does he work in a school? No, he doesn't.* Explain that we use **Do I/you/we/**

they and Does he/she/it to form questions in the present simple. Focus Ss' attention on the position of *do/does* (before the personal pronoun). We answer in short form with *Yes/No, I/you/we/they do/don't and he/she/it does/doesn't*.

- Ask Ss questions to check understanding.
  T: Do you work?
  S1: No, I don't. /Yes, I do.
  T: Does your mother work?
  S2: No, she doesn't./Yes, she does.
  T: Do we live in …?
  S3: Yes, we do. etc
- Ask Ss to read the table and then elicit examples from the dialogue.
- Elicit how we form the present simple negative.

Answer Key

present simple negative: I don't think
present simple interrogative: Hi Kim, do you know where Lucy is? What time does she leave college? Why don't you drop it off...? Does she live near here?
short answer: Yes, she does.
We form the present simple negative by writing do/ does not or don't/doesn't before the verb in its base form.

5 Aim To practise the present simple negative, interrogative & short answers

- Explain the task and give Ss time to complete it.
- Check Ss' answers around the class.

Answer Key

2 *Does, does*	5 *does, don't*
3 *Does, doesn't*	6 *Do, don't*
4 *Do, do*	7 *Do, don't*

6 a) Aim To present adverbs of frequency

- Read out the theory box and explain when we use adverbs of frequency.
- Elicit examples from the dialogue.

Answer Key

She usually eats in the cafeteria at noon.
It's never open after 2:30.
..., so she always leaves quite early ... .

b) Aim To practise adverbs of frequency

- Explain the task and read out the example.
- Give Ss time to complete the task.
- Check Ss' answers.

Suggested Answer Key

I rarely have football practice on Sundays.
I sometimes go jogging on Sundays.

I usually meet friends on Sundays.
I often go to the cinema on Sundays.
I always play baskctball on Sundays.
I sometimes eat out on Sundays.
I sometimes watch TV on Sundays.
I never cook dinner on Sundays.
I usually chat with friends online on Sundays.

7 Aim To talk about free-time and daily activities

- Explain the task and ask Ss to talk in pairs about how often they do the listed activities, following the example and using the adverbs of frequency.
- Monitor the activity around the class and then give Ss time to write a short paragraph about their partner's activities.
- Ask various Ss to read their paragraphs to the class.

Suggested Answer Key

A: How often do you go to the theatre?
B: I go to the theatre once a month.
A: How often do you cook?
B: I cook every Saturday.
A: How often do you go for long walks?
B: I go for long walks three times a month.
A: How often do you go out with your family?
B: I go out with my family once a week.
A: How often do you play computer games?
B: I never play computer games.
A: How often do you watch TV?
B: I watch TV every day.
A: How often do you meet your friends?
B: I meet my friends five days a week.

Tania goes swimming twice a week, and she goes to the theatre once a month. She cooks every Saturday and she goes for long walks three times a month. She goes out with her family once a week. She never plays computer games, but she watches TV every day and she meets her friends five days a week.

8 a) Aim To present love/like/hate + -ing

- Read out the theory box and explain that we use the verbs *love/like/hate* with *-ing* forms. Read out the examples.
- Elicit an example from the dialogue on p. 32.

Answer Key

She likes spending her break there.

b) Aim To practise love/like/hate + -ing

- Explain the task and read out the example.
- Give Ss time to complete the sentences.

• Check Ss' answers around the class.

Answer Key

2 *likes listening*
3 *hates going*
4 *doesn't like waking up*
5 *loves watching*

c) **Aim** To practise *love/like/hate* + *-ing* using personal examples

• Ask Ss to talk in pairs and practise *love/like/ hate* + *-ing*.
• Elicit answers from Ss around the class.

Suggested Answer Key

I love playing video games. I like reading books. I don't like going to the theatre. I hate cooking dinner.

9 **Aim** To present prepositions of time

Read out the theory box and elicit examples from the dialogue on p. 32.

Answer Key

at noon; On Thursdays; at four o'clock

Optional Game

Divide the class into two teams. Say days, months, times, etc. In teams, Ss have to add *at*, *in* or *on*. Each correct answer gets one point. The team with the most points is the winner.
e.g.   Teacher: Sunday.
       Team A S1: On Sunday.
          Teacher: Very good. Team A wins one point. March.
       Team B S1: In March.
          Teacher: Correct. One point to Team B. Eight o'clock.
       Team A S2: At eight o'clock.
          Teacher: Well done. etc

10 **Aim** To practise prepositions of time; to compare two people's daily routine

• Give Ss time to read the text and fill in the gaps with the appropriate preposition of time.
• Check Ss' answers.

Answer Key

1 at   3 at   5 At   7 at   9 On
2 in   4 at   6 In   8 On

Suggested Answer Key

Henry gets up at half past four in the morning, but my teacher gets up at half past seven. Henry has breakfast at half past six; Mr Smith has breakfast at half past eight before he goes to school. Mr Smith doesn't have lunch at noon like Henry. He has lunch at half past one. Then, he teaches until four o'clock. Like Henry,

sometimes Mr Smith watches TV, but he doesn't have a shower in the evening. He does that in the morning. He usually goes to bed around eleven o'clock, not at nine like Henry. Mr Smith doesn't like playing football, but he usually goes to the gym on Saturdays. Then, on Sundays, he often takes his family out to lunch.

4c Skills in Action

Vocabulary

1 a) **Aim** To present vocabulary for free-time activities

• Play the recording. Ss listen and repeat chorally and/or individually.
• Check Ss' pronunciation and intonation.

b) **Aim** To talk about your free time

• Ask Ss to ask and answer questions in pairs about their free-time activities.
• Monitor the activity around the class and then ask some pairs to tell the class.

Suggested Answer Key

A: *What do you usually do in your free time?*
B: *I meet friends and do yoga.*

Listening

2 **Aim** To listen for specific information (T/F statements)

• Ask Ss to read statements 1-4.
• Play the recording. Ss listen and mark the statements according to what they hear.
• Check Ss' answers.

Answer Key

1 T   2 F   3 F   4 T

Everyday English

3 **Aim** To listen and read for gist

• Ask Ss to read the phrases and then guess what the dialogue is about.
• Play the recording. Ss listen and read to find out.

Answer Key

The dialogue is about two friends arranging to do something on a Saturday.

4 **Aim** To match synonymous phrases

• Ask Ss to read the phrases and then read the dialogue again and find the synonymous ones.
• Check Ss' answers.

Answer Key

I'm afraid not. – Not really.
Probably. – I think so.
Meet you there. – See you there.
Make sure you're on time. – Don't be late.

5 **Aim** **To practise everyday English expressions for making arrangements**

- Explain the task and give Ss time to read through the language box. Then ask Ss to act out a similar dialogue to the one in Ex. 3 in pairs using the ideas.
- Write this diagram on the board for Ss to follow.

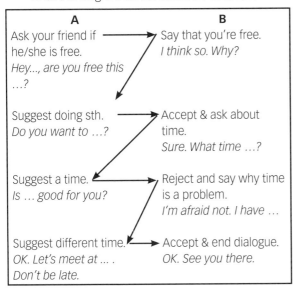

A	B
Ask your friend if he/she is free. *Hey…, are you free this …?*	Say that you're free. *I think so. Why?*
Suggest doing sth. *Do you want to …?*	Accept & ask about time. *Sure. What time …?*
Suggest a time. *Is … good for you?*	Reject and say why time is a problem. *I'm afraid not. I have …*
Suggest different time. *OK. Let's meet at … . Don't be late.*	Accept & end dialogue. *OK. See you there.*

- Monitor the activity around the class and offer assistance as necessary.
- Then ask some pairs to act out their dialogues in front of the class.

Suggested Answer Key

A: Hey Lisa, are you free this Monday?
B: I think so. Why?
A: Do you want to go to the cinema with me?
B: Sure. What time do you want to meet?
A: Is seven o'clock good for you?
B: I'm afraid not. I have a violin lesson until seven thirty.
A: OK. Let's meet at the cinema at eight, then. Don't be late.
B: OK. See you there.

Pronunciation

6 **Aim** **To pronounce** /s/, /z/, /ɪz/

- Play the recording. Ss listen and tick the correct boxes.
- Play the recording again with pauses for Ss to repeat chorally and/or individually.

Answer Key

	/s/	/z/	/ɪz/		/s/	/z/	/ɪz/
lives		✓		writes	✓		
walks	✓			washes			✓
goes		✓		watches			✓

Reading & Writing

7 a) **Aim** **To read for cohesion and coherence**

- Read out the **Study Skills** box and explain that this tip will help Ss to complete the task successfully.
- Direct Ss to the blog and give Ss time to read it and write an appropriate word to complete the gaps.

b) **Aim** **To listen for confirmation**

Play the recording for Ss to check their answers to Ex. 7a.

Answer Key

1	with	3	In	5	we	7	do
2	and	4	an	6	an		

8 **Aim** **To present opening/closing techniques**

- Read out the **Writing Tip** box and then elicit which technique Christy uses to start/end her blog.
- Check Ss' answers around the class.

Answer Key

Christy starts her article with a general thought ('Everyone loves Sunday') and by addressing the reader directly ('You see'). She ends her article by addressing the reader directly ('How do you spend your Sundays?').

Writing

9 **Aim** **To analyse a rubric; to prepare for a writing task**

- Ask Ss to read the rubric and look at the underlined words.
- Read out the **Study Skills** box. Then give Ss time to think of ideas and copy and complete the spidergram in their notebooks.
- Check Ss' answers.

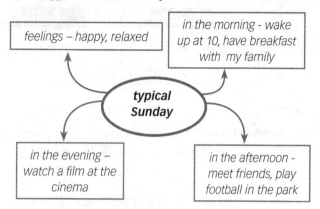

- feelings – happy, relaxed
- in the morning - wake up at 10, have breakfast with my family
- typical Sunday
- in the evening – watch a film at the cinema
- in the afternoon - meet friends, play football in the park

10 (Aim) **To write a blog entry about your typical Sunday**

- Give Ss time to write their blog entry using their notes from Ex. 9 and the plan to help them.
- Ask various Ss to share their answers with the class.
- Alternatively, assign the task as HW and check Ss' answers in the next lesson.

Suggested Answer Key

My typical Sunday

I really like Sundays, but who doesn't?
In the morning, I wake up at 10:00 and have breakfast with my family. In the afternoon, I meet my friends and we play football in the park. In the evenings, I often watch a film at the cinema with my friends. Sometimes, they come to my house and we watch a DVD. Sundays always make me feel really happy and relaxed.

Values

Ss try to explain the quotation in their mother tongue. If Ss have difficulty, explain the quotation. Ask Ss to memorise this quotation and check in the next lesson.
The quotation means that we should have a positive attitude every day.

Culture 4

Listening & Reading

1 (Aim) **To present vocabulary for sports; to talk about sports**

- Ask Ss to look at the pictures. Play the recording with pauses for Ss to listen and repeat chorally and/ or individually.
- Check Ss' intonation and pronunciation.
- Then ask various Ss around the class to answer the questions.

Suggested Answer Key

I play rugby and my friends play ice hockey. My favourite sport is rugby.

2 (Aim) **To listen and read for specific information**

- Read out the question.
- Play the recording. Ss listen and read the text to find out.

Answer Key

In Australia football, rugby and cricket are popular. So are surfing and swimming.
In Canada snowboarding, skiing, curling, rugby, cricket and baseball are popular. Ice hockey and lacrosse are popular, too.

- Refer Ss to the Word List to look up the meanings of the words in the **Check these words** box.

Background Information

Australia is a large continent and a country in the southern hemisphere. The capital city is Canberra. It has got a population of over 24 million people. It has got a wide range of ecosystems and wildlife.

Canada is a large country in North America. It has got ten provinces and three territories. It is surrounded by the Atlantic, Pacific an Arctic Oceans on three sides and has got a land border with the USA. The capital city is Ottawa and the population is over 35 million people.

Speaking & Writing

3 (Aim) (THINK) **To compare and contrast sports**

Ask various Ss around the class to offer comparisons and contrasting points about the sports people play in Australia and Canada.

Suggested Answer Key

In both Australia and Canada people play cricket and rugby. In Australia surfing is popular, but not in Canada. In Canada baseball, lacrosse, curling, ice hockey, skiing and snowboarding are popular, but they aren't popular in Australia.

4 (Aim) ICT **To write about popular sports in your country**

- Explain the task and give Ss time to work in pairs and research online to collect information about popular sports in their country.
- Give Ss time to use their information to write a short text.

- Then ask various Ss to read their texts to the class.
- Alternatively, assign the task as HW and ask Ss to read their texts in the next lesson.

Suggested Answer Key

I'm from China and in my country football, basketball, badminton and table tennis are popular sports. People play sports from a very young age in China and fitness is very important. People play sports for fun and they like watching professional sports events. Some of the world's great table tennis players are from China, such as Ma Long and Ding Ning.

Review 4
Vocabulary

1 **Aim** To practise vocabulary for daily routines

- Explain the task.
- Give Ss time to complete it.
- Check Ss' answers.

Answer Key

1 wakes	3 has	5 chats
2 gets	4 catches	

2 **Aim** To practise telling the time

- Explain the task.
- Give Ss time to complete it.
- Check Ss' answers.

Answer Key

2 It's half past eight. It's eight thirty.
3 It's (a) quarter to six. It's five forty-five.
4 It's (a) quarter past nine. It's nine fifteen.
5 It's twenty to three. It's two forty.
6 It's twenty-five past four. It's four twenty-five.

3 **Aim** To practise vocabulary for free-time activities

- Explain the task.
- Give Ss time to complete it.
- Check Ss' answers.

Answer Key

1 read	4 play	7 go	10 go
2 visit	5 watch	8 go	
3 meet	6 do	9 listen	

Grammar

4 **Aim** To practise the present simple and adverbs of frequency

- Explain the task.
- Give Ss time to complete it.

- Check Ss' answers.

Answer Key

1 always works	4 sometimes washes
2 is usually	5 never tidies
3 often play	

5 **Aim** To practise the present simple interrogative & short answers

- Explain the task.
- Give Ss time to complete it.
- Check Ss' answers.

Answer Key

1 Does, does	4 Do, do
2 Do, don't	5 Do, do
3 Does, doesn't	

6 **Aim** To practise prepositions of time

- Explain the task.
- Give Ss time to complete it.
- Check Ss' answers.

Answer Key

1 at	2 at	3 On	4 in	5 on

7 **Aim** To practise *like/love/hate* + *-ing* form

- Explain the task.
- Give Ss time to complete it.
- Check Ss' answers.

Answer Key

1 love having	4 likes chatting
2 likes going	5 doesn't like going
3 hates cleaning	

Everyday English

8 **Aim** To match questions and answers

- Explain the task.
- Give Ss time to complete it.
- Check Ss' answers.

Answer Key

1 C	2 D	3 A	4 E	5 B

Competences

Ask Ss to assess their own performance in the unit by ticking the items according to how competent they feel for each of the listed activities.

5 Birds of a feather

Go through the objectives box and tell Ss that these are the topics, skills and activities this unit will cover.

5a

Reading

1 **Aim** **To listen and read for specific information (T/F statements)**

- Read out the statements 1-4 and play the recording.
- Ss listen and read and mark them according to the texts. Then elicit answers to question from Ss around the class.
- Check Ss' answers.

Answer Key

1 F   2 T   3 F   4 T

Suggested Answer Key

The purpose of the text is to inform readers about two kinds of animals the Pohatu Marine Reserve protects.

- Play the video for Ss and elicit their comments.

2 **Aim** **To read for specific information (answer questions)**

- Give Ss time to read the texts again and answer the questions.
- Check Ss' answers around the class.
- Then elicit explanations for the words in bold.

Answer Key

1 Dolphins can swim very well.
2 Dolphins live in warm seas in many different parts of the world.
3 Dolphins live for about fifty/50 years.
4 Penguins are unusual birds because they can't fly.
5 Penguins have got thick feathers to keep them warm.

Suggested Answer Key

smile: *to make a happy expression with the corners of the mouth turned up*
weigh: *to be a certain number of kilos*
intelligent: *clever*
easily: *without much effort*
friendly: *nice*
lay eggs: *to produce oval-shaped shells with babies inside*
thick: *having a lot, dense*
warm: *quite hot*
funny: *strange*

- Refer Ss to the Word List to look up the meanings of the words in the **Check these words** box.

Background Information

Akaroa is a small town on Banks Peninsula in the Canterbury region of the South Island of New Zealand.

New Zealand is an island country in the southwestern Pacific Ocean. There are two main islands called the North Island and the South Island. The capital city is Wellington and most people speak English. It has got a population of about 4.8 million people.

Speaking

3 **Aim** **To complete a table and compare animals**

- Give Ss time to complete the table referring to the texts as necessary.
- Then ask various Ss around the class to offer comparisons between the two animals.

Answer Key

	Dolphins	Penguins
kind of animal:	mammals	birds
unusual because:	not fish but live in water	can't fly
they can:	swim very well, learn how to play games	swim very well
they've got:	grey skin, a big smile, fins and a tail	short legs, a short tail, thick feathers
they weigh:	70-500 kg	20 kg
they live:	in warm seas in many parts of the world	on the ice and in the seas around Antarctica
they eat:	fish	fish
they live for:	about 50 years	about 20 years

Suggested Answer Key

Dolphins are unusual because they are mammals that live in water. Penguins are unusual because they are birds, but they can't fly. Both dolphins and penguins can swim very well, but only dolphins can learn how to play games. Dolphins have got grey skin, a big smile, fins and a tail. Penguins have got a tail, too and they've got short legs and thick feathers.
Dolphins weigh a lot more than penguins – penguins weigh about 20kg and dolphins weigh between 70-500kg. Dolphins live in warm seas, but penguins live on the ice and in the seas around Antarctica. Both dolphins and penguins eat fish. Dolphins live longer than penguins – they live for about 50 years – but penguins only live for about 20 years.

Vocabulary

4 **Aim** **To present vocabulary for wild animals**

- Read out the **Study Skills** box and ask Ss to look at the pictures.
- Play the recording with pauses for Ss to repeat chorally and/or individually.
- Check Ss' pronunciation and intonation.

5 **Aim** **To classify animals**

- Ask Ss to look up the definitions of mammals, birds and reptiles in their dictionaries.
- Then give Ss time to classify the animals in Ex. 4.
- Check Ss' answers around the class.

Answer Key

Mammals: warm-blooded animals that give birth to live young and feed them on milk
Birds: warm-blooded animals that lay eggs, can fly and have feathers and a beak
Reptiles: cold-blooded animals that lay soft-shelled eggs and usually have dry, scaly skin

Mammals: zebra, bear, giraffe, monkey, elephant
Birds: flamingo
Reptiles: crocodile, snake

6 **Aim** **To present and practise vocabulary for parts of animals' bodies**

- Ask Ss to read the list of words and look at the pictures.
- Give Ss time to label the parts of the animals' bodies.
- Check Ss' answers.

Answer Key

1	feathers	3	neck	5	paws
2	beak	4	fur	6	tail

Speaking

7 a) **Aim** **To talk about parts of animals' bodies**

Read out the list of phrases and ask various Ss to use them to talk about the animals' bodies in Ex. 4.

Suggested Answer Key

The bear and the monkey have got thick fur.
The bear and the flamingo have got a short tail.
The crocodile has got a big mouth.
The giraffe and the flamingo have got long necks.
The elephant has got very big ears.
The snake has got a long body.
The flamingo has got feathers.
The flamingo has got wings.
The bear, the crocodile and the monkey have got claws.
The flamingo and the giraffe have got long legs.
The elephant has got a trunk.

b) **Aim** To describe animals

Ask various Ss to choose an animal from Ex. 4 and describe it to the class.

Suggested Answer Key

The flamingo has got a long neck, a beak, a tail, feathers, wings and very long legs.

8 **Aim** **THINK** To talk about your favourite animal

Ask various Ss to tell the class about their favourite animal and give reasons.

Suggested Answer Key

My favourite animal is the lion. I like it because it's very beautiful and strong and it can run very fast. Also, lions are very clever animals.

Writing

9 **Aim** **ICT** To write a fact file about an animal

- Explain the task and give Ss time to research online and find out about an animal from Ex. 4 and collect information under the headings in Ex. 3.
- Give Ss time to use the information to write their fact file.
- Ask various Ss to read their texts to the class.

Suggested Answer Key

Snakes	
kind of animal:	reptiles
unusual because:	Some give birth to live young.
they can:	swim, climb
they've got:	dry scaly skin
they weigh:	up to 250kg
they live:	in places all over the world except Antarctica, Iceland, Ireland, etc
they eat:	small animals/birds
they live for:	up to 50 years

Snakes are reptiles with long bodies and no legs. They are unusual because some of them lay eggs and some of them give birth to live young. They can swim well and climb. They have got dry, scaly skin and they can weigh up to 250kg. They live in places all over the world except Antarctica, Iceland, Ireland and some other countries. They eat many different types of small animals and birds and they live for about fifty years.

5b Grammar in Use

1 **Aim** To present modal verbs *must/mustn't, can/can't/could*

- Present the modal verbs.
- Explain that we use **must** to express obligation/duty and we use **mustn't** to express prohibition.
- Explain that we use **can/can't** to talk about permission.
- Explain that we use **could** to talk about permission in a more formal way.
- Direct Ss' attention to the table and ask various Ss to read the examples aloud.
- Then elicit examples from the webpage.

Answer Key

Visitors mustn't bring pets to the park.
Visitors must pay an entrance fee.
Visitors can take photos of the animals.
Visitors can bring their own food and have a picnic in the park.
Visitors can't drive through the park.
Visitors can come any day between 9:00 am and 5:00 pm.

Background Information

San Diego is a large city in California in the USA. About 1.4 million people live there. It is famous for its zoo which has over 3,700 animals. It was a pioneer in the idea of keeping animals in the open-air without cages to re-create natural animal habitats.

2 **Aim** To listen for specific information; to practise *must/mustn't*

- Explain the task and read out the example.
- Play the recording.
- Give Ss time to complete the table and then allow further time for Ss to write sentences for each item using **must/mustn't**.
- Check Ss' answers around the class.

Answer Key

Shark tank cleaners	must	mustn't
work alone		✓
enter a tank with sharks in it	✓	
clean tanks after meals	✓	
do over 1,000 dives a year	✓	
stay in the water very long		✓
use strong soap		✓

Shark tank cleaners must enter a tank with sharks in it.

5

Shark tank cleaners must clean tanks after meals.
Shark tank cleaners must do over 1,000 dives a year.
Shark tank cleaners mustn't stay in the water very long.
Shark tank cleaners mustn't use strong soap.

3 **Aim** To practise *must/mustn't*

- Explain the task and give Ss time to complete the sentences using the signs and referring to the theory box if necessary.
- Check Ss' answers.

Answer Key

1 *mustn't*	3 *mustn't*
2 *must*	4 *must*

4 **Aim** To practise *can/can't/could*

- Explain the task and read out the example.
- Give Ss time to complete the task in pairs and then ask some pairs to ask and answer in front of the class.

Answer Key

2 A: *Could I pick up a snake?*
  B: *No, you can't.*
3 A: *Could I go home early?*
  B: *Yes, you can.*
4 A: *Can I borrow your camera?*
  B: *No, you can't.*
5 A: *Can I open the window?*
  B: *Yes, you can.*
6 A: *Could I drive through the safari park?*
  B: *No, you can't.*

5 **Aim** To practise *must/mustn't, can/can't/could*

Elicit various sentences from Ss around the class.

Suggested Answer Key

You must hand your assignments in on time.
You mustn't be late for lessons/lectures.
You can't use your mobile phone in lessons/lectures.
I can watch TV at home.
I can relax at home.

6 **Aim** To present question words

- Read out the theory box and explain we use **what** to ask about things, **where** to ask about place, **when** to ask about time, **why** to ask about reason, **how long** to ask about length or time, **how tall** to ask about height, **how much** to ask about quantity and **how many** to ask about number and quantity.
- Elicit examples from the webpage.

Answer Key

Where is the Safari Park?
When is the park open?
How much does a ticket cost?

7 **Aim** To practise question words

- Explain the task and read out the example.
- Give Ss time to complete the task.
- Check Ss' answers and explain/elicit the meanings of any unknown words.

Answer Key

2 *How long*	5 *How much*	8 *What*
3 *How many*	6 *When*	
4 *Where*	7 *Why*	

8 **Aim** To practise question words

- Explain the task and go through the example.
- Give Ss time to complete it and then check their answers.

Suggested Answer Key

Where do kangaroos live? (Australia)
How tall are kangaroos? (about two metres tall)
How much do kangaroos weigh? (about sixty kilos)
How many back legs have kangaroos got? (two)
What can kangaroos do? (They can jump very high.)
When do kangaroos sleep? (during the day)
What do kangaroos eat? (leaves)
Where do kangaroos carry their babies? (in a pouch)
How long do kangaroos live? (for fifteen to twenty years)

9 **Aim** To talk about animals; to practise question words

- Explain the task and give Ss time to complete it in pairs.
- Monitor the activity around the class and then ask some pairs to ask and answer in front of the class.

Suggested Answer Key

1 A: *What is this animal?*
  B: *It's a sea lion.*
  A: *How much does it weigh?*
  B: *It weighs about 250 kilos.*
  A: *What does it eat?*
  B: *It eats fish.*
  A: *What can it do?*
  B: *It can swim very well.*
  A: *Where does it live?*
  B: *It lives in the Pacific Ocean.*
  A: *How long does it live?*
  B: *It lives for about 15 years.*

2 A: What is this animal?
   B: It's a tiger.
   A: How much does it weigh?
   B: It weighs about 200 kilos.
   A: What does it eat?
   B: It eats deer and monkeys.
   A: When does it sleep?
   B: It sleeps during the day.
   A: Where does it live?
   B: It lives in the forests in India.
   A: How long does it live?
   B: It lives for about 15 years.

10 **Aim** **ICT** **To create a quiz**

- Ask Ss to work in small groups and research online to collect information about various mammals, birds and reptiles and prepare a quiz.
- Then ask Ss to swap their quizzes with another group and try to complete it.
- Alternatively, assign the task as HW and have Ss swap quizzes in the next lesson.

Suggested Answer Key

1 How many legs does a ladybird have? (6)
2 Where do elephants live? (in Africa and southeast Asia)
3 What do caterpillars eat? (leaves)
4 When do lions sleep? (during the day)
5 How long do flamingos live? (25-30 years)
6 Why do kangaroos have strong back legs? (to help them jump)
7 How tall is an elephant? (about 3.3 m tall)
8 How long is a giraffe's neck? (about 1.8 m long)

5c Skills in Action

Vocabulary

1 **Aim** **To present vocabulary for farm animals**

- Ask Ss to look at the pictures. Play the recording. Ss listen and repeat chorally and/or individually.
- Check Ss' pronunciation and intonation.

Optional game

Divide the class into two teams. Allow Ss two or three minutes to memorise the names. Ss close their books. Ask questions, as in the examples below. The team which gives the correct answer first gets one point. The team with the most points is the winner.

e.g.   T: What animal is No. 6?
   Team A S1: Is it a rooster?
              T: No, it isn't.
   Team B S1: Is it a duck?
              T: No, it isn't.

Team A S2: It is a goose?
         T: Yes, it is. Team A wins one point. etc

Listening

2 **Aim** **To listen for specific information (T/F statements)**

- Ask Ss to read the statements 1-6 and then play the recording.
- Ss listen and mark the statements according to what they hear.
- Check Ss' answers.

Answer Key

1 T   2 T   3 F   4 F   5 F   6 T

3 **Aim** **To talk about farm animals**

- Explain the task and read out the example.
- Then have Ss ask and answer questions in pairs using the sizes and the animals in Ex. 1.
- Monitor the activity around the class and then ask some pairs to ask and answer in front of the class.

Suggested Answer Key

A: What is this animal?
B: It's a duck.
A: What colour is it?
B: It's white.
A: How big is it?
B: It's small.
A: How big is its beak?
B: It's quite big.
A: How long are its legs?
B: They're quite short. etc

Everyday English

4 **Aim** **To listen and read for gist**

- Ask Ss to read the first and the last exchange in the dialogue. Elicit what the dialogue is about and when Tony is free.
- Play the recording. Ss listen and read to find out.

Answer Key

The dialogue is about someone who would like to volunteer at a farm.
Tony is free on Saturday mornings.

5 **Aim** **To practise everyday English expressions for asking for/giving information; to act out a dialogue asking for information**

- Explain the task and give Ss time to read through the Useful Language box. Then ask Ss to act out a similar dialogue to the one in Ex. 4 in pairs.

48

- Write this diagram on the board for Ss to follow.

A	B
Greet B. Offer to help. → *Good ... . How can ...?*	Greet A. State what you're interested in. *Hello. I'm ... .*
Explain you need help. Ask for B's name. *Great! We need ... .* *What's ...?*	Say your full name. *I'm ... .*
Introduce yourself. Ask when B is available. *I'm ... . When ...?*	Say when you are free. *I'm free ... .*
Ask if B is available another day. *Can you also ...?*	Say if you are available or not. *Yes, .../I'm afraid I ... .*
Ask when B can start. *When can ... .*	Say when you can start. *This ... .*
Tell B what time to come & who to ask for. *Great! Come at ... .*	Thank A. *Thank you.*

- Monitor the activity around the class and offer assistance as necessary.
- Then ask some pairs to act out their dialogues in front of the class.

Answer Key

A: *Good morning. How can I help?*

B: *Hello. I'm interested in volunteering at the animal shelter.*

A: *Great! We need lots of help with the animals here. What's your name?*

B: *I'm Anna Smith.*

A: *I'm Nathan Marks, the manager. When are you available?*

B: *I'm free on Saturday and Sunday mornings.*

A: *Can you also come on Friday afternoons?*

B: *Yes, I can.*

A: *When can you start?*

B: *This weekend if it's OK with you.*

A: *Great! Come at 8:30 am on Saturday and ask for Rachel.*

B: *Thank you.*

Pronunciation

6 **Aim** To pronounce /e/, /ɜː/

- Play the recording with pauses for Ss to repeat chorally and/or individually.

- Check Ss' pronunciation and intonation.

Reading & Writing

7 **Aim** To read for gist

- Direct Ss to the form and give Ss time to read it and answer the questions.
- Check Ss' answers.

Answer Key

The form is a volunteer application form.

Michael Dawson writes the form. He is a student and he is interested in volunteering to help with cat care and fundraising events.

8 a) **Aim** To identify the main idea of a paragraph (matching headings)

- Ask Ss to read the headings A-E and give Ss time to read the form again and fill in the gaps with the correct heading.
- Check Ss' answers.

Answer Key

1 C	2 E	3 A	4 D	5 B

b) **Aim** THINK To express an opinion

- Give Ss time to study the application form again and consider their answers.
- Ask various Ss around the class to share their opinion with the rest of the class giving their reasons.

Suggested Answer Key

Yes, I think Michael Dawson is a good applicant because he has got previous experience working with animals. He has also got some useful skills. For example, he can drive a car and he knows first aid.

9 **Aim** To analyse a model application form

- Read out the ***Writing Tip*** box and refer Ss to the application form again.
- Read the rubric aloud and elicit answers to the questions. Check Ss' answers around the class.

Answer Key

He uses three full sentences. (I can drive a car and I know first aid. I am also interested in doing fundraising events. I am available Mondays 5 to 8 pm and Sundays 12 to 5 pm.)

He ticks boxes to show his age, employment status and interests. (✓ student)

He gives notes to show his education and volunteering experience. (A levels in Chemistry and English)

Writing

10 **Aim** To write/fill in a volunteer application form

- Explain the task. Then give Ss time to write and fill in a volunteer application form using the headings from Ex. 8a and the model in Ex. 7 to help them.
- Check Ss' answers.
- Alternatively, assign the task as HW and check Ss' answers in the next lesson.

Suggested Answer Key
PERSONAL DETAILS
Title: Miss
Name: Anna Carrillo
Address: Lamas Carvajal 12, Martín de la Jaran, Sevilla
Postcode: 41658
Telephone: 795 076 456
Email: m.carrillo@email.com
Age: … 16-17 yrs … 18-24 yrs ✓ 25+ yrs

STUDIES; EXPERIENCE
Education:
- *International Baccalaureate: 35 points*
- *now in third year of university studying Biology*
Volunteering experience:
- *six months working as a vet's assistant*
- *two weeks fundraising for a wildlife charity*
Skills: I can drive a car.

EMPLOYMENT
… full-time   … part-time … retired
… unemployed   ✓ student

INTERESTS
✓ dog walking   ✓ cat care
… charity shop   … helping hands
✓ other (please say what) I am interested in looking after animals at my home.

AVAILABILITY
I am available Mondays, Wednesdays and Fridays 4 pm-9 pm.

Signature: Anna Carrillo

Values

Ss try to explain the quotation in their mother tongue. If Ss have difficulty, explain the quotation. Ask Ss to memorise this quotation and check in the next lesson.
The quotation means that when we give something of ourselves such as when we volunteer our skills, kindness and time to others, then we get much more back in return which may include feelings of satisfaction, usefulness and achievement.

Culture 5

Listening & Reading

1 **Aim** To listen and read for specific information

- Ask Ss to look at the pictures and read out the questions.
- Play the recording. Ss listen and read the texts to find out.

Answer Key

The animals are from Australia. They are special because you cannot find them in other parts of the world.

- Play the video for Ss and elicit their comments.
- Refer Ss to the Word List to look up the meanings of the words in the **Check these words** box.

2 **Aim** To read for specific information (multiple matching)

- Ask Ss to read the questions 1-4 and then ask Ss to read the texts again and complete the task.
- Check Ss' answers.

Answer Key

1 D   2 A   3 B   4 C

Speaking & Writing

3 **Aim** **THINK** To talk about Australian animals

Ask various Ss around the class to say what they found interesting about the animals in the texts.

Suggested Answer Key

I think it's very interesting that emus lay green eggs, that kangaroos keep their babies in a pouch, that koalas only eat eucalyptus leaves and that a platypus is a mammal that lays eggs.

4 **Aim** **ICT** To write about unique animals in your country

- Explain the task and give Ss time to work in small groups. Ss can research online and collect information about unique animals in their country.
- Give Ss time to use their information to write a short magazine article or prepare a digital presentation.
- Then ask various Ss to read their magazine article or give a presentation to the class.
- Alternatively, assign the task as HW and ask Ss to read their articles or give their presentations in the next lesson.

Suggested Answer Key

ITALY'S UNIQUE ANIMALS

Apennine chamois – *It is a mammal that has got two horns on its head. The females and babies live in groups, but the males live alone. They feed on grass and plants. They can climb up and down steep hills and mountains very well.*

Spectacled salamander – *It is a reptile with black and red skin. It is unusual because it has four toes on its back legs instead of five. It sleeps in the day and the only time they go into the water is to lay eggs.*

Marsican brown bear – *It is a large mammal that is up to 2 metres tall. It weighs up to 230 kg and lives for about 20 years. It feeds on many different foods, for example, plants, fruit, honey, insects and small animals. Its favourite food is berries and it can smell them very well with its nose.*

Clouded Apollo butterfly – *This is an insect that can grow wings up to 7 cm. It has got clear wings with black spots on them. They live in meadows and near trees and flowers. Their favourite flowers are red and purple ones!*

Review 5

Vocabulary

1 **Aim** **To practise vocabulary for parts of animals' bodies**

- Explain the task.
- Give Ss time to complete it.
- Check Ss' answers.

Answer Key

1 D	2 C	3 B	4 E	5 F	6 A

2 **Aim** **To practise vocabulary for parts of animals' bodies**

- Explain the task.
- Give Ss time to complete it.
- Check Ss' answers.

Answer Key

1 stripes   3 fur   5 mouths
2 claws   4 neck

3 **Aim** **To practise vocabulary relating to animals**

- Explain the task.
- Give Ss time to complete it.
- Check Ss' answers.

Answer Key

1 reptiles   3 farm   5 wings
2 manes   4 mammals

4 **Aim** **To practise vocabulary relating to animals**

- Explain the task.
- Give Ss time to complete it.
- Check Ss' answers.

Answer Key

1 keep   3 lay   5 looks
2 weigh   4 has

Grammar

5 **Aim** **To practise modals verbs**

- Explain the task.
- Give Ss time to complete it.
- Check Ss' answers.

Answer Key

1 can, can   3 must, mustn't
2 Could, can't

6 **Aim** **To practise question words**

- Explain the task.
- Give Ss time to complete it.
- Check Ss' answers.

Answer Key

1 What   5 How long
2 Where   6 Why
3 How long   7 How many
4 How much   8 When

Everyday English

7 **Aim** **To match questions and answers**

- Explain the task.
- Give Ss time to complete it.
- Check Ss' answers.

Answer Key

1 E	2 D	3 B	4 C	5 A

Competences

Ask Ss to assess their own performance in the unit by ticking the items according to how competent they feel for each of the listed activities.

6 Come rain or shine

Topic	
In this unit, Ss will explore the topics of weather, seasons, months, activities and clothes	

6a Reading & Vocabulary	46-47
Lesson objectives: To learn vocabulary for weather, months & seasons, to talk about the weather, to listen for specific information (multiple matching), to read for specific information (T/F/DS), to compare the weather in three places, to write a blog post **Vocabulary:** Weather (*rainy, cloudy, windy, freezing cold, snowy, cold, foggy, warm, sunny, blowing, raining, shining, snowing, fog*); Months (*January, February, March, April, May, June, July, August, September, October, November, December*); Seasons (*winter, spring, summer, autumn*); Activities (*sailing a boat, sightseeing, holding an umbrella, snowboarding*), Nouns (*waterproof jacket, sand*); Adjective (*strange*); Phrase (*in fact*)	

6b Grammar in Use	48-49
Lesson objectives: To learn the present continuous, to compare the present simple and the present continuous, to write an email	

6c Skills in Action	50-51
Lesson objectives: To learn vocabulary for clothes, to listen for specific information, to describe clothes, to act out a dialogue and practise everyday English expressions for shopping for clothes; to pronounce /n/, /ŋ/, to read for specific information, to write a postcard **Vocabulary:** Clothing (*blouse, boots, scarf, trousers, cap, belt, dress, sandals, hat, top, jacket, skirt, tights, high-heeled shoes, shirt, suit, tie, shoes, jacket, gloves, jeans, T-shirt, shorts, socks, trainers*)	

Culture 6	52
Lesson objectives: To listen and read for specific information, to compare the climates in two cities, to create a calendar showing the weather **Vocabulary:** Nouns (*desert, protection*); Verb (*pack*)	

Review 6	53
Lesson objectives: To test/consolidate vocabulary and grammar learnt throughout the unit; to practise everyday English	

6a

Vocabulary

1 **Aim** **To present vocabulary related to weather**
- Go through the phrases in the list and explain/elicit the meanings of any unknown ones.
- Ask Ss to look at the photos and match the phrases to the weather in the photos.
- Check Ss' answers around the class.

Answer Key

A   cold and foggy
B   warm and sunny
C   freezing cold and snowy
D   rainy, cloudy and windy

2 **Aim** **To present vocabulary related to the weather**
- Ask Ss to read the sentences (1-4). Explain/Elicit the meanings of any unknown words in bold and then ask Ss to match them to the photos in Ex. 1.
- Check Ss' answers.

Answer Key

1 D   2 B   3 C   4 A

3 a) **Aim** **To present/revise and practise the months**
- Give Ss time to fill in the missing months and then check Ss' answers.
- If necessary, drill Ss by saying a month and then having Ss say the following month (e.g. T: March S1: April)

Answer Key

February – March – May – July – October

b) **Aim** **To present/revise the seasons**
Read out the question and elicit which months belong to which season from Ss around the class.

Suggested Answer Key

In my country, the winter months are December, January and February. The spring months are March, April and May. The summer months are June, July and August. The autumn months are September, October and November.

4 **Aim** To talk about the weather/seasons

- Ask Ss to work in pairs and ask and answer questions about the weather in different seasons following the example.
- Monitor the activity around the class and offer assistance as necessary.

Suggested Answer Key

B: What's the weather like in autumn?
A: It's cold and foggy. What's the weather like in winter?
B: It's freezing cold and snowy. What's the weather like in spring?
A: It's rainy, cloudy and windy.

5 a) **Aim** To present vocabulary for seasonal activities

- Explain/Elicit the meaning of any unknown words and then have Ss match the activities to the photos.
- Check Ss' answers.

Answer Key

1 B   2 A   3 D   4 C

b) **Aim** To describe pictures

- Have Ss describe the pictures using the vocabulary from Exs. 1-4, as in the example.
- Elicit descriptions from Ss around the class.

Suggested Answer Key

In photo B it's warm and sunny. The sun is shining and Mark is sailing a boat.
In photo C it's freezing cold and snowing. Laura is snowboarding.
In photo D, the wind is blowing and it's raining. Nancy is holding an umbrella.

Reading & Listening

6 **Aim** To listen for specific information

- Read out the statements 1-3 and play the recording.
- Ss listen and read and match the weather to the places.
- Check Ss' answers.

Answer Key

1 B   2 C   3 A

Background Information

Thailand is a country in Southeast Asia. The capital city is Bangkok and the population is about 69 million people. The language is Thai and the currency is the Baht.

Norway is a country in Scandinavia that borders Sweden to the east, Finland and Russia to the northeast and the Skagerrak Strait to the south. The capital city is Oslo and the population is 5.3 million people. Norway is one of the oldest still existing kingdoms in Europe.

The Maldives is an island nation in the Indian Ocean. The capital city is Malé and the population is around 440,000. It is a popular tourist destination and the smallest country in Asia.

7 **Aim** To skim a text

- Ask Ss to read the text quickly and focus only on the words relating to weather and clothes and make a note of them.
- Check Ss' answers around the class.

Answer Key

Weather: freezing cold, snow, a bit strange, it's warm, but it's raining, fantastic, It's very hot and the sun's shining., There isn't a cloud in the sky.
Clothes: heavy coat, hats and gloves, waterproof jackets

- Play the video for Ss and elicit their comments

8 **Aim** To read for specific information (T/F/DS)

- Read out the **Study Skills** box and explain that this tip will help Ss to complete the task successfully.
- Ask Ss to read the statements 1-6.
- Give Ss time to read the texts again and mark the statements according to what they read.
- Check Ss' answers around the class.
- Then elicit explanations for the words in bold.

Answer Key

1 T   2 DS   3 T   4 DS   5 F   6 T

Suggested Answer Key

freezing cold: *very cold*
in fact: *actually*
inside: *indoors, not outside*
strange: *odd*
Luckily: *Fortunately*
waterproof: *made with material that does not let water in*
sand: *a substance like powder you can see on beaches*

- Refer Ss to the Word List to look up the meanings of the words in the **Check these words** box.

Speaking

9 **Aim** To compare the weather in three places

- Play the recording. Ss listen and read the texts.

- Then ask Ss to compare the weather in the three places.
- Elicit comparisons from Ss around the class.

Suggested Answer Key

The weather is different in all three places. In Norway, it's freezing cold and there's snow. In Thailand, the weather is warm, but it's raining. In the Maldives, the weather is hot and sunny.

Writing

10 Aim THINK **To write a blog post**

- Ask Ss to imagine that they are Willis Weathers, the weather reporter, and ask them to write a blog entry about the weather in their country using the paragraphs in the texts as a model.
- Ask various Ss around the class to read out their blog entries.

Suggested Answer Key

Greetings from France! This is Willis Weathers and today I'm visiting Paris. The tourists aren't so lucky today because it's windy and it's raining. Luckily, I'm wearing a waterproof jacket and I have got an umbrella, so I can still see all the sights! I love it here!

6b Grammar in Use

1 Aim To present the present continuous (affirmative & negative)

- Present the present continuous.
- Explain that we form the present continuous affirmative with subject pronoun/noun + **am/is/are** + main verb + **-ing**. We form the present continuous negative with subject pronoun/noun + **am not/isn't/aren't** + main verb + **-ing**.
- Explain that we use this tense to talk about actions which are happening now or at the moment of speaking and for fixed arrangements in the near future.
- Direct Ss' attention to the theory box and have them study it and complete the rule.
- Then elicit examples from the text message.

Answer Key

Missing from the rule: *- ing*
Examples in the text: *Amelia and I aren't working, we are planning, we're taking*

2 Aim To practise forming the present continuous verb form

- Explain the task and give Ss time to complete it.
- Check Ss' answers around the class.

Answer Key

1	reading	7	fishing
2	sunbathing	8	skiing
3	shining	9	buying
4	doing	10	having
5	running	11	jogging
6	making	12	visiting

3 Aim To practise the present continuous (affirmative & negative)

- Explain the task and read out the example.
- Give Ss time to look at the pictures and correct the remaining sentences following the example.
- Check Ss' answers.

Answer Key

2 *No! Ann isn't playing games on her mobile. She's reading.*
3 *No! The dog isn't sleeping. It's running.*
4 *No! Peter isn't swimming. He's sunbathing.*
5 *No! Tom and Alex aren't having a barbecue. They're fishing.*

4 Aim To practise the present continuous (affirmative)

- Explain the task and read out the example.
- Give Ss time to complete the task and then check Ss' answers.

Answer Key

2	is/'s shining	5	is/'s buying
3	are/'re enjoying	6	is/'s taking
4	are/'re visiting		

Background Information

Lisbon is the capital and largest city in Portugal. It is one of the oldest cities in the world and has many historic buildings. It has a population of around 2.9 million people.

5 Aim To present the present continuous (interrogative & short answers)

- Present the present continuous interrogative.
- Explain that we form the present continuous interrogative with **am/is/are** + subject pronoun/noun + main verb + **-ing**. We form short answers with **Yes/No, I am [not], he/she/it/ is/isn't, we/you/they are/aren't**.
- Have Ss study the table and then elicit how we form the present continuous interrogative. Then elicit examples from the text message on p. 48.

Suggested Answer Key

*We form the interrogative of the present continuous by using the verb **to be** in the interrogative form and adding -ing to the base form of the main verb.*
***Example in the text:** Are you doing*

6 (Aim) **To practise the present continuous (interrogative & short answers)**

- Explain the task and give Ss time to complete it.
- Check Ss' answers around the class.

Answer Key

1 Is, she isn't
2 Are, they are
3 Are, I'm not/we aren't
4 Is, he is
5 Am, you aren't
6 Are, we are

7 (Aim) **To listen to audio cues and practise the present continuous interrogative & short answers**

- Explain the task and read out the example.
- Play the recording and have Ss tick the activities they hear.
- Then have Ss ask and answer questions in pairs following the example.
- Check Ss' answers and explain/elicit the meanings of any unknown words.

Answer Key

2 drive a car ✓
3 swim ✓
4 play computer games ✓
5 ride a motorbike ✓
6 play the guitar ✓
7 run ✓

Suggested Answer Key

B: *Is Stella having a shower?*
A: *No, she isn't. She's driving a car. Are Bob and Keith sleeping?*
B: *No, they aren't. They're swimming. Are they listening to music?*
A: *No, they aren't. They're playing computer games. Is James riding a horse?*
B: *No, he isn't. He's riding a motorbike. Is she playing the piano?*
A: *No, she isn't. She's playing the guitar. Are they walking?*
B: *No, they aren't. They're running.*

8 (Aim) **To compare the present simple and the present continuous**

- Explain/Elicit that we use the present simple for habits and daily routines and we use the present continuous for actions happening now, at the moment of speaking.

- Read the examples aloud and then ask Ss to complete the rules.
- Check Ss' answers and then elicit examples from the text message on p. 48.

Suggested Answer Key

*We use **the present simple** to talk about habits and daily routines.*
*We use **the present continuous** to talk about actions happening now, at the moment of speaking.*
Examples in the text in the present continuous: *Are you doing, Amelia and I aren't working, We are planning, we're taking.*
Examples in the text in the present simple: *Do you want to come, We usually go, Do you want me to come.*

9 (Aim) **To practise the present simple and the present continuous**

- Explain the task and read out the example.
- Give Ss time to complete the task following the example.
- Check Ss' answers.

Answer Key

2 Betty usually watches TV on Saturday morning. Right now, she is shopping for clothes.
3 James usually goes jogging in the morning. Right now, he is riding his bike.
4 Ben usually listens to music in the afternoon. Right now, he is reading a book.

10 (Aim) **To practise the present simple and the present continuous**

- Explain the task and give Ss time to complete it.
- Check Ss' answers.

Answer Key

1 are studying
2 are staying
3 rains
4 is snowing
5 go
6 put on
7 walk
8 is
9 are
10 is making
11 Are you enjoying
12 do you do

Background Information

Denmark is a small country in northern Europe. Its population is about 5.7 million people and its currency is the krone. It is a Scandinavian country and the capital city is Copenhagen. It has a monarchy and a prime minister.

11 **Aim** THINK **To write an email**

- Explain the task and give Ss time to compose an email in response to Alfie's email in Ex. 10.
- Remind Ss to include all the points in the rubric.
- Ask various Ss to read out the emails to the class.
- Alternatively, assign the task as HW and have Ss read out their emails in the next lesson.

Suggested Answer Key

Hi Alfie,

I'm in Rome. I am studying Italian on an exchange programme. I'm staying at my aunt's house. The weather's beautiful. It's warm and sunny. It almost never rains here! In the mornings, I go to my Italian lessons. In the afternoons, I walk about the city and take pictures. Life is exciting here and the people are very friendly. Anyway, I've got to go. My aunt is making pizza and I'm hungry!

Write back,

Tony

6c Skills in Action

Vocabulary

1 **Aim** **To present vocabulary for clothes**

- Ask Ss to look at the pictures.
- Then give Ss time to complete the task. Explain/ Elicit the meanings of any unknown words.
- Check Ss' answers.

Answer Key

1	scarf	3	blouse	5	boots
2	trousers	4	belt	6	cap

Optional game

Choose a person from the pictures. Say: *I spy someone. Who is it?* Ss ask questions to find the person.

e.g. S1: *Are they wearing a T-shirt?*

   T: *No, they aren't.*

   S2: *Are they wearing a suit?*

   T: *Yes, they are.*

   S3: *Is it D?*

   T: *Yes, it is.*

Choose another person and play the game again. Appoint a S to begin the game. Ss take turns guessing. Continue the game for a few rounds.

Listening

2 **a)** **Aim** **To listen for specific information**

- Ask Ss to look at the pictures again and then play the recording.

- Ss listen and number the pictures in the order they are described in the recording.
- Check Ss' answers.

Answer Key

1 F	2 C	3 A	4 D	5 B	6 E

b) **Aim** **To describe clothes**

Ask various Ss around the class to describe the clothes of the people in the pictures.

Suggested Answer Key

A *She is wearing a blue dress with a blue scarf and sandals.*

B *She is wearing a black top, a hat, a cardigan, white trousers and red sandals.*

C *She is wearing a green jacket, a colourful blouse, a black skirt, tights and high-heeled shoes.*

D *He is wearing a dark suit, a shirt, a belt, a grey tie and shoes.*

E *He's wearing a shirt, jeans, gloves, boots and a jacket.*

F *He is wearing a T-shirt, shorts, white trainers, socks and a cap.*

GAME

3 **Aim** **To describe clothes**

- Play the game according to the directions in the rubric.
- Continue as long as time allows.

Suggested Answer Key

A: *He's wearing blue jeans, a red T-shirt and a green jacket.*

B: *It's John!*

A: *That's right.*

B: *She's wearing a pink skirt, a black T-shirt and black trainers.*

C: *It's Lisa!*

B: *That's right. etc*

Everyday English

4 **a)** **Aim** **To read for cohesion and coherence; to listen for confirmation**

- Ask Ss to read the dialogue and think of an appropriate word/phrase to complete each gap.
- Play the recording. Ss listen and check their answers.

Answer Key

1	can	3	Do you have
2	small	4	What

56

b) **Aim** **To act out a dialogue shopping for clothes**

- Explain the task and ask Ss to act out a similar dialogue to the one in Ex. 4a in pairs using the clothes in the pictures.
- Write this diagram on the board for Ss to follow.

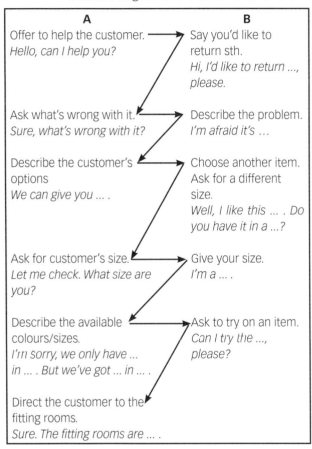

A	B
Offer to help the customer. *Hello, can I help you?*	Say you'd like to return sth. *Hi, I'd like to return ..., please.*
Ask what's wrong with it. *Sure, what's wrong with it?*	Describe the problem. *I'm afraid it's …*
Describe the customer's options *We can give you … .*	Choose another item. Ask for a different size. *Well, I like this … . Do you have it in a …?*
Ask for customer's size. *Let me check. What size are you?*	Give your size. *I'm a … .*
Describe the available colours/sizes. *I'm sorry, we only have … in … . But we've got … in … .*	Ask to try on an item. *Can I try the …, please?*
Direct the customer to the fitting rooms. *Sure. The fitting rooms are … .*	

- Monitor the activity around the class and offer assistance as necessary.
- Then ask some pairs to act out their dialogues in front of the rest of the class.

Suggested Answer Key

A: *Hello, can I help you?*
B: *Hi, I'd like to return this shirt, please.*
A: *Sure, what's wrong with it?*
B: *I'm afraid it's too small for me.*
A: *We can give you a refund, or you can pick another item.*
B: *Well, I like this shirt. Do you have it in a bigger size?*
A: *Let me check. What size are you?*
B: *I'm a large.*
A: *I'm sorry, we only have medium in blue. But we've got large in grey and red.*
B: *Can I try the grey one, please?*
A: *Sure. The fitting rooms are over there.*

A: *Hello, can I help you?*
B: *Hi, I'd like to return this skirt, please.*
A: *Sure, what's wrong with it?*
B: *I'm afraid it's too small for me.*
A: *We can give you a refund, or you can pick another item.*
B: *Well, I like this skirt. Do you have it in a bigger size?*
A: *Let me check. What size are you?*
B: *I'm a large.*
A: *I'm sorry, we only have medium in red. But we've got large in grey and black.*
B: *Can I try the grey one, please?*
A: *Sure. The fitting rooms are over there.*

A: *Hello, can I help you?*
B: *Hi, I'd like to return these trousers, please.*
A: *Sure, what's wrong with them?*
B: *I'm afraid they're too small for me.*
A: *We can give you a refund, or you can pick another item.*
B: *Well, I like these trousers. Do you have them in a bigger size?*
A: *Let me check. What size are you?*
B: *I'm a large.*
A: *I'm sorry, we only have medium in black. But we've got large in grey and red.*
B: *Can I try the grey ones, please?*
A: *Sure. The fitting rooms are over there.*

A: *Hello, can I help you?*
B: *Hi, I'd like to return this jumper, please.*
A: *Sure, what's wrong with it?*
B: *I'm afraid it's too small for me.*
A: *We can give you a refund, or you can pick another item.*
B: *Well, I like this jumper. Do you have it in a bigger size?*
A: *Let me check. What size are you?*
B: *I'm a large.*
A: *I'm sorry, we only have medium in grey. But we've got large in black and red.*
B: *Can I try the red one, please?*
A: *Sure. The fitting rooms are over there.*

5 **Aim** **To practise situational language for asking for an opinion about clothes**

- Read out the example exchange and then ask Ss to work in pairs and act out similar exchanges using the pictures.
- Monitor the activity around the class and then ask some pairs to act out their exchanges in front of the class.

Suggested Answer Key

A: *What do you think of these shoes?*
B: *Well, I think they're too small.*

A: *What do you think of these trousers?*
B: *Well, I think they're too short.*

A: *What do you think of this blouse?*
B: *Well, I think it's too big.*

A: *What do you think of this dress?*
B: *Well, I think it's too long.*

Pronunciation

6 **Aim** To pronounce /n/, /ŋ/

- Play the recording and have Ss tick the correct sounds.
- Play the recording again with pauses for Ss to repeat chorally and/or individually.
- Check Ss' pronunciation and intonation.

Answer Key

	/n/	/ŋ/		/n/	/ŋ/
wearing		✓	shine	✓	
rain	✓		fishing		✓
making		✓	run	✓	

Reading & Writing

7 **Aim** To read for specific information

- Direct Ss to the postcard and give Ss time to read it and answer the questions.
- Check Ss' answers.

Answer Key

1 *Aunt Dorothy*
2 *Natalie*
3 *Natalie is in York, UK, and Aunt Dorothy is in La Macarena, Colombia.*

Background Information

Colombia is a large country in the northern part of South America. The capital city is Bogota and it is home to some of the Amazon Rainforest.

8 a) **Aim** To understand addresses

- Read out the **Writing Tip** box and explain that this information will help Ss to write addresses correctly.
- Ask Ss to look at the address in the postcard and then give Ss time to match the letters (A-E) to the numbers (1-5).

- Check Ss' answers.

Answer Key

1 E   2 A   3 B   4 C   5 D

b) **Aim** To write an address

- Give Ss time to write the address correctly.
- Check Ss' answers.

Answer Key

Alice Denning
9 Napier Drive
Edinburgh
EH11 1RP
UK

9 **Aim** To learn to avoid repetition

- Read out the **Writing Tip** box and then ask Ss to read the text and replace the words in bold with appropriate alternatives to avoid repetition.
- Check Ss' answers around the class.

Answer Key

My cousin and I: *We*
on the beach: *here*
my cousin and I: *we*
John's boat: *It*
The islands near the beach: *They*
The local food: *It*

Background Information

Croatia is a country between central and southeast Europe. The capital city is Zagreb and it has twenty counties and a population of about 4.2 million people.

Writing

10 a) **Aim** To prepare for a writing task

- Ask Ss to imagine they are on holiday and answer the questions.
- Elicit answers from Ss around the class.

Suggested Answer Key

1 *Prague, Czech Republic*
2 *my cousin Kate*
3 *it's windy and rainy*
4 *mornings: walk around the city, afternoons: visit museums and eat at a restaurant*
5 *sitting in a café drinking coffee*
6 *a waterproof jacket, gloves, a hat*
7 *yes, it's great*

b) **Aim** To write a postcard

- Explain the task. Then give Ss time to write their postcard using their answers from Ex. 10a and the address from Ex. 8b to help them.
- Check Ss' answers.
- Alternatively, assign the task as HW and check Ss' answers in the next lesson.

Suggested Answer Key

Hi Alice,

Greetings from Prague in the Czech Republic! The weather is windy and rainy here, but I'm having a great time. I'm here with my cousin Kate. In the mornings, we walk around the city. In the afternoons, we visit museums and eat at a restaurant. Right now, I'm sitting in a café drinking coffee. I'm wearing a waterproof jacket, gloves and a hat to stay warm. It's great here!

See you,
Lynn

Alice Denning
9 Napier Drive
Edinburgh
EH11 1RP
UK

Values

Ss try to explain the quotation in their mother tongue. If Ss have difficulty, explain the quotation. Ask Ss to memorise this quotation and check in the next lesson.
The quotation means that when we travel, we learn about other places and other cultures. This knowledge is more valuable than any physical thing we could buy.

Culture 6

Listening & Reading

1 **Aim** To listen and read for specific information

- Ask Ss to look at the map and read out the questions.
- Play the recording. Ss listen and read the text to find out.

Suggested Answer Key

San Francisco is in western California, on the coast. Los Angeles is in southern California, on the coast.
The weather in San Francisco is dry and sunny from May to October. In spring and autumn, it's wet but warm and in winter (December and January) it is cool with temperatures of around 11°C.
The weather in Los Angeles is warm but not too hot in June, July, August and September. It is sunny all year round, and even in winter it doesn't get very cold (14-15°C).

- Play the video for Ss and elicit their comments.
- Refer Ss to the Word List to look up the meanings of the words in the **Check these words** box.

2 **Aim** To read for specific information

- Ask Ss to read the text again and copy and complete the table in their notebooks.
- Check Ss' answers. Then ask Ss to explain the words in bold.

Answer Key

Season	San Francisco		Los Angeles	
	Winter	**Summer**	**Winter**	**Summer**
Weather	*cool*	*dry and sunny*	*not very cold*	*warm, not too hot*
Temperature	*11°C*	*15 – 17°C*	*14 – 15°C*	*20 – 30°C*
Must bring	*jumpers, trousers, boots, hat, good coat*	*T-shirts, light clothes*	*jumper*	*hat, T-sirts, shorts, sandals*

size: *how big or small sth is*
pack: *put clothes in luggage*
foggy: *misty*
wet: *not dry*
cool: *pleasantly cold; not warm*
protection: *safety*

Speaking & Writing

3 **Aim** THINK To compare climates in two cities

Ask various Ss around the class to offer comparisons between the two cities using the information in the table in Ex. 2.

Suggested Answer Key

Los Angeles and San Francisco have quite different climates. Los Angeles is sunny all year round. In summer it doesn't get very hot and in winter it doesn't get very cold. San Francisco is usually sunny in summer, but sometimes foggy. In spring, autumn and winter it's rainy. It's not very cold, but it rains a lot.

4 **Aim** ICT To create a calendar showing the weather where you live for each season

- Explain the task and ask Ss to work in small groups and research online to find out about the weather in each season where they live.

- Give Ss time to use their information to create a calendar.
- Then ask various Ss to present their calendar to the class.
- Alternatively, assign the task as HW and ask Ss to present their calendars in the next lesson.

Suggested Answer Key

Season	Weather	Temperature
Winter	cold and snowy	0-5°C
Spring	rainy, windy	5-15°C
Summer	warm, sunny	15-25°C
Autumn	foggy, cool	10-15°C

Review 6

Vocabulary

1 **Aim** To practise vocabulary related to weather

- Explain the task.
- Give Ss time to complete it.
- Check Ss' answers.

Answer Key

1 freezing   3 blowing   5 windy
2 foggy   4 raining   6 sunny

2 **Aim** To practise vocabulary for clothing

- Explain the task.
- Give Ss time to complete it.
- Check Ss' answers.

Answer Key

1 blouse   4 jacket   7 boots
2 sandals   5 trainers
3 suit   6 cap

Grammar

3 **Aim** To practise -ing forms

- Explain the task.
- Give Ss time to complete it.
- Check Ss' answers.

Answer Key

1 shining   4 skiing   7 jogging
2 running   5 buying   8 visiting
3 making   6 having

4 **Aim** To practise the *present continuous*

- Explain the task.
- Give Ss time to complete it.
- Check Ss' answers.

Answer Key

1 are/'re planning   4 am/'m shopping
2 is not/isn't snowing   5 is/'s enjoying
3 Are you playing   6 is not/isn't doing

5 **Aim** To practise the present continuous

- Explain the task.
- Give Ss time to complete it.
- Check Ss' answers.

Answer Key

1 a   2 b   3 a   4 a   5 a

6 **Aim** To practise the present continuous and the present simple

- Explain the task.
- Give Ss time to complete it.
- Check Ss' answers.

Answer Key

1 go, am going   5 are eating, eat/are
2 does, is doing   having, have
3 are playing, play   6 is snowing, snow
4 are having, have/are
    eating, eat

Everyday English

7 **Aim** To match questions and answers

- Explain the task.
- Give Ss time to complete it.
- Check Ss' answers.

Answer Key

1 C   2 A   3 D   4 E   5 B

Competences

Ask Ss to assess their own performance in the unit by ticking the items according to how competent they feel for each of the listed activities.

Values: Environmentalism

1 **Aim** To listen and read for specific information

- Ask Ss to look at the title, the pictures and the headings, and elicit ideas from Ss about how we can help animals in danger.
- Play the recording. Ss listen and read the text to find out.

Answer Key

We can help animals in danger by putting water out, being careful with rubbish, growing plants that animals can eat, reporting strays and driving carefully.

- Play the video for Ss and elicit their comments.

2 **Aim** To read for specific information (answer questions)

- Ask Ss to read the questions and then give them time to read the text again and answer them.
- Check Ss' answers.

Answer Key

1   *Because dogs, cats, birds and hedgehogs get hot and thirsty.*
2   *By making sure the bin has a lid they can't open.*
3   *They can choke on it or it can poison them.*
4   *They run special programmes to help them.*
5   *By driving carefully and slowly.*

3 **Aim** **THINK** To understand the purpose of the text

- Explain that different texts have different purposes. Some entertain the reader by being interesting or funny *(e.g. magazine articles, blogs)*, some inform the reader by providing them with information or facts *(e.g. newspaper articles, notices, memos)* and others try to persuade the reader to believe or do something by using persuasive language *(e.g. advertisements)*.
- Ask Ss to decide what the purpose of the text is and then elicit answers with reasons from various Ss.

Answer Key

The purpose of the webpage is to inform and to persuade. The webpage says it has interesting ways to help animals. Then, it gives a list of ways to help them and things we should and shouldn't do. It wants to persuade us to do these things.

4 **Aim** ICT To expand the topic

- Ask Ss to work in small groups and research online and collect information about other ways to protect animals in their area.
- Then give Ss time to use this information and write about their ideas using the text in Ex. 1 as a model.
- Ask various groups of Ss to present their ideas to the class.
- Alternatively, assign the task as HW and ask Ss to present their ideas in the next lesson.

Suggested Answer Key

Give and collect money

You can give money to an animal shelter. You can collect money for an animal shelter, too. They can use the money in different ways to help animals in your neighbourhood.

Spread the word

Tell other people how they can help. You can put up posters or give people pamphlets.

5 **Aim** To give a talk

- Give Ss time to prepare a talk using their answers in Ex. 4 to help them and then ask various Ss around the class to give their talk to the class.
- Encourage the class to give feedback to each S.

Suggested Answer Key

Hello everyone. I'm Juanita Galliano. They're big or small, short or tall, and we love them all! What are they? … Animals! There are many animals that live in our neighbourhood, and we can help them in many ways.

First, we should make sure our rubbish bins have a lid that animals can't open. It is usual for animals to look for food in rubbish bins, but it is dangerous for them as they can choke on rubbish or it can poison them.

We can give money to an animal shelter and we can collect money for an animal shelter too. The animal shelter can use the money in different ways to help animals in our neighbourhood.

Finally, we can tell other people how they can help. We can put up posters or give people pamphlets. After all, we love the animals in our neighbourhood, don't we? Thank you for listening.

Public Speaking Skills

1 a) **Aim** **To present a public speaking task**

Ask Ss to read the task.

b) **Aim** **To analyse a model for content**

- Play the recording. Ss listen and read the model.
- Then ask Ss to copy the spidergram into their notebooks and complete it.

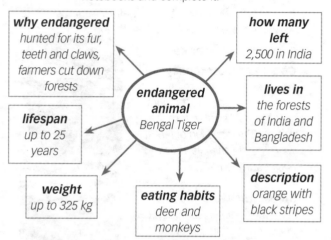

why endangered
hunted for its fur, teeth and claws, farmers cut down forests

how many left
2,500 in India

lifespan
up to 25 years

endangered animal
Bengal Tiger

lives in
the forests of India and Bangladesh

weight
up to 325 kg

eating habits
deer and monkeys

description
orange with black stripes

- Play the recording again if necessary.

Suggested Answer Key

2 **Aim** **To present opening techniques**

Elicit which opening technique is used in the model and then elicit suggestions for an alternative opening technique. Refer them back to Public Speaking Skills A (p. 29) if they can't remember the techniques.

Answer Key

Opening technique: humour/asking a riddle

Suggested Answer Key

(Address the audience directly.) Can you guess which animal is the king of the big cats and it's disappearing?

3 **Aim** **To present closing techniques**

- Ask Ss to read the theory and then elicit which closing technique is used in the model.
- Then elicit suggestions for an alternative closing technique.

Answer Key

Closing technique: a quote/saying

Suggested Answer Key

(a 'what if' question) What if the Bengal tiger disappears? We must try to help them so that doesn't happen.

4 **Aim** **To give a presentation**

- Ask Ss to copy the spidergram from Ex. 1b into their notebooks and give them time to complete it with information about an endangered animal in their country or another country.
- Then ask Ss to use their notes and the model to help them prepare a presentation on the endangered animal.
- Ask various Ss to give their presentation to the class.
- Alternatively, assign the task as HW and have Ss give their presentations in the next lesson.

Suggested Answer Key

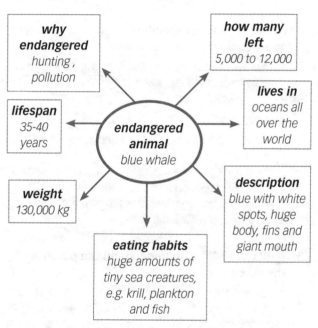

why endangered
hunting, pollution

how many left
5,000 to 12,000

lifespan
35-40 years

endangered animal
blue whale

lives in
oceans all over the world

weight
130,000 kg

eating habits
huge amounts of tiny sea creatures, e.g. krill, plankton and fish

description
blue with white spots, huge body, fins and giant mouth

Hi everyone. My name is Erin Jansen. It's the biggest animal that ever existed. What is it? It's a blue whale! The blue whale is endangered, and the number of blue whales around the world is only between 5,000 and 12,000.

The blue whale lives in oceans all over the world. It is blue with white spots. It has got a huge body, fins and a giant mouth. It eats huge amounts of tiny sea creatures like krill, plankton and fish. It weighs over 130,000 kg, and its lifespan is around 35 to 40 years.

The first reason why the blue whale is endangered is hunters. They hunt the blue whales for their oil and meat. Pollution is also a threat. Pollution kills many of the small sea creatures the blue whale eats. So, without food, the blue whale also can't survive.

The blue whale is an amazing animal and we must not let it disappear. In the words of Jim Murphy, "There are a number of things everyone can do to help protect whales."

Thank you for listening.

Topic

In this unit, Ss will explore the topics of types of food/drink, cutlery, tableware, meals, ways to cook and food preparation

7a Reading & Vocabulary   56-57

Lesson objectives: To learn vocabulary for food/drinks, to talk about food/drinks, to act out dialogues about food/drinks, to listen and read for specific information (sentence completion), to talk about dishes, to learn vocabulary for cutlery and tableware, to write about a typical dish and drink in your capital city

Vocabulary: Food & Drinks (*pear, strawberries, pineapple, coconut, bananas, grapes, orange, apple, cherries, coffee, cola, orange juice, tea, water, chocolate cake, ice cream, apple pie, pancakes, biscuits, lettuce, pepper, salad, carrots, onion, garlic, cabbage, potatoes, cereal, rice, pasta, noodles, bread, eggs, cheese, butter, milk, salt & pepper, mustard & ketchup, chicken, lamb, beef, fish, crab, prawns*); Food categories (*vegetables, meat & poultry, fruit, grains, sweets, drinks, dairy & eggs, seafood, seasoning & sauces*); Cutlery & Tableware (*knife, fork, plate, bowl, tablespoon, teaspoon*); Nouns (*cuisine, culture, speciality, sauce, chopsticks, ingredient, powder, tip, weight*); Adjectives (*salty, refreshing, insulting*)

7b Grammar in Use   58-59

Lesson objectives: To learn countable-uncountable nouns, to learn phrases of quantity, to learn *a lot of/much/many – how much/how many – a few/a little*, to act out a dialogue making a shopping list, to decide on a menu and write a shopping list

Vocabulary: Phrases of quantity (*bottle, loaf, piece [of], glass, packet, carton, slice, cup, bowl, bag, pot, box*)

7c Skills in Action   60-61

Lesson objectives: To learn vocabulary for ways to cook, to listen for specific information (gap fill), to act out a dialogue and practise everyday English expressions for ordering food, to pronounce /g/, /dʒ/, to listen and read for specific information, to learn the *imperative*, to write a restaurant review

Vocabulary: Ways to cook (*boil, fry, bake, roast, grill*)

Culture 7   62

Lesson objectives: To learn vocabulary for food preparation, to listen and read for specific information, to talk about how to make a dish, to write a recipe

Vocabulary: Nouns (*recipe, baking powder, instructions, towel, frying pan, pot*); Verb (*season*)

Review 7   63

Lesson objectives: To test/consolidate vocabulary and grammar learnt throughout the unit; to practise everyday English

Go through the objectives box and tell Ss that these are the topics, skills and activities this unit will cover.

7a

Vocabulary

1 Aim To present vocabulary for food/drinks

- Go through the food/drinks in the pictures and then give Ss time to match the sections A-I to the correct headings.
- Play the recording for Ss to listen and check their answers.

Answer Key

A	fruit	F	dairy & eggs
B	drinks	G	seasoning & sauces
C	sweets	H	meat & poultry
D	vegetables	I	seafood
E	grains		

2 Aim To talk about food/drinks

Ask Ss to read the questions and then elicit answers from various Ss around the class.

Suggested Answer Key

1 *I like strawberries, pineapple, and ice cream. I also like orange juice. I don't like peppers or coffee.*
2 *I eat strawberries and pineapple every week and I eat ice cream twice a month. I drink orange juice every day.*
3 *For breakfast you can have fruit, cereal with milk, bread with butter, eggs, pancakes, coffee or orange juice. For a light meal you can have noodles, rice or pasta, a salad with chicken, a small dish of meat or poultry, water or tea. For dessert you can have chocolate cake, ice cream or apple pie.*

Speaking

3 Aim To act out dialogues relating to food/drinks

- Play the recording and ask Ss to listen and read the dialogues.
- Then ask Ss to work in pairs and act out similar dialogues using the prompts.
- Monitor the activity around the class and then ask some pairs to act out the dialogues in front of the class.

Suggested Answer Key

A: *I'm thirsty. Is there anything to drink?*
B: *Would you like some coffee?*
A: *No, thanks. I don't like coffee.*
B: *How about some tea?*
A: *Oh, yes, please!*

A: *I'm thirsty. Is there anything to drink?*
B: *Would you like some cola?*
A: *No, thanks. I don't like cola.*
B: *How about some water?*
A: *Oh, yes, please!*

A: *I'm hungry. Is there anything to eat?*
B: *Would you like some pasta?*
A: *No, thanks. I don't like pasta.*
B: *How about some fish?*
A: *Oh, yes, please!*

A: *I'm hungry. Is there anything to eat?*
B: *Would you like some chicken?*
A: *No, thanks. I don't like chicken.*
B: *How about some noodles?*
A: *Oh, yes, please!*

Reading & Listening

4 **Aim** To listen and read for specific information

- Read out the questions in the rubric and play the recording.
- Ss listen and read to find the answers.
- Check Ss' answers.

Answer Key

In picture A, the dish is Goi Cuon. We use prawns, meat, vegetables and noodles inside rice paper to make it.
In picture B, the dish is Okonomiyaki. We use a pancake with cabbage, meat and any other ingredient to make it.

- Play the video for Ss and elicit their comments.

Background Information

Ho Chi Minh City is the largest city in Viet Nam. It used to be called Saigon. It gets its name from the revolutionary leader Ho Chi Minh. Around 9 million people live there.

Viet Nam is a country in Southeast Asia. It is the most eastern country in the area. The capital is Hanoi. The currency is the dong and about 96 million people live there.

Tokyo is the capital city of Japan. It is a financial centre and many businesses have headquarters there. About 13.5 million people live there and it has also been ranked as one of the safest, cleanest and most liveable cities in the world.

Japan is an island country in East Asia in the Pacific Ocean. It is also known as the 'Land of the Rising Sun'. The capital city is Tokyo and the population is 127 million people.

5 **Aim** To read for specific information (sentence completion)

- Ask Ss to read sentences 1-6.
- Give Ss time to read the texts again and complete the sentences according to what they read.
- Check Ss' answers around the class.

Answer Key

1 speciality
2 coconut milk
3 chopsticks
4 yourself (at your table)
5 cold
6 leave a tip (in a restaurant)

- Refer Ss to the Word List to look up the meanings of the words in the **Check these words** box.

6 **Aim** **THINK** To express an opinion; to talk about dishes

Elicit answers from Ss around the class and ask Ss to provide reasons to support their opinion.

Suggested Answer Key

I would like to try the Japanese pizza, Okonomiyaki, because it looks very interesting and tasty. I also like the idea of a pancake with cabbage and meat.

7 **Aim** To present vocabulary for cutlery and tableware

- Read out the words in the list and explain/elicit the meanings of any unknown words.
- Then give Ss time to complete the sentences using the words.
- Check Ss' answers.

Answer Key

1 tablespoon
2 plate
3 knife
4 fork
5 bowl
6 teaspoon

Writing

8 **Aim** **ICT** To write about a typical dish and drink from the capital city in your country

- Ask Ss to research online and find out information about a typical dish and drink in the capital city of their country.
- Then give Ss time to use the information to write a short text about them using the subheadings in Ex. 4 to help them.

- Ask various Ss around the class to read out their texts.
- Alternatively, assign the task as HW and have Ss read out the texts in the next lesson.

Suggested Answer Key

Madrid, Spain

What to eat and drink *Tortilla de patata is a typical Spanish dish. It is an omelette with potatoes and eggs and sometimes onions. They serve it hot or cold. Café con leche is a popular drink. It is coffee with cold or hot milk.*

Culture Tip *Don't leave a big tip in a Spanish restaurant. Spanish people tip, but not a lot of money.*

Did you know? *You can find this dish in most restaurants.*

7b Grammar in Use

1 **Aim** To present countable – uncountable nouns

- Ss read the dialogue.
- Explain that some nouns can be counted (*e.g. egg, car, apple, etc*) and these are countable, and some nouns can't be counted (*e.g. milk, water, coffee, etc*). These are uncountable nouns.
- Explain that we use **a/an** with countable nouns and **some** with uncountable nouns.
- Direct Ss' attention to the theory box and have them study it and then elicit examples from the dialogue.

Answer Key

Examples: *some ingredients, some bananas, an orange, any pears, a pineapple, some strawberries.*

2 a) **Aim** To practise countable/uncountable nouns

- Explain the task and give Ss time to complete it.
- Check Ss' answers around the class.

Answer Key

honey U, some	*tomato C, a*
jam U, some	*burger C, a*
coffee U, some	*egg C, an*
cherry C, a	*meat U, some*
sugar U, some	*flour U, some*
sandwich C, a	*butter U, some*
soup U, some	*peach C, a*
lemon C, a	

b) **Aim** To practise plurals

- Give Ss time to write the plurals of the countable nouns in Ex. 2a.

- Check Ss' answers around the class.

Answer Key

tomato: *tomatoes*
burger: *burgers*
cherry: *cherries*
egg: *eggs*
sandwich: *sandwiches*
lemon: *lemons*
peach: *peaches*

3 **Aim** To present phrases of quantity

- Ask Ss to study the theory and read out the items 1-12.
- Then elicit examples from the dialogue on p. 58.

Answer Key

a pot of yoghurt, a carton of milk

4 **Aim** To practise phrases of quantity

- Explain the task and read out the example.
- Give Ss time to complete the task and then check Ss' answers.

Answer Key

2 a glass of milk	*5 a box of cereal*
3 five pieces of cake	*6 three cartons of fruit*
4 two bottles of olive oil	* juice*

5 **Aim** To present *a lot of/lots of – much/many – how much/how many – a few/a little*

- Read out the table and ask various Ss to read the examples.
- Explain that we use **a lot of/lots of** with countable nouns in the affirmative, **much** with uncountable nouns in the negative and interrogative, **many** with countable nouns in the negative and interrogative, **how much** and **a little** with uncountable nouns and **how many** and **a few** with countable nouns.
- Ask Ss to study the theory and then elicit examples from the dialogue on p. 58.

Answer Key

Examples: *how many people, few peaches, How many peaches, a little yoghurt, How much yoghurt*

6 **Aim** To practise *a lot of/much/many – how much/how many – a few/a little*

- Explain the task and give Ss time to complete it.
- Check Ss' answers.

Answer Key

1	How much	6	much
2	a few	7	much, a little
3	a lot of	8	any, a lot
4	an	9	a few
5	some	10	much

7 **Aim** **To listen for specific information; to practise *a lot of/much/many – how much/how many – a few/a little***

- Explain the task and play the recording. Ss listen and tick the items.
- Check Ss' answers.
- Then have Ss ask and answer questions using the shopping list and following the example.
- Monitor the activity around the class.

Answer Key

2 kilos of meat ✓	2 bags of flour ✓
1 kilo of cheese ✓	3 bottles of cola ✓
20 slices of ham ✓	1 carton of orange juice
2 loaves of bread ✓	8 bananas
1 kilo of tomatoes	

Suggested Answer Key

A: How much cheese does he need?
B: He needs a kilo of cheese. How much ham does he need?
A: He needs 20 slices of ham. How much bread does he need?
B: He needs 2 loaves of bread. How many tomatoes does he need?
A: He doesn't need any tomatoes. How much flour does he need?
B: He needs 2 bags of flour. How much cola does he need?
A: He needs 3 bottles of cola. How much orange juice does he need?
B: He doesn't need any orange juice. How many bananas does he need?
A: He doesn't need any bananas.

8 **Aim** **To act out dialogues**

- Explain the task and ask Ss to read the dialogue. Then have Ss work in pairs and act out similar dialogues using the prompts.
- Monitor the activity around the class and then have some pairs act out their dialogues in front of the class.

Suggested Answer Key

A: Would you like some orange juice?
B: Yes, please, I'd love some. Would you like some chocolate?

A: No, thanks. I don't like chocolate.
A: Would you like some tea?
B: Yes, please, I'd love some. Would you like some biscuits?
A: No, thanks. I don't like biscuits.

A: Would you like some pizza?
B: Yes, please, I'd love some. Would you like some soda?
A: No, thanks. I don't like soda.

9 **Aim** **To practise *a/an, some/any, a lot of/much/many – how much/how many – a few/a little***

- Explain the task and go through the example and then give Ss time to complete the task.
- Check Ss' answers.

Answer Key

2	a = some	10	any = some
3	any = some	11	much = a lot of/many
4	an = a	12	a little = a few
5	many = any/much	13	How many = How much
6	a lot of = much	14	How much = How many
7	sugars = sugar	15	many = some/much
8	How many = How much		
9	a few = some/a little		

Optional Game

Divide the class into two teams. Call out nouns from p. 56. In teams Ss add ***a/an*** or ***some***. Each correct answer wins one point. The team with the most points is the winner.

e.g.   T: *Banana.*
Team A S1: *A banana.*
          T: *Very good. Team A gets one point. Milk.*
Team B S1: *Some milk, etc.*

10 **Aim** **THINK** **To decide on a menu and write a shopping list**

- Have Ss discuss in pairs what they can put on the menu for a dinner party for their friends.
- Monitor the activity around the class and then give Ss time to write a shopping list.
- Ask various Ss to read out their lists to the class.
- Alternatively, assign the shopping list as HW and have Ss read out their lists in the next lesson.

Suggested Answer Key

Shopping list

For the meat and pasta bake: *3 kilos of meat, 3 packets of pasta, 1 kilo of tomatoes, 5 onions, 1/2 kilo of cheese*

For the salad: *2 cabbages, 5 carrots, 1 onion, a bottle of oil*
Drinks: *5 bottles of cola, 6 bottles of water*

7c Skills in Action

1 a) **Aim** **To present vocabulary for ways to cook**
- Ask Ss to look at the pictures.
- Play the recording. Ss listen and repeat chorally and/or individually. Check Ss' pronunciation and intonation.

b) **Aim** **To expand vocabulary**

Ss work in pairs. Elicit answers.

Suggested Answer Key

cake: *bake*
eggs: *boil, fry*
fish: *boil, fry, grill*
pasta: *boil*
chicken: *boil, roast, fry, grill*
potatoes: *boil, bake, roast, fry*
steak: *fry, grill*

Listening

2 a) **Aim** **To predict content**
- Go through the advert with Ss. Explain that in this task Ss have to identify the part of speech each gap asks for. Ss work on their own. Go round the class and help if necessary. Ss in pairs compare their answers. Check Ss' answers.

Answer Key

0 adjective	2 noun	4 number
1 noun	3 noun	5 time

b) **Aim** **To listen for specific information**
- Ask Ss to look at the gapped text again and then play the recording.
- Ss listen and fill the gaps according to what they hear.
- Check Ss' answers.

Answer Key

6 Long	8 ice cream	10 twelve/
7 burgers	9 30	12 midnight

Everyday English

3 **Aim** **To read for cohesion and coherence; to listen for confirmation**
- Ask Ss to read the dialogue and think of an appropriate word to complete each gap.

- Play the recording. Ss listen and check their answers.

Answer Key

1 for	3 for	5 like
2 at	4 Would	6 slice

4 **Aim** **To act out a dialogue ordering food**
- Explain the task and ask Ss to act out a similar dialogue to the one in Ex. 3 in groups of three using the items on the menu.
- Write the diagram on the board for Ss to follow.

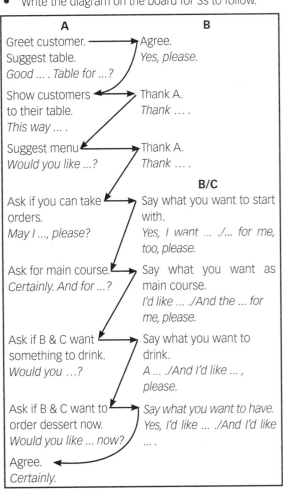

- Monitor the activity around the class and offer assistance as necessary.
- Then ask some pairs to act out their dialogues in front of the class.

Suggested Answer Key

Waiter: *Good evening sir. Table for two?*
A: *Yes, please.*
Waiter: *This way, please.*
B: *Thank you.*
Waiter: *Would you like to look at the menu?*
B: *Thanks.*

		Waiter:	May I take your order, please?
A:	Yes, I want the onion soup, to start with.
B:	Onion soup for me, too, please.
Waiter:	Certainly. And for the main course?
A:	I'd like prawns with rice.
B:	And the fried fish for me, please.
Waiter:	Of course. Would you like something to drink?
B:	A glass of orange juice, please.
A:	And I'd like a glass of water, please.
Waiter:	Very well. Would you like to order your dessert now?
A:	Yes. I'd like the carrot cake.
B:	And I'd like some fresh fruit.
Waiter:	Certainly.

Pronunciation

5 (Aim) **To pronounce /g/, /dʒ/**

- Play the recording and have Ss tick the correct sounds.
- Play the recording again with pauses for Ss to repeat chorally and/or individually.
- Check Ss' pronunciation and intonation.

Answer Key

	/g/	/dʒ/		/g/	/dʒ/
sugar	✓		burger	✓	
ingredient	✓		glass	✓	
orange		✓	fridge		✓

Reading & Writing

6 (Aim) **To listen and read for specific information**

- Direct Ss to the review and play the recording.
- Ss listen and read to complete the table.
- Check Ss' answers.

Answer Key

Location: 10 Bridge Street
Starters: fresh salads, spicy soups
Main courses: pepper steak, roast chicken, fish with rice
Sides: garlic bread
Desserts: apple pie, homemade ice cream
Service: excellent, helpful and friendly waiters
Cost: £25
Opening hours: 12 noon to 12 midnight
Recommendation: a great restaurant for any occasion, very busy so don't forget to book a table

7 (Aim) **To present and practise adjectives used in restaurant reviews**

- Read out the **Writing Tip** box and explain that this information will help Ss when they have to write a restaurant review.

- Explain the task and read out the example.
- Give Ss time to complete the task and then check their answers.

Answer Key

2	tasty	5	superb	8	helpful,
3	fresh	6	homemade		friendly
4	spicy	7	excellent		

8 (Aim) **To present the imperative**

- Explain that we use the imperative to give orders or instructions and we use the base form of the verb without a personal pronoun with **do/don't**.
- Read out the theory box and the examples and elicit examples from the review in Ex. 6.

Answer Key

Examples: Try the Cookhouse's garlic bread, have a slice, don't forget to book a table first

9 (Aim) **To practise the imperative**

- Explain the task and give Ss time to compete it.
- Check Ss' answers around the class.

Answer Key

| 1 | Try | 3 | order | 5 | Don't |
| 2 | Don't miss | 4 | Make | | forget |

Writing

10 a) (Aim) **To prepare for a writing task**

- Ask Ss to copy the table in Ex. 6 into their notebooks and give them time to complete it with information about a restaurant they like.
- Elicit answers from Ss around the class.

Suggested Answer Key

Name/Type: Tony's/Italian
Location: 94 Bridge Road, London
Starters: pasta dishes
Main courses: roast chicken
Sides: cheese salad
Desserts: lemon cheesecake
Service: superb, friendly waiters
Cost: £30
Opening hours: noon - 11 pm
Recommendation: great restaurant, busy, so don't forget to book

b) (Aim) **To write a restaurant review**

- Explain the task. Then give Ss time to write their review using their answers from Ex. 10a and the plan to help them.
- Remind Ss to check their punctuation.

- Check Ss' answers.
- Alternatively, assign the task as HW and check Ss' answers in the next lesson.

Suggested Answer key

Tony's is an amazing Italian restaurant at 94 Bridge Road, London.

There are a lot of tasty dishes to choose from. For starters, there are delicious pasta dishes. The best main course is roast chicken. Try their cheese salad – it's delicious. For dessert, have lemon cheesecake.

The service is superb with friendly waiters. A meal for two costs £30 and the opening hours are noon - 11 pm. Tony's is a great restaurant, but it's very busy, so don't forget to book.

Values

Ss try to explain the proverb in their mother tongue. If Ss have difficulty, explain the proverb. Ask Ss to memorise this proverb and check in the next lesson.

The proverb means that we should only eat enough to live a healthy life and not make eating so important in our lives so that we overeat and become unhealthy.

Culture 7

Vocabulary

1 **Aim** **To present vocabulary relating to food preparation**

- Play the recording. Ss listen and repeat chorally and/or individually.
- Check Ss' pronunciation and intonation.

Listening & Reading

2 **Aim** **To listen and read for specific information**

- Ask Ss to look at the dishes on the webpage and read out the questions.
- Play the recording. Ss listen and read to find out.

Answer Key

The dishes are from Ireland. The Irish potato pancakes (Boxty) have an egg. The Irish stew has onions.

- Refer Ss to the Word List to look up the meanings of the words in the **Check these words** box.
- Play the video for Ss and elicit their comments.

Background Information

Ireland is an island country in the British Isles. The capital city is Dublin. It has a population of about 4.7 million. The country has a long history and Irish culture has had a great influence on many other cultures.

Speaking & Writing

3 **Aim** **To talk about dishes**

- Ask Ss to work in pairs and ask and answer questions about one of the dishes in the texts, what ingredients you need and how to make it.
- Monitor the activity around the class.

Suggested Answer Key

A: *What ingredients do you need for Boxty?*
B: *You need 4 large potatoes, 1 egg, 100 g of flour, 150 ml of milk, baking powder and salt.*
A: *How do you make it?*
B: *Firstly, peel and grate the potatoes into small pieces and put them into a towel. Then, squeeze all the juice out of the potatoes. Then, mix the flour, salt and baking powder together. After this, beat the egg and then mix the flour, salt and baking powder with the egg and potatoes. Use a tablespoon to get part of the mixture and put it in a hot frying pan. Then, fry until cooked on both sides. Finally, repeat with the rest of the mixture.*

A: *What ingredients do you need for Irish stew?*
B: *You need a kilo of lamb, 6 potatoes, 4 onions, 4 carrots, water, salt and pepper.*
A: *How do you make it?*
B: *Firstly, cut the lamb into large pieces and season with salt and pepper. Then, fry the lamb pieces in a large pot until they are brown. After this, put the meat aside and cut the onions, carrots and potatoes into large pieces. Cook in the pot until they are brown. Put the meat into the pot and add water. Finally, cook for an hour.*

4 **Aim** **ICT** **To write a recipe for a traditional dish in your country**

- Explain the task and ask Ss to research online to find out about traditional dishes from their country.
- Give Ss time to write the recipe and add photos.
- Then ask various Ss to present their recipes to the class.
- Alternatively, assign the task as HW and ask Ss to present their recipes in the next lesson. Also, ask Ss to cook the recipe at home and record themselves and show the class.

Suggested Answer Key

Spanish omelette
Ingredients
4 eggs
4 potatoes
1 onion
4 tbsp olive oil
salt

Instructions

First, peel the potatoes. Then put them in a pan and boil them for 5 minutes. Next, cut the onions and potatoes into small pieces. Now, beat the eggs and add a little salt. Then, mix everything together in a bowl and fry the mixture in a pan with some olive oil until cooked on both sides. You can also bake it in the oven.

Review 7

Vocabulary

1 Aim To practise vocabulary for food/drinks

- Explain the task.
- Give Ss time to complete it.
- Check Ss' answers.

Answer Key

1 apple pie	3 cheese	5 soup
2 orange	4 pepper	6 salt

2 Aim To practise vocabulary for cutlery and tableware

- Explain the task.
- Give Ss time to complete it.
- Check Ss' answers.

Answer Key

1 glass	3 tablespoon	5 fork
2 knife	4 plate	6 bowl

3 Aim To practise vocabulary for ways to cook and food preparation

- Explain the task.
- Give Ss time to complete it.
- Check Ss' answers.

Answer Key

1 Boil	4 Fry	7 Roast
2 bake	5 Peel	8 Beat
3 Squeeze	6 Add	

4 Aim To practise vocabulary relating to food

- Explain the task.
- Give Ss time to complete it.
- Check Ss' answers.

Answer Key

1 bowl	5 seafood
2 recipe	6 ingredients
3 waiters	7 desserts
4 grains	

Grammar

5 Aim To practise countable/ uncountable nouns

- Explain the task.
- Give Ss time to complete it.
- Check Ss' answers.

Answer Key

1 U	3 U	5 C	7 U	9 C
2 C	4 U	6 C	8 U	10 C

6 Aim To practise phrases of quantity

- Explain the task.
- Give Ss time to complete it.
- Check Ss' answers.

Answer Key

1 loaf	4 pot	7 piece	10 carton
2 bottle	5 slice	8 glass	
3 bowl	6 cup	9 packet	

7 Aim To practise *much, many, little, few, some, any*

- Explain the task.
- Give Ss time to complete it.
- Check Ss' answers.

Answer Key

1 any	3 some	5 some	7 few
2 any	4 little	6 many	8 much

Everyday English

8 Aim To match questions and answers

- Explain the task.
- Give Ss time to complete it.
- Check Ss' answers.

Answer Key

1 D	2 C	3 E	4 A	5 B

Competences

Ask Ss to assess their own performance in the unit by ticking the items according to how competent they feel for each of the listed activities.

New places, new faces

Topic

In this unit, Ss will explore the topics of places to visit and tourist attractions.

8a   Reading & Vocabulary   64-65

Lesson objectives: To learn adjectives describing places, to compare two places, to skim a text, to listen for confirmation, to read for specific information (comprehension questions), to talk about LA as an ideal destination, to write comparisons between two places
Vocabulary: Adjectives describing places *(quiet, noisy, clean, dirty/polluted, tall, small, cheap, expensive, modern, old, exciting, boring, sunny, fashionable, unforgettable, fascinating)*; Nouns *(star, stall)*; Phrases *(close to, home to, along with, suit everyone's budget)*

8b   Grammar in Use   66-67

Lesson objectives: To learn the comparative and superlative, to compare two cities, to learn comparatives with adverbs of degree, to act out dialogues comparing places, to talk about your town/city

8c   Skills in Action   68-69

Lesson objectives: To learn vocabulary for tourist attractions, to listen for specific information (multiple matching), to act out a dialogue and practise everyday English expressions for making suggestions, to pronounce /s/, /ʃ/, to read for specific information, to write an article about a place
Vocabulary: Tourist attractions *(restaurant, museum, art gallery, sports stadium, theme park, theatre, gift shop, park)*

Culture 8   70

Lesson objectives: To listen and read for specific information, to read for specific information (comprehension questions), to order places according to level of interest, to write shorts texts about two places of natural beauty
Vocabulary: Nouns *(trekking)*; Adjective *(must-see)*

Review 8   71

Lesson objectives: To test/consolidate vocabulary and grammar learnt throughout the unit; to practise everyday English

---

Go through the objectives box and tell Ss that these are the topics, skills and activities this unit will cover.

8a

Vocabulary

1 **(Aim)** **To present adjectives for describing places**

- Explain the task and read out the example.
- Go through the list of adjective-noun collocations and explain/elicit the meanings of any unknown words.
- Then elicit sentences about York and Los Angeles following the example from Ss around the class.

Answer Key

York has got clean streets, while LA has got dirty/ polluted streets.
There are tall buildings/houses in LA and small buildings/houses in York.
There are cheap shops/hotels/restaurants in York and expensive shops/hotels/restaurants in LA.
LA is a modern city, while York is an old city.
LA has got an exciting nightlife, while York has got a boring nightlife.

> ### Background Information
> **York** is a historic city in Yorkshire in England. It is over 2,000 years old and has played an important role in English history.

2 **(Aim)** **To compare two places**

- Read out the adjectives and explain/elicit any unknown words.
- Explain the task and read out the examples.
- Elicit comparisons from Ss around the class.

Answer Key

York is cleaner than LA.
York is quieter than LA.
LA is more modern than York.
LA is more polluted than York.
York is cheaper than LA.
York is older than LA.
LA is more crowded than York.

Reading

3 **Aim** To skim a text; to listen for confirmation

- Read out the statements 1-5 and ask Ss to read the text quickly and decide which of the statements are true.
- Play the recording for Ss to listen and check their answers.

Answer Key

Sentences 4 & 5 are true.

- Play the video for Ss and elicit their comments.

4 **Aim** To read for detailed understanding (comprehension questions)

- Ask Ss to read the questions 1-5.
- Give Ss time to read the text again and answer the questions.
- Check Ss' answers around the class.

Suggested Answer Key

1 *You can stay at a hotel. The hotels next to special bus stops are special because you can get rides to the city sights.*
2 *You can see handprints of famous actors outside Grauman's Chinese Theatre.*
3 *You can find cheap modern clothes on Melrose Avenue.*
4 *You can eat at one of the 37 stalls which offer tasty dishes from all over the world.*
5 *You can watch a basketball match at the Staples Centre.*

- Refer Ss to the Word List to look up the meanings of the words in the **Check these words** box.

5 **Aim** To consolidate vocabulary and information from a text

- Read out the words in the list and explain/elicit the meaning of any unknown words.
- Give Ss time to complete the phrases. Check Ss' answers and then give them time to write sentences with them based on the text.
- Elicit answers from Ss around the class.

Answer Key

1 film	4 street	7 outdoor
2 sunny	5 designer	8 sports
3 heavy	6 expensive	

Suggested Answer Key

1 *You can see the handprints and footprints of film stars outside Grauman's Chinese Theatre.*
2 *LA has got sunny weather.*
3 *There is heavy traffic in LA.*
4 *There are street performers in Venice Beach.*
5 *You can find designer clothes on Rodeo Drive.*
6 *There are expensive shops on Rodeo Drive.*
7 *The Hollywood Bowl is a big outdoor theatre.*
8 *There is a huge sports stadium in the Staples Centre.*

6 **Aim** To consolidate new vocabulary

- Give Ss time to match the words in bold in the text to the synonymous words in the list.
- Check Ss' answers around the class.

Answer Key

sunny: *bright*
close to: *near*
fashionable: *trendy*
unforgettable: *memorable*
tasty: *delicious*
fascinating: *interesting*

Speaking

7 **Aim** To give reasons for choice

Ask various Ss to tell the class three reasons why LA is an ideal holiday destination and elicit how many other Ss in the class agree.

Suggested Answer Key

LA is an ideal city for a holiday because there are fascinating places to visit like Venice Beach and Universal Studios. There are also great shops with cheap and expensive clothes. Also, there are a lot of restaurants where you can eat tasty dishes from all over the world.

Writing

8 **Aim** **THINK** To compare places

- Give Ss time to compare their city/town/village to LA and write a few sentences following the examples.
- Ask Ss to read out their sentences to the class.

Suggested Answer Key

Mexico City is crowded and noisy. LA is crowded and noisy, too. Both cities are polluted.
In LA, the shops, hotels and restaurants are expensive. Shops in Mexico City are not that expensive.
LA has got lots of restaurants. Mexico City has got lots of restaurants, too.

8b Grammar in Use

1 **Aim** To present the comparative/superlative

- Ss read the advert.
- Present the comparative/superlative.
- Read out the examples in the theory box and explain that they are the adjective, the comparative form of the adjective and the superlative form of the adjective.
- Explain that adjectives describe a quality that sb/sth has; comparatives show that sb/sth has more of the quality than sth/sb else and superlatives show that sb/sth has the most of a quality than the others in a group.
- Direct Ss' attention to the theory box and elicit how we form the comparative and superlative forms of adjectives.
- Then elicit examples from the advert.

Answer Key

*With one-syllable adjectives, we add **-(e)r** to form the comparative and **-(e)st** to form the superlative.*
*With one-syllable adjectives ending in a vowel + consonant we double the consonant and then add **-(e)r/-(e)st**.*
*With two-syllable adjectives, we form the comparative with **more** + adjective and the superlative with **most** + adjective. For two syllable adjectives ending in a consonant + **-y**, we replace **-y** with **-i** and add **-er/-est**. Then, there are irregular adjectives which do not follow the above rules e.g. good – better – the best.*
***Examples from advert:** the tallest building, the biggest city, larger ... than, more popular ... than, the busiest places, the most exciting, better ... than.*

Background Information

New York City is the most populated city in the USA with a population of over 8.5 million people. It is a major centre for commerce, entertainment, technology, politics, education and sport. Its nickname is 'the Big Apple'.

2 **Aim** To practise forming the comparative/ superlative

- Explain the task and give Ss time to complete it.
- Check Ss' answers around the class.

Answer Key

adjective	comparative	superlative
tall	taller	**the tallest**
big	bigger	**the biggest**

large	**larger**	*the largest*
popular	**more popular**	*the most popular*
busy	busier	**the busiest**
exciting	more exciting	**the most exciting**
good	**better**	*the best*

3 **Aim** To practise the comparative

- Explain the task.
- Give Ss time to complete the task.
- Check Ss' answers.

Answer Key

1 hotter	4 cheaper
2 more fashionable	5 tastier
3 worse	6 nicer

4 **Aim** To practise the comparative/ superlative

- Explain the task.
- Give Ss time to complete the task.
- Check Ss' answers.

Answer Key

1 larger than, the largest
2 warmer than, the warmest
3 noisier than, the noisiest
4 more expensive than, the most expensive

5 **Aim** To compare cities

- Explain the task and ask Ss to work in pairs and compare cities in their country using the adjectives in the list and following the example.
- Monitor the activity around the class and then ask some pairs to share their comparisons with the rest of the class.

Suggested Answer Key

A: *In Italy, Varese is colder than Rome.*
B: *Bolzano is the coldest city in Italy.*
A: *Parma is smaller than Florence.*
B: *Scandicci is the smallest of all.*
A: *I think Florence is quieter than Rome.*
B: *Lucca is the quietest city.*
A: *Verona is cheaper than Bologna to visit.*
B: *Well, Florence is the cheapest city to visit.*
A: *Milan is larger than Pisa.*
B: *Rome is the largest city.*
A: *Sorrento is sunnier than Nicastro.*
B: *Siracuse is the sunniest of all.*

73

8

6 **Aim** **To practise superlative forms**

- Explain the task and give Ss time to fill in the superlative forms and choose their answers.
- Play the recording for Ss to listen and check.

Answer Key

1 *the largest – A*	4 *the driest – A*
2 *the highest – C*	5 *the smallest – C*
3 *the longest – C*	6 *the tallest – B*

7 **Aim** **To present and practise comparatives with adverbs of degree**

- Give Ss time to read the table and explain when we use adverbs of degree (*too, very, quite, etc*) with comparatives.
- Then ask Ss to look at the table for the means of transport and read out the example sentences.
- Ask Ss to make sentences using comparatives with adverbs of degree following the examples.
- Check Ss' answers around the class.

Suggested Answer Key

Taxis aren't as safe as trains.
Trains are much safer than taxis.
Trains are very safe in Britain.
Taxis in Britain are too dangerous.
Buses are safe enough to travel on.

Buses aren't as fast as trains.
Taxis are much faster than buses.
Taxis are quite fast in Britain.
Buses in Britain are too slow.
Taxis in Britain are fast enough.

Taxis aren't as comfortable as trains.
Trains are much more comfortable than buses.
Taxis are quite comfortable in Britain.
Buses are too uncomfortable in Britain.
Taxis in Britain are comfortable enough.

8 **Aim** **To practise the comparative**

- Explain the task and read out the examples.
- Ask Ss to read the sentences and then play the recording for Ss to decide if the sentences are true or not. Then have Ss make sentences following the examples.
- Ask various Ss to share their answers with the class.

Answer Key

3 F *That's false. Edinburgh isn't as noisy as London. London is much noisier than Edinburgh.*

4 T *That's true. Edinburgh isn't as polluted as London. London is much more polluted than Edinburgh.*

5 F *That's false. London isn't as cheap as Edinburgh. Edinburgh is much cheaper than London.*

Background Information

Edinburgh is the capital city of Scotland. It is in the southeast of Scotland on the Firth of Forth. It is a centre for education and its cultural and historical attractions make it a popular tourist destination. Over 500,000 people live there.

London is the capital city of England and the United Kingdom. It is in the southeast of the country on the River Thames and it is over 2,000 years old. It is a popular tourist destination and has a number of World Heritage sites, museums, palaces and famous landmarks. More than 8 million people live there.

9 a) **Aim** **To practise the comparative with adverbs of degree**

- Explain the task and go through the key.
- Give Ss time to complete the task and then check Ss' answers.

Answer Key

1 *very*   2 *too*   3 *much*   4 *quite*

b) **Aim** **To act out dialogues**

- Explain the task and ask Ss to act out dialogues in pairs following the example in Ex. 9a.
- Monitor the activity around the class and then ask some pairs to act out their dialogues in front of the class.

Suggested Answer Key

A: *Shall we go to Johannesburg for our summer holidays?*
B: *Well, it looks very exciting, but I think it's too crowded for us.*
A: *Why don't we go to Cape Town then? It's much more beautiful than Johannesburg and quite quiet.*
B: *OK, let's go there then.*

A: *Shall we go to San Jose for our summer holidays?*
B: *Well, it looks very interesting but I think it's too noisy for us.*
A: *Why don't we go to Drake Bay then? It's much prettier than San Jose and quite peaceful.*
B: *OK, let's go there then.*

10 **Aim** **To practise comparisons**

- Explain the task and read out the example.
- Ask Ss to work in pairs following the example.

- Monitor the activity around the class and then ask some pairs to act out their dialogues in front of the class.

Suggested Answer Key

A: *Which is the oldest building in Astana?*
B: *I think the Merchant House is the oldest building in my city. Which is the largest Park in Bangkok?*
A: *Rama IX Park is the largest park. Which is the busiest road in Astana?*
B: *I think Tashenov is. Which is the most popular café in your city?*
A: *It is The Snooze Coffee House. Which is the most expensive restaurant in your city?*
B: *I'm not sure. I think it is the Most Restaurant. Which is the most famous square in your city?*
A: *Siam Square is the most famous. Which is the prettiest building in your city?*
B: *I think it is the Khan Shatyr Entertainment Centre.*

8c Skills in Action

Vocabulary

1 a) Aim To present vocabulary for tourist attractions

- Ask Ss to look at the pictures.
- Then give Ss time to complete the task. Explain/Elicit the meanings of any unknown words.
- Check Ss' answers.

Suggested Answer Key

We can try local dishes in a restaurant.
We can see statues in a museum.
We can see paintings in an art gallery.
We can watch a football match in a sports stadium.
We can go on rides in a theme park.
We can watch a performance in a theatre.
We can buy souvenirs in a gift shop.
We can go for a walk in a park.

b) Aim To practise vocabulary for tourist attractions

Elicit which of the places in Ex. 1a there are in Ss' city.

Suggested Answer Key

In my city Astana, there are a lot of restaurants where people can try local dishes. There are also amazing museums with gift shops. There are many green parks and theatres, too. My city is also home to the Astana Arena, a large sports stadium.

Listening

2 Aim To listen for specific information (multiple matching)

- Ask Ss to read the lists and then play the recording.
- Ss listen and match the people to the places.
- Check Ss' answers.

Answer Key

1 G   2 A   3 E   4 C   5 B

Everyday English

3 Aim To listen and read for specific information

- Read the question aloud and then play the recording.
- Ss listen and find out the answer.

Answer Key

They decide to go to the Universal Studios theme park.

4 Aim To act out a dialogue making suggestions; to practise situational language for making suggestions and accepting/refusing suggestions

- Explain the task and ask Ss to act out a similar dialogue to the one in Ex. 3 in pairs using the useful language in the box and the prompts in the list.
- Write this diagram on the board for Ss to follow.

- Monitor the activity around the class and offer assistance as necessary.
- Then ask some pairs to act out their dialogues in front of the class.

Suggested Answer Key

A: *Morning, Ralph. The hotel's amazing, isn't it?*

B: *Hi Helen! Yes, it's very comfortable. Now, what's the plan for our first day in LA?*

A: *Why don't we go to the Los Angeles Theatre? They have great shows there.*

B: *That doesn't sound like fun. How about visiting the Aquarium of the Pacific?*

A: *I don't really feel like going there. I don't like aquariums. What do you say to visiting the LA Galaxy stadium? We can see a football match.*

B: *No, let's not do that. I can see a match at home. Shall we visit Grand Park? We can go for a nice walk there.*

A: *That sounds great!*

Pronunciation

5 **Aim** To pronounce /s/, /ʃ/

- Play the recording and have Ss tick the correct sounds.
- Play the recording again with pauses for Ss to repeat chorally and/or individually.
- Check Ss' pronunciation and intonation.

Answer Key

	/s/	/ʃ/		/s/	/ʃ/
shopping		✓	shall		✓
sunbathing	✓		fashionable		✓
sightseeing	✓		sunny	✓	

Reading & Writing

6 **Aim** To analyse a rubric

- Ask Ss to read the task and pay attention to the underlined parts. Then give Ss time to complete the sentences.
- Check Ss' answers.

Answer Key

1 *article, a popular tourist destination in my country, what visitors can see and do there*
2 *travel website*
3 *80-120*

7 a) **Aim** To read for detailed understanding

- Direct Ss to the article and give them time to read it.
- Ask Ss to copy and complete the spidergram in their notebooks using the information in the article.
- Check Ss' answers on the board.

Suggested Answer Key

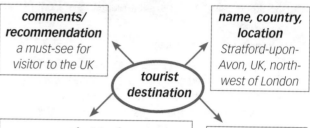

comments/ recommendation
a must-see for visitor to the UK

name, country, location
Stratford-upon-Avon, UK, north-west of London

tourist destination

what to do
eat at a restaurant next to the river, go for a walk and see traditional houses, visit Shakespeare's home, go to the Royal Shakespeare Theatre and watch one of his plays

what to see
peaceful parks, wide River Avon

Background Information

William Shakespeare (1564-1616) was one of the greatest writers and playwrights in the English language and he has been called the national poet. Some of his works are *Romeo & Juliet*, *Othello*, and *King Lear*.

b) **Aim** THINK To identify the author's purpose

Elicit why Ss think the author wrote the text.

Answer Key

The author's purpose is to encourage readers to visit Stratford-upon-Avon.

8 **Aim** To identify adjectives

Elicit the adjectives the author uses to describe the places in the list.

Answer Key

historic town
peaceful parks
wide River Avon
local restaurants
traditional houses
old home
popular plays

9 **Aim** To identify appropriate adjectives

- Explain the task and give Ss time to complete it.
- Check Ss' answers around the class.

Answer Key

1 *sandy*   3 *warm*
2 *delicious*   4 *long*

Writing

10 a) (**Aim**) **ICT To develop research skills; to identify key information & make notes**

- Read out the **Writing Tip** box and explain that this information will help Ss to complete the writing task successfully.
- Ask Ss to copy the spidergram from Ex. 7a into their notebooks and give them time to research online and collect information about a popular tourist destination in their country and complete the spidergram.

Suggested Answer Key

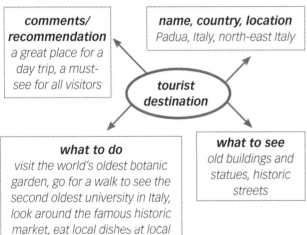

comments/ recommendation
a great place for a day trip, a must-see for all visitors

name, country, location
Padua, Italy, north-east Italy

tourist destination

what to do
visit the world's oldest botanic garden, go for a walk to see the second oldest university in Italy, look around the famous historic market, eat local dishes at local restaurants or cafés

what to see
old buildings and statues, historic streets

b) (**Aim**) **To write an article about a place**

- Explain the task. Then give Ss time to write their articles using their answers from Ex. 10a and the plan to help them.
- Check Ss' answers.
- Alternatively, assign the task as HW and check Ss' answers in the next lesson.

Suggested Answer Key

Padua

In Italy? Don't know where to go? Do you want to see something special? Then pay a visit to Padua, in the north-east of the country.

This pretty city is full of old buildings and statues as well as interesting historic streets. There is so much you can do there! You can visit the world's oldest botanic garden or go for a walk to see the second oldest university in Italy. You can also look around the famous historic market, too! Of course, you can eat local dishes at one of the local restaurants or cafés.

Padua is a great place for a day trip and a must-see for all visitors. Go to Padua now!

Values

Ss try to explain the quotation in their mother tongue. If Ss have difficulty, explain the quotation. Ask Ss to memorise this quotation and check in the next lesson.

The quotation means that when we visit a place we should try to experience everything that place has to offer and show interest and enthusiasm and make every trip an adventure.

Culture 8

Listening & Reading

1 (**Aim**) **To listen and read for specific information**

- Ask Ss to look at the photos and read out the questions.
- Play the recording. Ss listen and read the text to find out.

Answer Key

a volcano – picture B
a waterfall- picture C
a lake – picture D
a fjord – picture A
In Tongariro National Park you can see a volcano, lakes and waterfalls.

- Play the video for Ss and elicit their comments.
- Refer Ss to the Word List to look up the meanings of the words in the **Check these words** box.

2 (**Aim**) **To read for detailed understanding (comprehension questions)**

- Ask Ss to read the questions and then give them time to read the text again and answer them.
- Check Ss' answers.

Answer Key

1 *Up to a million people visit Milford Sound every year.*
2 *Visitors to Milford Sound can see clear water, beautiful waterfalls and fantastic views.*
3 *Visitors can go camping, skiing and mountain biking in Tongariro National Park.*
4 *In Maori, New Zealand's name means the land of the long white cloud.*

Speaking & Writing

3 (**Aim**) (**THINK**) **To compare places**

- Ask Ss to discuss in pairs which place is more interesting to them and why and order the places accordingly.
- Ask some pairs to share their answers with the class.

Suggested Answer Key

Milford Sound is the most interesting place to me followed by Tongariro National Park. I would like to visit Milford Sound because I would like to see the clear water of the fjord, the beautiful waterfalls and the fantastic views there. I would also like to go on a boat cruise.

4 **Aim** **ICT** **To develop research skills; to write shorts text abut places of natural beauty**

- Explain the task and ask Ss to research online to find out information about two places of natural beauty in their country or in another country.
- Give Ss time to use their information to write short texts describing the places and answering the questions.
- Then ask various Ss to present their texts to the class. If Ss prefer they can prepare a digital presentation and present that to the class.
- Alternatively, assign the task as HW and ask Ss to present their texts/presentations in the next lesson.

Suggested Answer Key

The Nærøyfjord is one of the most famous and beautiful fjords in Norway. Visitors from all around the world go there to see its beauty. There are tall mountains on its sides and amazing waterfalls running down them. The tops of the mountains have snow on them too. Visitors can go on a boat cruise and kayaking.

Trollheimen mountain range is where visitors can see some of Norway's most amazing mountains. It's like no place in the world. There, visitors can find some of the tallest mountains in Norway and beautiful lakes as well as popular trekking trails. Visitors can go trekking, skiing and cycling.

Review 8

Vocabulary

1 **Aim** **To practise vocabulary from the unit**

- Explain the task.
- Give Ss time to complete it.
- Check Ss' answers.

Answer Key

1 shops	3 weather	5 traffic
2 clothes	4 buildings	

2 **Aim** **To practise vocabulary from the unit**

- Explain the task.
- Give Ss time to complete it.
- Check Ss' answers.

Answer Key

1 fashionable	3 delicious	5 crowded
2 fascinating	4 noisy	

3 **Aim** **To practise vocabulary for tourist attractions**

- Explain the task.
- Give Ss time to complete it.
- Check Ss' answers.

Answer Key

1 gallery	3 shop
2 stadium	4 park

4 **Aim** **To practise vocabulary from the unit**

- Explain the task.
- Give Ss time to complete it.
- Check Ss' answers.

Answer Key

1 go	3 go	5 watch
2 watch	4 buy	6 see

Grammar

5 **Aim** **To practise the comparative and superlative**

- Explain the task.
- Give Ss time to complete it.
- Check Ss' answers.

Answer Key

1 more	4 noisiest
2 most luxurious	5 best
3 cheaper	

6 Aim To practise the comparative/superlative

- Explain the task.
- Give Ss time to complete it.
- Check Ss' answers.

Answer Key

1	the most expensive	4	taller
2	the hottest	5	more crowded
3	as interesting		

7 Aim To practise the comparative with adverbs of degree

- Explain the task.
- Give Ss time to complete it.
- Check Ss' answers.

Answer Key

1	very	3	too	5	quite
2	too	4	much		

Everyday English

8 Aim To practise functional language

- Explain the task.
- Give Ss time to complete it.
- Check Ss' answers.

Answer Key

1 C	2 D	3 A	4 E	5 B

Competences

Ask Ss to assess their own performance in the unit by ticking the items according to how competent they feel for each of the listed activities.

9 Times change

Topic

In this unit, Ss will explore the topics of features in a place, places/buildings in a town/city, and transport.

9a Reading & Vocabulary	72-73

Lesson objectives: To learn vocabulary for features in a place, to listen and read for detail, to read for specific information (comprehension questions), to talk about Inishmore, to compare two places
Vocabulary: Features in a place *(fishing boats, a souvenir shop, a stone cottage, a ferry boat, an airport, a guest house)*, Nouns *(coast, islander)*; Verb *(seem)*; Phrase *(get around)*

9b Grammar in Use	74-75

Lesson objectives: To learn the past simple of the verb *to be*, to learn the past simple of the verb *have*, to learn the past simple of the verb *can*, to listen for specific information, to compare yourself to Inca children, to create a quiz

9c Skills in Action	76-77

Lesson objectives: To learn vocabulary for places/ buildings in a town/city, to listen for specific information (gap filling), to act out a dialogue and practise everyday English expressions for asking for/giving directions; to pronounce /l/ pronounced or silent, to read for coherence, to write an article about a place then and now
Vocabulary: Places/Buildings in a town/city *(bus stop, museum, park, hotel, bank, post office, petrol station, fire station, supermarket, department store, restaurant, school, cinema, police station, hospital, café, train station)*

Culture 9	78

Lesson objectives: To listen and read for specific information, to present streets in the UK, to present street names and their meaning, to create your own city and street names
Vocabulary: Nouns *(poultry, honour)*; Adjectives *(straight, royal)*

Review 9	79

Lesson objectives: To test/consolidate vocabulary and grammar learnt throughout the unit; to practise everyday English

Go through the objectives box and tell Ss that these are the topics, skills and activities this unit will cover.

9a

Vocabulary

1 **Aim** **To present vocabulary for features in a place**
- Go through the items in the list and explain/elicit the meanings of any unknown words.
- Ask Ss to look at the pictures and match the phrases to the pictures.
- Check Ss' answers around the class.

Answer Key

1 A   2 D   3 B   4 F   5 E   6 C

2 **Aim** **To listen and read for detail**
- Ask Ss to read the summary and try to guess which are the four mistakes.
- Explain to the Ss that they will listen and read the main text, and not the summary, to find out if they are right.
- Play the recording. Ss listen and check.
- Check Ss' answers.

- Play the video for Ss and elicit their comments.

Answer Key

1 west coast (not east coast)
2 donkeys (not bicycles)
3 houses didn't have running water
4 aren't any green fields (Yes, there are)

Reading

3 a) **Aim** **To read for specific information (comprehension questions)**
- Ask Ss to read the questions (1-5) and then give Ss time to read the text and answer them.
- Check Ss' answers.
- Refer Ss to the Word List to look up the meanings of the words in the **Check these words** box.

Answer Key

1 Inishmore is off the west coast of Ireland.
2 Seventy years ago, tourists couldn't reach the island because there wasn't an airport or any ferry boats.
3 The islanders got around on donkeys or small fishing boats.
4 Tourists can reach Inishmore by aeroplane or by ferry boats today.
5 He thinks it is a beautiful island and that life is easier now than it was seventy years ago.

b) **Aim** THINK **To suggest an alternative title for the text**

Elicit suitable alternative titles from Ss around the class.

Suggested Answer Key

Inishmore: How Times Change

4 **Aim** **To consolidate vocabulary and information from a text**

- Read out the words in the list and give Ss time to use them to complete the phrases.
- Check Ss' answers and then give Ss time to use the completed phrases to write sentences based on the text.

Answer Key

1	boats	3	water	5	shops
2	cottages	4	houses	6	fields

Suggested Answer Key

People used to get around in small fishing boats.
Houses in the past were small stone cottages.
They didn't have running water or electricity.
There weren't any guest houses in the past. Today there are souvenir shops.
There are still lots of green fields on Inishmore.

5 **Aim** **To match adjectives to their opposites**

- Explain the task and give Ss time to complete it.
- Check Ss' answers and then have Ss write sentences using the phrases.
- Ask Ss around the class to share their sentences with the rest of the class.

Answer Key

1 big   2 same   3 busy   4 easy

Suggested Answer Key

Inishmore is a little island, but Ireland is a big island.
In some ways, Inishmore is a different place, but in others, it's still the same place.
Inishmore is still a quiet place. It is not a busy place.
People had a difficult life in the past, but today they have an easy life.

6 **Aim** **To consolidate new vocabulary**

- Have Ss explain the words in bold in the text, using their dictionaries as necessary.
- Elicit definitions from Ss around the class.

Suggested Answer Key

exactly: *in every way, completely*
in fact: *in reality/really*

reach: *travel/get to*
getting around: *travelling from one place to another*
electricity: *energy to power appliances and devices*
back then: *at that time in the past*
working hard: *doing a lot of work*

Speaking & Writing

7 **Aim** **To identify key information; to make notes and talk about Inishmore then and now**

- Ask Ss to copy the table into their notebooks and complete it with information about Inishmore then and now from the text in Ex. 2.
- Then ask various Ss around the class to talk about Inishmore then and now.

Suggested Answer Key

THEN	NOW
There weren't any tourists.	There are up to 2,000 tourists a day.
There wasn't an airport or ferry boats.	There is an airport.
There were only donkeys and fishing boats.	They have cars, buses, bicycles and big ferry boats.
Life was difficult.	Life is easy.
People didn't have much money.	People have a lot of money.
They had small stone cottages.	They have got new, modern houses.
They didn't have electricity or running water.	They have got electricity and running water.
It was very quiet.	It is very busy.
There weren't any guest houses or restaurants.	There are guest houses, restaurants and lots of souvenir shops.

There wasn't an airport on Inishmore then. There were only donkeys and fishing boats. Life was difficult then. People didn't have much money and they had small stone cottages. Now they have lots of money and new, modern houses. Now, they've also got electricity and running water, but they didn't have it back then. There weren't any guest houses or restaurants then, but now they have guest houses, restaurants and souvenir shops.

8 **Aim** THINK **To make comparisons**

- Give Ss time to think of comparisons between Inishmore and the place they live, and then write some sentences.
- Ask various Ss to share their sentences with the class.

9

Suggested Answer Key

Where I live is similar to Inishmore because there were only donkeys and fishing boats in the past, but now we have got cars, buses and trains. Also, in the past, people used to have small stone houses, but now they have got modern flats. Where I live, it still hasn't got many guest houses, but it has got some souvenir shops.

9b Grammar in Use

1 **Aim** **To listen for specific information**

- Ask Ss to try and answer the quiz questions.
- Play the recording. Ss listen and check their answers.

Answer Key

1 A	2 B	3 A	4 C

2 **Aim** **To present *was/were* (the past simple of the verb *to be*)**

- Present the past simple affirmative of the verb **to be**. Say then write on the board: *I was at home yesterday.* Underline *was* and explain that this is the verb **to be** in the past simple. Point to a S and say: *You were at home yesterday.* Then write it on the board. Point to a male S and say: *He was at home yesterday.* Then write it on the board. Present the other persons in the same way. Elicit that the verb is **was** in the first and third person and **were** in the second person.
- Present the past simple negative of the verb **to be**. Say then write on the board: *I was not/wasn't at home yesterday.* and *You were not/weren't at home yesterday.* Underline *I was not/wasn't* in the first sentence and *You were not/weren't* in the second sentence. Explain that we use **wasn't/ weren't** + base form of the verb in all persons to form the negative of the past simple.
- Present the past simple interrogative of the verb **to be**. Say then write on the board: *Was I at home yesterday? Yes, I was. No, I wasn't* and *Were you at home yesterday? Yes, you were./No, you weren't.* Explain that we use **was/were** + subject to form questions in the past simple. Point out that we answer in the short form with **Yes/No,** + personal pronoun + **was(n't)/were(n't)**.
- Ask Ss to read the table and then elicit examples in the quiz.

Answer Key

Examples in the text: *London buses weren't red until ..., The first city where people could use an underground train was ..., The Wright Brothers were the first ...*

3 **Aim** **To practise the past simple of the verb *to be***

- Explain the task and give Ss time to complete it.
- Check Ss' answers around the class.

Answer Key

1 was
2 were, weren't, were, were
3 was, wasn't, was
4 was

4 a) **Aim** **To practise the past simple of the verb *to be***

- Explain the task and give Ss time to complete it.
- Check Ss' answers.

Answer Key

1 Were	5 was	9 were	13 was
2 wasn't	6 was	10 was	
3 was	7 was	11 Were	
4 were	8 wasn't	12 wasn't	

b) **Aim** **To develop speaking skills**

- Explain the task. Ask Ss to work in pairs and act out a similar dialogue to the one in Ex. 4a using the prompts.
- Monitor the activity around the class and then ask some pairs to act out their dialogue in front of the class.

Suggested Answer Key

A: *Were you at home last night?*
B: *No, I wasn't. I was at a restaurant.*
A: *Who were you with?*
B: *I was with Sharon.*
A: *How was the food?*
B: *It wasn't very nice. It was horrible. Where were you?*
A: *I was at home.*
B: *Were you with Craig?*
A: *No, I wasn't. He was at a football match.*

5 **Aim** **To practise the past simple of the verb *to be***

- Explain the task and read out the example.
- Ask Ss to work in pairs and ask and answer questions about London using the prompts and following the example.

- Monitor the activity around the class and then ask some pairs to act out their dialogue, in front of the class.

Suggested Answer Key

A: Were there any post offices in London 150 years ago?
B: Yes, there were. Were there any blocks of flats?
A: No, there weren't. Were there any horses?
B: Yes, there were. Was there any electricity?
A: No, there wasn't. Were there any phone boxes?
B: No, there weren't. Were there any tea rooms?
A: Yes, there were. Was there an airport?
B: No, there wasn't. Were there any theatres?
A: Yes, there were. Was there a football stadium?
B: No, there wasn't.

6 **Aim** **To present the past simple of the verb** *have*

- Present the past simple of the verb *have*. Say and write on the board: *I had fun yesterday.* Underline *had* and explain that **had** is the past tense of the verb **have**. Explain that it is the same in all persons. Explain that the negative form is **didn't have** for all persons. Explain that the interrogative form is **Did** + subject + **have** for all persons.
- Ask Ss to read the table and then elicit an example from the quiz, in Ex. 1.

Answer Key

The first cars didn't have

7 **Aim** **To practise the past simple of the verb** *have*

- Explain the task and give Ss time to complete it.
- Check Ss' answers around the class.

Answer Key

1 had, have
2 have, had
3 didn't have, had, have
4 didn't have, have

8 a) **Aim** **To practise the past simple of the verb** *have*

- Explain the task and read out the example exchange.
- Give Ss time to tick the items and then have Ss complete the task in pairs following the example.
- Monitor the activity around the class and then ask some pairs to act out their dialogue, in front of the class.

Answer Key

hot-air balloons ✓   computers ✗
mobile phones ✗   telephones ✓
GPS devices ✗   cars ✓
typewriters ✓   USB flash drives ✗

Suggested Answer Key

A: Did they have hot-air balloons?
B: Yes, they did. Did they have mobile phones?
A: No, they didn't. Did they have GPS devices?
B: No, they didn't. Did they have typewriters?
A: Yes, they did. Did they have computers?
B: No, they didn't. Did they have telephones?
A: Yes, they did. Did they have cars?
B: Yes, they did. Did they have USB flash drives?
A: No, they didn't.

b) **Aim** **To practise the past simple of the verb** *have*

- Explain the task and read out the example.
- Check Ss' answers around the class.

Answer Key

People had hot-air balloons 100 years ago.
People didn't have mobile phones 100 years ago.
People didn't have GPS devices 100 years ago.
People had typewriters 100 years ago.
People didn't have computers 100 years ago.
People had telephones 100 years ago.
People had cars 100 years ago.
People didn't have USB flash drives 100 years ago.

9 **Aim** **To present the past simple of the verb** *can*

- Present the past simple of the verb **can**. Say and write on the board: *I could ride a bike when I was young.* Underline *could* and explain that **could** is the past tense of the verb **can**. Explain that it is the same in all persons. Explain that the negative form is **couldn't** for all persons. Explain that the interrogative form is **Could** + subject for all persons.
- Ask Ss to read the table and then elicit an example from the quiz in Ex. 1.

Answer Key

The first city where people could use ...

10 a) **Aim** **To listen for specific information and practise the past simple of the verb** *can*

- Explain the task, read out the example and then play the recording.
- Ss listen and fill in the ages.
- Then give Ss time to make sentences following the example.

Answer Key

	Paul	Doug
talk	1	2
count	**2**	3
read	2	5
walk	2	**3**
ride a bicycle	**3**	10
swim	**4**	**10**

Suggested Answer Key

Paul could count when he was two, but Doug couldn't count until he was three.

Paul could read when he was two, but Doug couldn't read until he was five.

Paul could walk when he was two, but Doug couldn't walk until he was three.

Paul could ride a bicycle when he was three, but Doug couldn't ride a bicycle until he was ten.

Paul could swim when he was four, but Doug couldn't swim until he was ten.

b) Aim To practise the past simple of the verb *can* using personal examples

Elicit sentences from Ss around the class.

Suggested Answer Key

I could walk when I was one, but I couldn't talk until I was two. I could count when I was three, but I couldn't read until I was six. I could swim when I was five but I couldn't ride a bicycle until I was seven.

11 Aim To practise the past simple of the verbs *to be*, *have* and *can*

- Explain the task and give Ss time to complete it.
- Check Ss' answers.

Answer Key

1	were	8	was	15	had
2	had	9	were	16	had
3	weren't	10	could	17	was
4	weren't	11	couldn't	18	had
5	had	12	were	19	couldn't
6	didn't have	13	were	20	had
7	were	14	were		

12 a) Aim To do a quiz and listen for specific information

- Ask Ss to try and answer the quiz questions.
- Play the recording. Ss listen and check their answers.

Answer Key

1	B	2	A	3	A	4	B

b) Aim To make comparisons

- Explain the task and read out the example.
- Elicit comparisons from children around the class.

Suggested Answer Key

When I was eight I had lots of paper books. Inca children didn't have any paper books. They had wooden toys. When I was eight, I could read and write. Inca children couldn't read or write. They could cook, farm and fish. When I was eight, my favourite food was meat. Inca children's favourite food wasn't meat. Inca children's favourite food was potatoes and corn. When I was eight my favourite games were board games. Inca children's favourite games were board games, too!

13 Aim ICT To create a quiz

- Ask Ss to work in groups and research online to collect information about another ancient civilization and prepare a quiz.
- Have groups exchange their quizzes and try to complete them.

Suggested Answer Key

1 Maya children…
  A helped their parents.
  B went to school.
2 Maya children didn't have…
  A tools for their jobs.
  B toys to play with.
3 The Maya children ate…
  A fish and chips.
  B corn and beans.
4 Maya children became adults when they were…
  A 13.
  B 15.

9c Skills in Action

Vocabulary

1 a) **Aim** **To present vocabulary for places/ buildings in a town/city**

- Ask Ss to look at the map.
- Then give Ss time to complete the task. Explain/ Elicit the meanings of any unknown words.
- Check Ss' answers.

Answer Key

1 next to	3 opposite	5 on
2 between	4 in front of	

b) **Aim** **To practise locating places on a map/ describing location**

- Explain the task and ask Ss to complete the task in pairs.
- Ask some pairs to tell the class.

Suggested Answer Key

The hospital is opposite the police station.
The bank is opposite the school.
The petrol station is opposite the park.
The department store is opposite the museum.
The restaurant is next to the café.
The train station is opposite the restaurant.
The hotel is between the museum and the café.

Listening

2 **Aim** **To listen for specific information (gap filling)**

- Ask Ss to look at the gapped text and then play the recording.
- Ss listen and complete the gaps.
- Check Ss' answers.

Answer Key

1 Grand Hotel	4 Hill	
2 up	5 left	
3 400		

Everyday English

3 **Aim** **To read for cohesion and coherence; to listen for confirmation**

- Ask Ss to look at the map, read the dialogue and choose the correct words.
- Play the recording. Ss listen and check their answers.

Answer Key

1 right	2 right	3 left

4 **Aim** **To act out a dialogue asking for/giving directions**

- Explain the task and ask Ss to act out a similar dialogue to the one in Ex. 3 in pairs using the prompts and the Useful Language.
- Write this diagram on the board for Ss to follow.

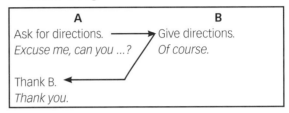

- Monitor the activity around the class and offer assistance as necessary.
- Then ask some pairs to act out their dialogues in front of the rest of the class.

Suggested Answer Key

From the hotel to the post office
A: *Excuse me, can you tell me how to get to the post office?*
B: *Of course. Walk down Hill Street and turn right onto King Street. It's on the right, opposite the supermarket.*
A: *Thank you.*

From the café to the petrol station
A: *Excuse me, I'm looking for the petrol station.*
B: *Okay. Walk down Hill Street and turn left onto King Street. Then walk down King Street and the petrol station is on the left opposite the park.*
A: *Thank you.*

From the cinema to the supermarket
A: *Could you tell me the way to the supermarket?*
B: *Of course. Go up Hill Street and turn left onto King Street. Then, go up King Street and the supermarket is on your left. It's opposite the post office.*

Pronunciation

5 **Aim** **To pronounce /l/**

- Play the recording and have Ss circle the words in which the /l/ is silent.
- Play the recording again with pauses for Ss to repeat chorally and/or individually.
- Check Ss' pronunciation and intonation.

Answer Key

could, talk, walk

Reading & Writing

6 **Aim** **To read for coherence**

- Give Ss time to read the article and put the paragraphs into the correct order.
- Check Ss' answers.

Answer Key

A 2   B 1   C 4   D 3

7 **Aim** **To present and practise linkers**

- Read out the *Writing Tip* box and explain that this information will help Ss understand how to use linkers.
- Give Ss time to complete the task using the correct linkers.
- Check Ss' answers.

Answer Key

1 because	3 because	5 so
2 so	4 so	6 because

8 **Aim** **To elicit understanding of a text**

- Ask Ss to complete the table with information about Canary Wharf then and now.
- Then ask various Ss around the class to talk about Canary Wharf then and now.

Answer Key

Then: *dirty, empty, many, much, nice*
Now: *cleaner, flats, lovely, train(s)*

Suggested Answer Key

Fifty years ago, Canary Wharf was a dirty area. There were empty warehouses and there weren't many shops. Nowadays, it is a lot cleaner and there are flats, lots of shops, offices and restaurants. Back then, people didn't have much money and they didn't have cars or nice houses. They could only travel by bus or on foot. Today, people have got more money and they've got cars and lovely houses. They can also travel by train or plane.

9 **Aim** **ICT** **To develop research skills; to identify key information and make notes**

Ask Ss to research online and collect information about what the place they live was like then and now and complete a table like the one in Ex. 8.

Suggested Answer Key

THEN	NOW
Athens was quieter.	*Athens is busier.*
There weren't many shops, restaurants or cafés.	*There are lots of shops, restaurants, offices and cafés.*
There weren't many tourists.	*There are a lot of tourists.*
People had small houses.	*People have flats.*
People could only get around by bus, train or on foot.	*People can get around by bus, trolley, metro and tram.*

Writing

10 **Aim** **To write an article about place then and now**

- Explain the task. Then give Ss time to write their article using their answers from Ex. 9 and the plan to help them.
- Check Ss' answers.
- Alternatively, assign the task as HW and check Ss' answers in the next lesson.

Suggested Answer Key

Athens is the capital city of Greece. Today, the city is different to how it was fifty years ago.

Athens was quieter. There weren't many shops, restaurants or cafés and there weren't many tourists. People had small houses and could only get around by bus, train or on foot.

Nowadays, Athens is much busier. There are lots of shops, restaurants, offices and cafés. There are also a lot of tourists. People live in flats and can get around by bus, trolley, metro and tram.

Athens has got so much to offer. It is a great place to live in.

Values

Ss try to explain the quotation in their mother tongue. If Ss have difficulty, explain the quotation. Ask Ss to memorise this quotation and check in the next lesson.

The quotation means that the more effort or hard work you put into something then the more rewarding it is. This may be in terms of personal satisfaction or other rewards such as money or praise.

Culture 9

Listening & Reading

1 **Aim** **To listen and read for specific information**

- Ask Ss to look at the signs and read out the question.
- Play the recording. Ss listen and read the text to find out.

Answer Key

Streets in the UK get their names from work names, descriptions of streets and from the royal family.

- Play the video for Ss and elicit their comments.
- Refer Ss to the Word List to look up the meanings of the words in the **Check these words** box.

2 **Aim** **To read for detailed understanding**

- Ask Ss to read the text again and elicit explanations for the street names in the photos.
- Check Ss' answers.

Answer Key

Castle Hill gets its name from a castle nearby.
Curtain Road gets its name because of shops there that made or sold curtains.
Prince Avenue got its name from a prince in the royal family.

Speaking & Writing

3 **Aim** **To consolidate information in a text**

Ask various Ss around the class to present streets in the UK and the meaning of their names using the signs.

Suggested Answer Key

In the UK, streets names have interesting stories behind them. Some might describe places of work that were on the street. For example, on Curtain Road there were lots of shops where people made or sold curtains. Other streets have names that describe them. For example, Castle Hill is a street that is close to a castle. Other roads can have names from the royal family, for example Prince Avenue.

4 **Aim** **ICT** **To present street names in your country**

- Explain the task and ask Ss to work in small groups and research online to find out about street names in their country.
- Give Ss time to use the information and prepare a presentation.
- Then ask various Ss to present their information to the class.

- Alternatively, assign the task as HW and ask Ss to present their information in the next lesson.

Suggested Answer Key

There are streets in Italy that get their names from important people. For example, Via Abramo Lincoln, Via Garibaldi or Via Matteotti. In this way, people are able to honour people from Italy's past.
Some Italian street names get their names from important dates in Italian history. For example; Via XXV Aprile, or Via 1 Maggio which are also national holidays in Italy.
Also in most Italian towns there is a street called Via Roma which leads to Rome.

5 **Aim** **THINK** **To create your own city**

- Give Ss time to create their own city and name the streets.
- Ask various Ss to present their city to the class and explain where the streets get their names from.

Suggested Answer Key

In my city there are streets that get their names from a description of the street. For example, Ocean View Road – from this street you can see the ocean. I also have 1st May Avenue because in my country, 1st May is an important national holiday. Next, we have Greengrocer's Lane. This street gets its name from all of the shops selling fruit and vegetables there. Finally, we have Tower Hill, this street goes up to the famous city tower. etc

Review 9

Vocabulary

1 **Aim** **To practise vocabulary from the unit**

- Explain the task.
- Give Ss time to complete it.
- Check Ss' answers.

Answer Key

1 fishing	3 stone	5 green
2 running	4 west	

2 **Aim** **To practise vocabulary from the unit**

- Explain the task.
- Give Ss time to complete it.
- Check Ss' answers.

Answer Key

1 big	3 different	5 difficult
2 busy	4 quiet	

3 **Aim** To practise vocabulary for places/ buildings in a town/city

- Explain the task.
- Give Ss time to complete it.
- Check Ss' answers.

Answer Key

1 C	3 J	5 B	7 F	9 A
2 D	4 E	6 H	8 G	10 I

Grammar

4 **Aim** To practise the past simple of the verbs *to be, have, can*

- Explain the task.
- Give Ss time to complete it.
- Check Ss' answers.

Answer Key

1 Were, wasn't	4 Was, was
2 have, didn't	5 Did, did
3 Could, could	

5 **Aim** To practise the past simple of the verbs *to be, have, can*

- Explain the task.
- Give Ss time to complete it.
- Check Ss' answers.

Answer Key

1 is, wasn't	4 have got, haven't got
2 are, were	5 was, weren't
3 Could, couldn't, can	

Everyday English

6 **Aim** To complete a dialogue

- Explain the task.
- Give Ss time to complete it.
- Check Ss' answers.

Answer Key

1 Excuse	4 corner
2 Walk	5 opposite
3 turn	

Competences

Ask Ss to assess their own performance in the unit by ticking the items according to how competent they feel for each of the listed activities.

Values: Respect

1 **Aim** To listen and read for specific information

- Ask Ss to look at the title of the text.
- Elicit how travellers can show respect to local cultures.
- Play the recording. Ss listen and read the text and find out.

Answer Key

People can show respect to local cultures by asking before taking pictures, respecting the local dress code, leaving things how they find them and being careful what they buy.

- Play the video for Ss and elicit their comments.

2 **Aim** (THINK) **To understand the author's purpose**

- Ask Ss to consider the author's purpose in writing the text.
- Elicit Ss' answers and ask Ss to say how the information can help them.

Suggested Answer Key

The purpose of the text is to persuade people to show respect when they travel and to inform them how they can do this. The information can help me the next time I go abroad. I'll try hard to respect the local culture.

3 **Aim** (THINK) **To discuss how visitors can show respect in their country**

- Ask Ss to work in small groups and discuss how visitors can show respect in their country.
- Monitor the activity around the class and then ask various groups to share their answers with the class.

Suggested Answer Key

A: *Every country has different types of etiquette. My country, Egypt, is no different! First, it is common to wear clothes that cover your shoulders. So visitors should make sure they wear clothes that show respect for the culture.*

B: *Yes, and people should take off their shoes when they enter someone's home. This shows respect, too.*

C: *Also, people should use their right hand to shake hands, take food and accept gifts. The left hand is unclean in Egypt so it is rude to use it for these things.*

A: *That's right, and visitors can bring a gift to someone's home, but don't bring flowers. Flowers are for funerals and weddings. Instead, they can bring sweets or other small gifts.*

B: *That's true. Every country is different, and the rules of etiquette in Egypt are not the same as the rules in other countries.*

C: *Yes. I think if you follow these rules and show respect, you can have a great time in Egypt without being rude.*

Public Speaking Skills

1 a) **(Aim)** **To understand a public speaking task**

- Ask Ss to read the task to identify what the presentation will be about.
- Elicit who the speaker is (a student), who the audience will be (other students) and what the presentation will be about (present a historic landmark from S's country).

b) **(Aim)** **To analyse a model public speaking task**

- Play the recording. Ss listen and read the model.
- Then ask Ss to copy the spidergram into their notebooks and complete it.
- Play the recording again if necessary.

Suggested Answer Key

comments/feelings: special because other pyramids have paintings and objects, but Great Pyramid doesn't, it was one of the Seven Wonders of the Ancient World, Egyptians are proud, it is a symbol of the start of Egypt's civilisation

where: at Giza, near Cairo in Egypt

Landmark the Great Pyramid

purpose: no one is sure, but people think it was a tomb for King Khufu

description: 146 metres tall, 230 metres wide at the bottom, over 2 million blocks of stone, 4,500 years old

2 (Aim) To learn about getting feedback from the audience

Ask Ss to read the **Study Skills** box and then elicit which method of getting feedback from the audience is used in the model.

Answer Key

Feedback technique: *pop quiz style questions in teams*

3 (Aim) ICT To prepare and give a presentation on a historic landmark

- Ask Ss to copy the spidergram from Ex. 1b into their notebooks and give them time to complete it with information about a historic landmark in their country.
- Then ask Ss to use their notes and the model to help them prepare a presentation on the historic landmark.

- Ask various Ss to give their presentation to the class.
- Alternatively, assign the task as HW and have Ss give their presentations in the next lesson.

Suggested Answer Key

Landmark: *the Eiffel Tower*
where: *Paris, France*
description: *324 metres tall, made out of 18,000 pieces of iron, 5 billion lights on it, designed by Gustave Eiffel, almost 130 years old*
purpose: *made for World's Fair, at first, people thought it was ugly, but soon became a symbol of the city of Paris*
comments/feelings: *people come to Paris from all over the world to see the beautiful Eiffel tower, proud of symbol of Paris*

Hi, everyone! I'm Jacques Trudeau. What is the most famous landmark in the world? … The Taj Mahal in India? The Colosseum in Rome? Good answers! But there's one place that stands out more than those famous landmarks: it's the Eiffel Tower!

The Eiffel Tower is in Paris, France. It's 324 metres tall and it's made out of 18,000 pieces of iron. There are five billion lights on it, too! An engineer named Gustave Eiffel designed it and they built it in 1889, so now it's almost 130 years old.

Gustave Eiffel made the Eiffel Tower for the 1889 World's Fair. At first, people thought it was ugly, but soon it became a symbol of the city of Paris. Today, people come to Paris from all over the world to see the beautiful Eiffel Tower. I feel proud of this symbol of Paris, and so do all French people! In the words of Ernest Hemingway, "There are only two places in the world where we can live happy: at home and in Paris." My home is in Paris, so I'm very happy!

Now, please get into groups of three and talk about this question: What impresses you the most about the Eiffel Tower and why? …

Thank you for your time.

Their stories live on

Topic

In this unit, Ss will explore the topics of famous people and their achievements, jobs, and feelings/reactions.

10a Reading & Vocabulary	82-83

Lesson objectives: To learn vocabulary for jobs, to read dates, to listen and read for specific information (T/F statements), to read for specific information (multiple matching), to talk about jobs, to talk about famous people, to write about and present famous people from your country
Vocabulary: Jobs *(painter, physicist, teacher, politician, lawyer, actor, model, inventor, engineer, zoologist)*; Nouns *(robbery, crash, theory of relativity, equation)*; Verb *(fire)*

10b Grammar in Use	84-85

Lesson objectives: learn the past simple, to act out dialogues, to learn prepositions of movement, to tell a story

10c Skills in Action	86-87

Lesson objectives: To learn vocabulary for feelings/reactions, to listen for order of events, to act out a dialogue and practise everyday English expressions for narrating an event, to learn intonation in yes/no questions, to learn linkers, to learn adjectives and adverbs, to write a story
Vocabulary: Feelings/Reactions *(frightened, happy, upset, worried, shocked, excited, proud, confused)*

Culture 10	88

Lesson objectives: To listen and read for specific information, to read for specific information (T/F/DS statements), to talk about William Shakespeare, to write a short article about a famous writer from your country
Vocabulary: Noun *(leather)*; Verb *(inspire)*; Adverb *(definitely)*

Review 10	89

Lesson objectives: To test/consolidate vocabulary and grammar learnt throughout the unit; to practise everyday English

Go through the objectives box and tell Ss that these are the topics, skills and activities this unit will cover.

10a

Vocabulary

1 **Aim** To present vocabulary for jobs
- Ask Ss to look at the people in the pictures. Elicit whether Ss are familiar with any of them.
- Explain/Elicit the meanings of the jobs in the fact files.
- Ask Ss to read the fact files and match the people in the pictures to them.
- Check Ss' answers.

Answer Key

1 F   2 D   3 C   4 A   5 E   6 B

2 **Aim** To learn to read dates
- Read out the ***Study Skills*** box and explain how we read dates.
- Then explain the task and read out the example.
- Have Ss work in pairs and ask and answer questions following the example to practise reading dates using the information in the fact files.
- Monitor the activity around the class.

Suggested Answer Key

B: Who was Roger Moore?
A: He was a British actor and model.
B: When was he born?
A: He was born on the 14th of October, 1927.
B: When did he die?
A: He died on the 23rd of May, 2017. Who was Dian Fossey?
B: She was an American zoologist.
A: When was she born?
B: She was born on the 16th of January, 1932.
A: When did she die?
B: She died on the 26th of December, 1985. Who was Mahatma Gandhi?
A: He was an Indian politician and lawyer.
B: When was he born?
A: He was born on the 2nd of October, 1869.
B: When did he die?
A: He died on the 30th of January, 1948. Who was Albert Einstein?
B: He was a German physicist and teacher.
A: When was he born?
B: He was born on the 14th of March, 1879.
A: When did he die?
B: He died on the 18th of April, 1955. Who was Frida Kahlo?
A: She was a Mexican painter.

91

B: When was she born?
A: She was born on the 6th of July, 1907.
B: When did she die?
A: She died on the 13th of July, 1954.

Reading

3 Aim To read for specific information (T/F statements)

- Ask Ss to read the sentences.
- Play the recording. Ss listen and read the text and mark the statements as true or false.
- Check Ss' answers.

Answer Key

1 F	2 F	3 T

4 Aim To read for specific information (multiple matching)

- Give Ss time to read the text again and decide who each statement refers to and write the correct letters.
- Check Ss' answers.

Answer Key

1 AE	2 RM	3 FK	4 RM

- Play the video for Ss and elicit their comments.
- Refer Ss to the Word List to look up the meanings of the words in the **Check these words** box.

5 Aim To distinguish between words easily confused (*work/job*)

- Read out the sentences and give Ss time to complete them with either *work* or *job*.
- Check Ss' answers.

Answer Key

1 job	3 job	5 job
2 work	4 work	

6 Aim To skim a text; to describe job duties

- Ask Ss to scan the text and find five jobs and then explain them to their partner.
- Ask some pairs to share their answers with the class.

Suggested Answer Key

A police officer protects people and looks into crimes to find out who did them.
A film director tells actors what to do when making a film.
A doctor treats people when they are sick or injured.
A teacher helps students learn.
An inventor comes up with new inventions.

Speaking

7 Aim THINK To express an opinion; to talk about famous people

Elicit answers from Ss around the class and ask Ss to provide reasons to support their opinion.

Suggested Answer Key

I think the luckiest person in the text was Roger Moore because a film director offered him a part and he didn't have to work hard to get it.

8 Aim THINK ICT To develop research skills; to write about famous people from your country

- Ask Ss to research online and find information about six famous people from the past from their country.
- Then give Ss time to find photos and label them with their names and the other information required in the rubric.
- Ask various Ss around the class to present their famous people to the class.
- Alternatively, assign the task as HW and have Ss present the people in the next lesson.

Suggested Answer Key

Hi everyone! I'm Giuseppe Russo. Do you know the most famous people from Italy's history? Well, let me tell you about some of them.

This is Leonardo da Vinci. He was a famous Italian painter. He was born on the 15th of April, 1452. He died on the 2nd of May, 1519.

This is Christopher Columbus. He was a famous Italian explorer. He was born in 1451 and died on the 20th of May, 1506.

Another famous Italian person was Marco Polo. He was a famous Italian explorer. He was born in 1254. He died on the 8th of January, 1324.

Next, this is Galileo Galilei. He was a famous Italian astronomer. He was born on the 15th of February, 1564. He died on the 8th of January, 1642.

This is Maria Montessori. She was a famous Italian educator. She was born on the 31st of August, 1870. She died on the 6th of May, 1952.

Finally, this is Jean-Baptiste Lully. He was a famous Italian composer. He was born on the 28th of November, 1632. He died on the 22nd of March, 1687.
These are just a few of the most famous people in my country's history. Thank you.

10b Grammar in Use

1 a) Aim To present the past simple

- Present the past simple.
- Say then write on the board: *I watched TV yesterday.* Underline *watched* and explain that this verb is in the past simple. Point to a S and say: *You watched TV yesterday.* Then write it on the board. Point to a male S and say: *He watched TV yesterday.* Then write it on the board. Present the other persons in the same way. Elicit that the verb is the same in all persons.
- Explain/Elicit the spelling rules of the past simple for regular verbs by writing the verbs *work, love, play, study, travel* and their past simple forms on the board: *work – worked* (most verbs take **-ed** to form their past simple form), *love – loved* (verbs ending in **-e** add **-d**), *study – studied* (verbs ending in a consonant + **-y** lose **-y** and take **-ied**), *play – played* (verbs ending in a vowel + **-y** add **-ed**), *travel – travelled* (verbs ending in a vowel + **l**, **p**, **k**, **b**, etc, double the consonant and add **-ed**).
- Say, then write on the board: *Did I watch TV yesterday? No, I didn't.* and *Did you watch TV yesterday? No, you didn't.* Explain that we use **Did** + personal pronoun + base form of the main verb to form questions in the past simple. Focus Ss' attention on the position of **did** (before the personal pronoun). Point out that we answer in the short form with **Yes,/No,** + personal pronoun + **did/didn't**.
- Say, then write on the board: *I didn't watch TV yesterday.* and *She didn't watch TV yesterday.* Underline *I didn't* in the first sentence and *She didn't* in the second sentence. Explain that we use **didn't** in all persons to form the negative of the past simple. Point out that the verb is the same in all persons.
- Direct Ss' attention to the theory box and have them study it and then elicit examples from the text message.

Answer Key

Examples: *was born, he went to England, his father died, he could join, mother taught, Tolkien learned to love books, she died too, he was 12, friend of the family raised him, Tolkien studied, he married Edith Bratt, but left in the same year, He left the army, started his academic career, also wrote stories, Tolkien began 'The Hobbit', It made him very famous, he wrote 'The Lord of the Rings', It took him, He died on*

Background Information

South Africa is the largest and most southernmost country in Africa. It is a multi-ethnic country and has 11 official languages. The capital city is Pretoria and the population is around 55 million people.

b) Aim To practise the past simple and identify regular/irregular verbs

- Explain the task and read out the example.
- Give Ss time to complete the task.
- Check Ss' answers around the class.

Answer Key

2 died – regular	9 left – irregular
3 could – irregular	10 started – regular
4 taught – irregular	11 wrote – irregular
5 learned – regular	12 began – irregular
6 raised – regular	13 made – irregular
7 studied – regular	14 took – irregular
8 married – regular	

2 a) Aim To practise the past simple and identify regular/irregular verbs

- Give Ss time to read the text and complete the task.
- Check Ss' answers and elicit the irregular verbs from Ss around the class.

Answer Key

1 was – irregular	7 discovered – regular
2 studied – regular	8 received – regular
3 returned – regular	9 died – regular
4 worked – regular	10 was – irregular
5 married – regular	11 died – regular
6 had – irregular	12 buried – regular

b) Aim To consolidate information in a text and practise the past simple

- Explain the task and read out the example.
- Then ask Ss to complete the task in pairs following the example.

- Ask various pairs to ask and answer in front of the class.

Answer Key

2   A: Did he work as a doctor?
    B: No, he didn't. He worked as a professor.

3   A: Did he marry Mary Marion McElroy?
    B: No, he didn't. He married Sarah Marion McElroy.

4   A: Did he/they have a daughter?
    B: No, he/they didn't. He/They had a son.

5   A: Did he discover radium?
    B: No, he didn't. He discovered penicillin.

6   A: Did he receive the Nobel Prize for Science?
    B: No, he didn't. He received the Nobel Prize for Medicine.

7   A: Did he die in 1965?
    B: No, he didn't. He died in 1955.

3 **Aim** **To practise the past simple interrogative forms**

- Explain the task and read out the example.
- Then give Ss time to complete the task.
- Check Ss' answers around the class.

Answer Key

2   Elvis Presley got his first guitar on his eleventh birthday.

3   Elvis Presley recorded his first hit in 1954.

4   Elvis Presley didn't write his own songs.

5   Elvis Presley made 31 films.

6   Elvis Presley didn't perform concerts in Europe.

Background Information

Elvis Presley (1935-1977) was a very famous singer, musician and actor. He was a cultural icon of the 20th century and he was known as the 'King of Rock and Roll'.

4 **Aim** **To practise the past simple**

- Explain the task and read out the example.
- Give Ss time to complete the task in pairs using the time expressions and the prompts.
- Monitor the activity around the class and then ask some pairs to act out their dialogues in front of the class.

Suggested Answer Key

B: When was the last time you posted a video online?
A: The last time I posted a video online was yesterday. How about you?
B: The last time I posted a video online was a week ago.

A: When was the last time you went shopping?
B: The last time I went shopping was two days ago. How about you?
A: The last time I went shopping was yesterday evening.

B: When was the last time you got a gift?
A: The last time I got a gift was last Tuesday. How about you?
B: The last time I got a gift was two weeks ago.

A: When was the last time you updated your social media profile?
B: The last time I updated my social media profile was two days ago. How about you?
A: The last time I updated my social media profile was yesterday morning.

B: When was the last time you lent money to a friend?
A: The last time I lent money to a friend was a week ago. How about you?
B: The last time I lent money to a friend was six weeks ago.

A: When was the last time you ate at a restaurant?
B: The last time I ate at a restaurant was three days ago. How about you?
A: The last time I ate at a restaurant was six weeks ago.

B: When was the last time you met a famous person?
A: The last time I met a famous person was ten years ago. How about you?
B: The last time I met a famous person was five years ago.

5 **Aim** **To practise the past simple; to identify sentence cohesion**

- Explain the task and ask Ss to read items 1-6 and a-f.
- Give Ss time to complete the past simple forms and then match the items.
- Check Ss' answers.

Answer Key

1   gave > d – adopted
2   met > a – became
3   designed > f – agreed
4   was > e – left
5   returned > b – led
6   died > c – was

6 **Aim** **To present prepositions of movement**

- Use the pictures to explain prepositions of movement.
- Then give Ss time to read the text and fill in the gaps with the prepositions of movement from the pictures.

- Then ask Ss to put the pictures in order according to the story.
- Check Ss' answers and then ask various Ss to tell the story using the pictures.

Answer Key

2	through	5	down	8	across
3	towards	6	past	9	over
4	up	7	over	10	into

Order: 1 – e, 2 – h, 3 – b, 4 – d, 5 – a, 6 – f, 7 – c, 8 – i, 9 – g

Suggested Answer Key

Ralph went horse-riding in the countryside. First, he went along the road and through a tunnel. Then, he went towards the forest. Next, he went up and down a hill. After, he went past a cottage and under a bridge. Finally, he went across a field. A tractor scared the horse, and it jumped over the fence. Then, Ralph fell into the lake. He got very wet!

7 **Aim** **To practise prepositions of movement; to narrate a story**

- Explain the task and ask Ss to work in pairs and take turns telling the story with three mistakes for their partner to correct.
- Monitor the activity around the class.

Suggested Answer Key

A: *Ralph went horse-riding in the countryside. First, he went along a road and past a tunnel.*

B: *No! He didn't go past a tunnel. He went through a tunnel.*

A: *That's right, he went through a tunnel. Then, he went towards a forest. Next, he went up and down a hill. After, he went into a cottage.*

B: *No! He didn't go into a cottage. He went past a cottage.*

A: *Yes, he went past a cottage. Next, he went under a bridge. Finally, he went across a field. A tractor scared the horse, and it jumped through a fence.*

B: *No! It didn't jump through a fence. It jumped over a fence.*

A: *Yes, it jumped over a fence. Then, Ralph fell into a lake. He got very wet!*

10c Skills in Action

Vocabulary

1 **a)** **Aim** **To present vocabulary for feelings/ reactions**

- Ask Ss to look at the pictures.

- Play the recording. Ss listen and repeat chorally and/or individually. Check Ss' pronunciation and intonation.
- Elicit which feelings are negative and which are positive.

Answer Key

Positive feelings: *happy, excited, proud*
Negative feelings: *frightened, upset, worried, shocked, confused*

b) **Aim** **To practise vocabulary for feelings/ reactions**

- Explain the task and read out the example.
- Ask Ss to work in pairs and set a two-minute time limit for the task.
- Check Ss' answers around the class.

Suggested Answer Key

I visited a friend I didn't see for a long time. I felt happy.
My team lost the football match yesterday. I felt upset.
I didn't study for my exam. I felt worried.
I saw a snake. I felt shocked.
I met my favourite actor. I felt excited.
I won a science award. I felt proud.
I didn't understand a question on my test. I felt confused.

Listening

2 **a)** **Aim** **To predict content of a listening task**

Play the recording and elicit what Ss think the story is going to be about based on the sounds.

Suggested Answer Key

I think someone's car breaks down in a dangerous situation with wild animals nearby, but they manage to get away.

b) **Aim** **To listen for order of events**

- Ask Ss to read the events.
- Play the recording.
- Ss listen and put the events in the correct order.
- Check Ss' answers.

Answer Key

2 *They stopped to take pictures of lions.*
3 *The lions scared Claire.*
4 *The car wouldn't start.*
5 *Smoke and flames came out of the engine.*
6 *They tried to attract someone's attention.*
7 *A ranger scared away the lions.*
8 *They climbed into the ranger's truck.*

Everyday English

3 **Aim** To practise the past simple; to listen for confirmation

- Ask Ss to read the dialogue and put the verbs in brackets into the past simple.
- Play the recording. Ss listen and check their answers.

Answer Key

1	*Did you enjoy*	5	*saw*
2	*had*	6	*did you do*
3	*met*	7	*went*
4	*did that happen*	8	*asked*

4 **Aim** To narrate an event

- Explain the task and read out the example.
- Ask Ss to act out similar exchanges in pairs using the phrases in the Useful Language box.
- Write this diagram on the board for Ss to follow.

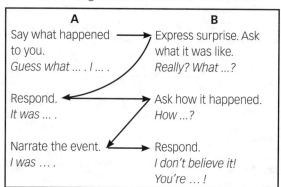

A	B
Say what happened to you. *Guess what … . I … .*	Express surprise. Ask what it was like. *Really? What …?*
Respond. *It was … .*	Ask how it happened. *How …?*
Narrate the event. *I was … .*	Respond. *I don't believe it! You're … !*

- Monitor the activity around the class and offer assistance as necessary.
- Then ask some pairs to act out their exchanges in front of the class.

Suggested Answer Key

B: *Guess what happened to me. I met my favourite pop star, Lady Gaga!*
A: *Really? What was it like?*
B: *It was fantastic.*
A: *How did it happen?*
B: *I was at a small café and she walked by the window! I went outside and asked her for a selfie with her.*
A: *I don't believe it! You're so lucky!*

Intonation

5 **Aim** To practise intonation in *yes/no* questions

- Play the recording with pauses for Ss to repeat chorally and/or individually.
- Check Ss' pronunciation and intonation.

Reading & Writing

6 **Aim** To present and practise linkers

- Read out the theory box and ask Ss to read the examples aloud.
- Then give Ss time to read the story and choose the correct linking words.
- Check Ss' answers.

Answer Key

1	*and*	4	*because*	7	*and*
2	*when*	5	*so*		
3	*but*	6	*then*		

7 **Aim** To present and practise adjectives and adverbs used in stories

- Read out the **Writing Tip** box and explain that this information will help Ss when they have to write a story.
- Explain the task and give Ss time to complete it.
- Check Ss' answers.

Answer Key

day: *warm autumn*
friend: *close*
road: *wide*
cry: *frightened*
face: *pale*
voice: *low*

8 **Aim** To form adverbs; consolidate understanding of use of adjectives and adverbs

- Explain the task and give Ss time to complete the table with the adverbs formed from the adjectives.
- Check Ss' answers and then elicit which adverbs the writer used in the story and which adjectives they come from.

Answer Key

Adjective	Adverb	Adjective	Adverb
hard	*hard*	*fast*	*fast*
strange	*strangely*	*easy*	*easily*
happy	*happily*	*good*	*well*
desperate	*desperately*	*quick*	*quickly*

Adverbs in the story:	Adjectives in the story:
beautifully	*beautiful*
loudly	*loud*
suddenly	*sudden*
fast	*fast*
quickly	*quick*
hard	*hard*
happily	*happy*

Writing

9 a) **Aim** To analyse the setting of a scene in a story

- Ask Ss to look at the picture, read the text and then answer the questions.
- Check Ss' answers around the class.

Answer Key

1 a cold winter afternoon
2 cold
3 on the beach
4 the writer and his dog Rex
5 Rex began to bark loudly.

b) **Aim** To listen for order of events

- Ask Ss to read the events A-F. Play the recording. Ss listen and put the events in order according to what they hear.
- Check Ss' answers.

Answer Key

2 A	3 E	4 D	5 B	6 C

10 **Aim** To develop narrative skills; to write a story;

- Explain the task. Then give Ss time to write their story using the ideas in Ex. 9 and the plan to help them.
- Check Ss' answers.
- Alternatively, assign the task as HW and check Ss' answers in the next lesson.

Suggested Answer Key

One cold winter afternoon, Bill took his dog, Rex, for a walk on the beach.
Suddenly, Rex began to bark loudly. There was a woman further down the beach shouting, "Help! Help!" Bill ran towards her. Then, he heard her shout, "The sea! He's in the sea!"
Bill quickly looked and saw a child. Bill dived into the water. He swam out to the boy fast and brought him back to shore.
They brought the boy back home. He soon felt better. The boy's nanny felt so happy that the boy was alright. Bill felt proud that he saved him.

Values

Ss try to explain the quotation in their mother tongue. If Ss have difficulty, explain the quotation. Ask Ss to memorise this quotation and check in the next lesson.
The quotation means that we shouldn't wait for other people to change things, we should make changes ourselves and keep trying to make the world a better place.

Culture 10

Listening & Reading

1 **Aim** To present vocabulary relating to Shakespeare

- Ask Ss to read the names in the list and try to guess how they are related to Shakespeare.
- Play the recording. Ss listen and read the text to find out.

Answer Key

Stratford-Upon-Avon: where Shakespeare was born
Anne Hathaway: Shakespeare's wife
Susanna: Shakespeare's oldest daughter and oldest child
Hamnet and Judith: Shakespeare's twin children
London: Shakespeare moved to London in 1592
The Lord Chamberlain's Men: the company of actors Shakespeare worked with
Henry V: one of Shakespeare's historical plays
Romeo and Juliet: one of Shakespeare's tragedies

2 **Aim** To read for specific information (T/F/DS statements)

- Ask Ss to read the sentences (1-6) and then give them time to read the text again and mark them according to what they read.
- Check Ss' answers.

Answer Key

1 DS	2 F	3 T	4 F	5 DS	6 T

- Play the video for Ss and elicit their comments.
- Refer Ss to the Word List to look up the meanings of the words in the **Check these words** box.

3 **Aim** THINK To consolidate new vocabulary

- Give Ss time to explain the words in bold using their dictionaries as necessary.
- Check Ss' answers around the class.

Suggested Answer Key

cared for: took care of
childhood: the time in life when you are a child
twins: two siblings born at the same time
joined: became part of
forever: for all of time
common: popular

Speaking & Writing

4 **Aim** THINK To develop critical thinking skills

Give Ss time to consider their answers and then ask various Ss to share their answers with the class.

Suggested Answer Key

William Shakespeare is an important figure in the English language because he added about 1,700 words to it and created many common phrases.

5 **Aim** ICT **To develop research skills; to write a short article about a famous writer**
- Explain the task and ask Ss to research online to find out about a famous writer from their country.
- Give Ss time to use the information to write a short article including all the points in the rubric.
- Then ask various Ss to read their articles to the class.
- Alternatively, assign the task as HW and ask Ss to read their articles out in the next lesson.

Suggested Answer Key

Name: *James Joyce*
What famous for: *writing novels and poems*
When/Where born: *Dublin, Ireland, on 2nd February, 1882*
Early years: *the oldest of 10 children, lived in poverty*
Studies: *was a good student, went to University College Dublin to get a degree*
Family: *met wife Nora Barnacle in 1904, had children George and Lucia*
Achievements: *wrote famous novels like Ulysses and Finnegan's Wake, inspired new writing style*
When/Where died: *13th January 1941 in Zurich, Switzerland*

James Joyce is a famous Irish writer of novels and poems. He was born in Dublin, Ireland on 2nd February, 1882. He was the oldest of 10 children and lived in poverty. Joyce was a good student. He earned his degree at University College Dublin.
James Joyce met his wife Nora Barnacle in 1904. They had two children: George and Lucia. Joyce is most famous for writing famous novels like 'Ulysses' and 'Finnegan's Wake'. Also, he inspired a new writing style. He died in Zurich, Switzerland on 13th January, 1941.

Review 10

Vocabulary

1 **Aim** **To practise vocabulary for jobs**
- Explain the task.
- Give Ss time to complete it.
- Check Ss' answers.

Answer Key

1	politician	3	zoologist	5	lawyer
2	actor	4	physicist	6	painter

2 **Aim** **To practise vocabulary for feelings/reactions**
- Explain the task.
- Give Ss time to complete it.
- Check Ss' answers.

Answer Key

1	frightened	3	excited	5	worried
2	proud	4	upset	6	shocked

Grammar

3 **Aim** **To practise the past simple**
- Explain the task.
- Give Ss time to complete it.
- Check Ss' answers.

Answer Key

1	married	4	watched	7	enjoyed
2	cared	5	took	8	said
3	made	6	died		

4 **Aim** **To practise the past simple**
- Explain the task.
- Give Ss time to complete it.
- Check Ss' answers.

Answer Key

1	felt	5	didn't play	9	did he
2	Did they fly	6	watched		leave
3	wrote	7	didn't pass	10	went
4	travelled	8	did he work		

5 **Aim** **To practise adjectives and adverbs**
- Explain the task.
- Give Ss time to complete it.
- Check Ss' answers.

Answer Key

1	suddenly	3	fast	5	good
2	beautiful	4	happily		

Everyday English

6 **Aim** **To practise functional language**
- Explain the task.
- Give Ss time to complete it.
- Check Ss' answers.

Answer Key

1 D	2 C	3 A	4 B	5 E

Competences

Ask Ss to assess their own performance in the unit by ticking the items according to how competent they feel for each of the listed activities.

<table>
<tr><td colspan="2">

Topic

In this unit, Ss will explore the topics of the environment and summer plans.
</td></tr>
</table>

11a Reading & Vocabulary	**90-91**

Lesson objectives: To learn vocabulary relating to the environment, to listen and read for specific information, to read for specific information (sentence completion), to talk about the future, to learn vocabulary relating to helping the environment, to give advice, to write a leaflet

Vocabulary: Environment (*Wild animals will disappear. There will be more pollution from cars. The rainforests will disappear. Everyone will have electric cars. There will be lots of rubbish. People will live in smart houses. People will recycle all their rubbish. People will plant more trees.*); Helping the environment (*Turn off lights. Use cloth shopping bags. Buy food from the market. Give old clothes to charity. Walk or ride a bike. Have a shower, not a bath. It saves water. Cars cause pollution. Clothes don't end up in the rubbish. It saves electricity. Plastic bags are bad for the environment. It doesn't have plastic packaging.*); Nouns (*environmental club, planting, pollution*); Verb (*recycle*); Adjectives (*miserable, sad, wild*); Phrase (*up to*)

11b Grammar in Use	**92-93**

Lesson objectives: To learn *will*, to learn *be going to*, to compare *be going to* and the present continuous, to learn *it – there*, to write about future activities

11c Skills in Action	**94-95**

Lesson objectives: To learn vocabulary for summer plans, to listen for specific information (multiple choice), to act out a dialogue and practise everyday English expressions for inviting – accepting/refusing invitations, to pronounce *'ll – won't*, to read for specific information, to write an email about your summer plans

Vocabulary: Summer plans (*move house, have French lessons, start a computer course, go windsurfing, go hiking, work part-time in an animal sanctuary, join a gym, volunteer for an environmental group*)

Culture 11	**96**

Lesson objectives: To listen and read for author's purpose, to read for specific information (T/F/DS), to talk about the Arbor Day Foundation, to present a charity from your country

Vocabulary: Nouns (*donation*); Verbs (*care for, raise, volunteer, inspire, support*); Adjective (*amazing*); Phrase (*fundraising event*)

Review 11	**97**

Lesson objectives: To test/consolidate vocabulary and grammar learnt throughout the unit; to practise everyday English

Go through the objectives box and tell Ss that these are the topics, skills and activities this unit will cover.

11a

Vocabulary

1 **Aim** **To present vocabulary relating to the environment**

- Go through the items in the predictions and explain/elicit the meanings of any unknown words.
- Read out the examples and elicit which ones Ss think will come true in 50 years' time.

Suggested Answer Key

I don't think there will be more pollution from cars.
I think the rainforests will disappear.
I think everyone will have electric cars.
I don't think there will be lots of rubbish.
I don't think people will live in smart houses.
I think people will plant more trees.

Reading

2 **Aim** **To listen and read for specific information**

- Ask Ss to guess which predictions will appear in the text.
- Play the recording. Ss listen and find out.

Answer Key

There will be more pollution from cars.
There will be lots of rubbish.
The rainforests will disappear.
Wild animals will disappear.
Everyone will have electric cars.
People will recycle all their rubbish.

- Play the video for Ss and elicit their comments.

3 **Aim** **To read for specific information (sentence completion)**

- Ask Ss to read the sentence stems 1-4 and then give Ss time to read the text and complete them.
- Check Ss' answers.

Answer Key

1. *will disappear*
2. *an environmental club*
3. *of pollution (from cars)*
4. *to recycle (all their rubbish)*

- Then give Ss time to explain the words in bold using their dictionaries as necessary.
- Check Ss' answers around the class.

Suggested Answer Key

sad: *bad in a way that makes you feel upset or angry*
wild: *(of animals) living independently of humans*
planting: *to put a seed, a plant or a tree into the ground so that it will grow*
up to: *sb's responsibility*

- Refer Ss to the Word List to look up the meanings of the words in the **Check these words** box.

Speaking

4 (Aim) (THINK) To develop critical thinking skills; to make decisions

Read out the question. Give Ss time to tell their partners. Elicit answers from various Ss around the class.

Suggested Answer Key

I will help make our future a bright one by riding my bike and walking instead of taking my car. This will help the environment because cars cause pollution. I will use cloth shopping bags because plastic shopping bags are bad for the environment.

5 (Aim) To present vocabulary relating to helping the environment

- Read out the lists of advice and reasons and explain/elicit the meanings of any unknown words.
- Then give Ss time to match the advice to the reasons.
- Check Ss' answers.

Answer Key

1 d   2 e   3 f   4 c   5 b   6 a

6 (Aim) To practise new vocabulary

- Read out the Giving Advice box and ask various Ss to read out the example sentences.
- Explain that we use **should/shouldn't** to give advice. Then explain the task and read out the example.
- Give Ss time to complete the task using the sentences in Ex. 5 and the useful language in the box.
- Then ask Ss around the class to share their sentences with the rest of the class.

Suggested Answer Key

Why don't you use cloth shopping bags? Plastic bags are bad for the environment.
I think it's a good idea to buy food from the market. It doesn't have plastic packaging.
I don't think it's a good idea to throw clothes in the rubbish. You should give old clothes to charity instead.
You shouldn't drive a car. Walk or ride a bike because cars cause pollution.
You should have a shower, not a bath. It saves water.

Writing

7 (Aim) ICT To develop research skills; to select information; to write a leaflet about helping the environment

- Explain the task and give Ss time to research online and collect more ideas about helping the environment. Then they use their ideas to write a leaflet.
- Remind Ss to use **should/shouldn't**.
- Ask Ss to present their leaflets in class. If they want to, they can then hand them out at their college/ university.
- Alternatively, assign the task as HW and ask Ss to present their leaflets in the next lesson.

Suggested Answer Key

Ways to Help the Environment

1   You should drink tap water instead of bottled water. Plastic bottles are bad for the environment.

2   You should compost vegetable waste. The compost soil is good for the environment.

3   You should use low energy light bulbs. They save electricity.

4   You should turn off your computer or TV when you're not in the room. It saves electricity.

5   You should drive slower. It uses less petrol and makes less air pollution.

11b Grammar in Use

1 (Aim) To present *will* (the future simple)

- Present the future simple tense **will**.
- Say then write on the board: *I'm thirsty. I will drink some water.* and *Next week he will buy a new laptop.* Underline *I will drink* and *he will buy* and explain that these verbs are in the future simple. Explain that we use **will** + the base form of the main verb to form the affirmative. Explain that we use this tense to talk about on-the-spot decisions and predictions based on what we think.
- Say then write on the board: *Will you go out tonight? No, it's raining. I will not/won't go out tonight.* Underline *Will you go* and *I will not/won't go* and explain that these are the interrogative and negative

forms of the future simple. Give examples for all persons and explain that we form the negative with **will** + **not** + the base form of the main verb and the interrogative with **will** + subject + the base form of the verb.

- Ask Ss to read the theory box and then elicit examples in the dialogue.

Answer Key

Examples in the dialogue: *there won't be enough food, I'll come with you, there will be lots of people*

2 (**Aim**) **To consolidate the uses of will**

- Explain the task and give Ss time to read the sentences 1-5 and decide the use of the verb in each one.
- Check Ss' answers around the class.

Answer Key

1 b	2 a	3 a	4 b	5 a

3 (**Aim**) **To practise *will/won't***

- Explain the task and give Ss time to complete it.
- Check Ss' answers.

Answer Key

2 Will, will	4 will, won't
3 will, will	5 will, won't

4 a) (**Aim**) **To listen for specific information**

- Explain the task and ask Ss to read the predictions 1-9.
- Play the recording. Ss listen and mark the predictions according to what they hear.
- Check Ss' answers around the class.

Answer Key

1 W	3 X	5 X	7 X	9 X
2 W	4 W	6 M	8 M	

b) (**Aim**) **To practise *will/won't* for predictions**

- Explain the task and read out the example exchange.
- Give Ss time to ask and answer questions following the example.
- Monitor the activity around the class and then ask some pairs to ask and answer in front of the class.

Suggested Answer Key

B: *Will people live in underwater cities?*
A: *No, they won't. Will life be more expensive?*
B: *Yes, it will. Will people go on holiday to the Moon?*

A: *No, they won't. Will there be more people in the world?*
B: *Yes, there will. Will pollution be worse?*
A: *Yes, it will. Will there be enough trees?*
B: *No, there won't. Will people use oxygen masks to breathe?*
A: *Yes, they will. Will there be food pills instead of fresh food?*
B: *No, there won't.*

5 (**Aim**) **To practise *will/won't* for on-the-spot decisions**

- Explain the task and ask Ss to read the prompts and the on-the-spot decisions.
- Read out the example and then give Ss time to make sentences following the example.
- Elicit sentences from Ss around the class.

Suggested Answer Key

It's raining. I'll put on my raincoat.
It's cold. I'll close the window.
I'm tired. I'll go to bed.
I'm hungry. I'll have a sandwich.
It's hot. I'll open the window.
The house is on fire. I'll call the fire brigade.

6 (**Aim**) **To present *be going to***

- Present ***be going to***. Say then write on the board: *I am going to buy a smartphone.* Explain that we use ***be going to*** + infinitive to talk about plans and future intentions. Say then write on the board: *Look out! You're going to fall!* Explain that we also use ***be going to*** for predictions based on what we can see.
- Ask Ss to read the theory box and then elicit an example in the dialogue.
- Then elicit from Ss which use of ***be going to*** in the theory box the sentence expresses.

Answer Key

Example in the dialogue: *I'm going to get a job like that when I leave university.*
The example expresses an intention.

7 a) (**Aim**) **To practise *be going to***

- Explain the task and read out the example.
- Give Ss time to complete the task and then check Ss' answers around the class.

Answer Key

1 is going to watch	4 aren't going to study
2 am going to visit	5 is going to take
3 isn't going to have	6 isn't going to go

101

b) **Aim** To practise *be going to*

- Explain the task and read out the example exchange. Then have Ss work in pairs and ask and answer following the example.
- Monitor the activity around the class and then have some pairs ask and answer in front of the class.

Suggested Answer Key

B: *Is Stan going to watch a film this weekend?*
A: *Yes, he is. Am I going to visit my cousin in New York this weekend?*
B: *Yes, you are. Is Jo going to have a meal with Sam this weekend?*
A: *No, she/he isn't. Are Michael and Tom going to study for their French exam this weekend?*
B: *No, they aren't. Is Peter going to take his dog to the vet's this weekend?*
A: *Yes, he is. Is Tania going to go to a concert this weekend?*
B: *No, she isn't.*

8 **Aim** To compare *be going to* and the present continuous

- Ask Ss to read the theory box and then elicit how the two tenses differ.
- Elicit examples of the present continuous for future arrangements in the dialogue on p. 92.

Answer Key

'Be going to' is used to talk about future plans and intentions and the present continuous is used to talk about fixed future arrangements.
Examples in the dialogue: *Are you going to the gym, I'm not going to the gym, I'm attending a presentation*

9 **Aim** To practise the present continuous for future arrangements

- Explain the task and read out the example exchange. Then have Ss work in pairs and ask and answer following the example.
- Monitor the activity around the class and then have some pairs ask and answer in front of the class.

Suggested Answer Key

B: *What is Tom doing at eleven o'clock?*
A: *He's meeting Frank for coffee at eleven o'clock. What is Tom doing at one o'clock?*
B: *He's having lunch with Jane at one o'clock. What is Tom doing at five o'clock?*
A: *He's catching the train to London at five o'clock.*

10 **Aim** To practise the future simple, *be going to* and the present continuous

- Explain the task give Ss time to complete it.
- Check Ss' answers and ask Ss to identify the uses.

Answer Key

1 *will have (prediction)*
2 *is going to work (intention)*
3 *is starting (fixed future arrangement)*
4 *will be (prediction)*
5 *won't work (on-the-spot decision)*
6 *are leaving (fixed future arrangement)*
7 *is going to win (prediction based on evidence)*
8 *aren't going to stay (future plan)/are not staying (fixed future arrangement)*

11 **Aim** To present and practise *it – there*

- Explain that when a sentence has no clear subject we can use **there** or **it** as a subject pronoun instead, with the verb **to be** and a noun phrase. With the future simple we use **it will be** + adjective and **there will be** + noun.
- Ask Ss to read the theory box and elicit an example from the dialogue on p. 92.
- Then give them time to read the gapped sentences 1-5 and fill in the correct word.
- Check Ss' answers.

Answer Key

Example in the dialogue: *there will be lots of people*

1 *It*	3 *It*	5 *There*
2 *There*	4 *It*	

12 **Aim** **THINK** To develop critical thinking skills; to make predictions

- Explain the task. Give Ss time to consider their answers and then write their sentences.
- Ask various Ss around the class to share their answers with the rest of the class.

Suggested Answer Key

I think people will live in space in 50 years.
I think there will be more pollution in 50 years.
I think the oceans will rise in 50 years.
I'm going to travel to Spain next year.
I'm going to graduate from college next year.
I'm watching a film at the cinema tonight.

11c Skills in Action

Vocabulary

1 a) Aim To present vocabulary for summer plans

- Ask Ss to look at the pictures.
- Explain/Elicit the meanings of any unknown words.
- Then elicit answers from Ss around the class.

Answer Key

A   *Mary isn't going to move house in the summer.*
B   *Mary isn't going to have French lessons in the summer.*
C   *Mary is going to start a computer course in the summer.*
D   *Mary is going to go windsurfing in the summer.*
E   *Mary isn't going to go hiking in the summer.*
F   *Mary is going to work part-time in an animal sanctuary in the summer.*
G   *Mary isn't going to join a gym in the summer.*
H   *Mary is going to volunteer for an environmental group in the summer.*

b) Aim To talk about your summer plans

Read out the question and elicit answers from Ss around the class.

Suggested Answer Key

I'm going to go scuba diving this summer. I'm going to take an English language course this summer, too.

Listening

2 Aim To listen for specific information (multiple choice)

- Ask Ss to read the questions and answer choices.
- Ask them to predict what the recording will be about and then play it.
- Ss listen and choose their answers according to what they hear.
- Check Ss' answers.

Answer Key

1 C   2 A   3 A   4 B

Everyday English

3 Aim To listen and read for specific information

- Read out the question and play the recording.
- Ss listen and find out the answer.

Answer Key

Emily and Lyn are going to meet for dinner on Sunday evening.

4 Aim To substitute everyday English expressions for inviting, accepting/refusing invitations

- Explain the task and give Ss time to complete it using the phrases/sentences in the Useful Language box.
- Check Ss' answers around the class.

Suggested Answer Key

Would you like to: *Why don't you ...?*
I'd love to, but I can't: *I'm afraid I can't.*
That's all right.: *Never mind!*
Why don't we: *Do you want to ...?*
Sure, why not!: *Sounds great.*

5 Aim To act out a dialogue inviting – accepting/refusing invitations

- Explain the task and ask Ss to act out similar dialogues to the one in Ex. 3 in pairs, taking turns to invite and using the prompts and the language box.
- Write this diagram on the board for Ss to follow.

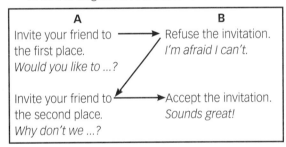

- Ask Ss to record themselves.
- Monitor the activity around the class and offer assistance as necessary.
- Then ask some pairs to act out their dialogues in front of the class.

Suggested Answer Key

A: *Hi! I'm going to the mall on Saturday afternoon. Would you like to come with me?*
B: *I'm afraid I can't. I'll be at the zoo with my cousin.*
A: *Never mind! Why don't we go to the cinema on Sunday evening?*
B: *Sounds great!*

A: *Hi! I'm going to the museum on Saturday morning. Would you like to come with me?*
B: *I'd love to, but I can't. I'm going shopping.*
A: *That's a pity! Why don't we go to the market on Saturday afternoon then?*
B: *Sounds good.*

Pronunciation

6 **Aim** To pronounce *'ll – won't*

- Play the recording with pauses for Ss to repeat chorally and/or individually.
- Check Ss' pronunciation and intonation.

Reading & Writing

7 **Aim** To read for specific information

- Give Ss time to read the email and then complete the table with the missing information.
- Check Ss' answers.

Answer Key

PLANS/INTENTIONS	REASON/PURPOSE
they/travel to Wroclaw Lena/show **Sarah around the city** they/go hiking in **Tatra National Park** they/join her family in **Sopot**	Lena wants Sarah to meet her family it's a **very interesting place** it's very **beautiful** Lena wants to **relax a bit**
FIXED ARRANGEMENTS	
Sarah's flight/land on **25th June**	

Background Information

Poznan is a city in central Poland. It is one of the oldest and largest cities in Poland. It is an important business and cultural centre and a popular tourist destination. About 550,000 people live there.

8 **Aim** To learn to express reason, result or purpose

- Read out the **Writing Tip** box and explain that this information will help Ss understand how to express reason, result or purpose.
- Explain the task and read out the example.
- Then ask Ss to work in pairs and talk about Lena's plans/intentions using *because* or the *to-infinitive* following the example.
- Monitor the activity around the class and then as some Ss to share their answers with the class.

Suggested Answer Key

Lena is going to show Sarah around Wroclaw because it's a very interesting place.
They are going to go hiking in Tatra National Park because it's very beautiful.
They are going to join her family in Sopot to relax a bit.

9 **Aim** To practise expressing reason, result or purpose

- Explain the task and read out the example.
- Give Ss time to read the intentions and results, match them and then make sentences following the example.
- Check Ss' answers.

Answer Key

2 d	3 e	4 a	5 b

Tony is going to join a gym so he can get fit.
Tony is going to have French lessons so he can learn a new language.
Tony is going to go windsurfing so he can do something exciting.
Tony is going to volunteer for a charity so he can help people.

Writing

10 a) **Aim** To prepare for a writing task

- Ask Ss to copy and complete the table in Ex. 7 into their notebooks and complete it with their plans for their summer holidays.
- Give Ss time to complete it.
- Ask various Ss to share their answers with the class.

Suggested Answer Key

PLANS/INTENTIONS	REASON/PURPOSE
travel to LA, USA, with Paul show Paul Los Angeles go surfing at Zuma Beach sunbathe on the beach	visit my aunt and uncle it's an interesting city it's very exciting I want to relax
FIXED ARRANGEMENTS	
our flight/land on the 30th of June	

b) **Aim** To write an email about your summer plans

- Explain the task. Then give Ss time to write their email using their answers from Ex. 10a and the plan to help them.
- Check Ss' answers.
- Alternatively, assign the task as HW and check Ss' answers in the next lesson.

Suggested Answer Key

Hi Paul,
How are you? I'm so excited about our summer holidays! I've got some fantastic plans for us.
Our flight is landing in Los Angeles on 30th June. I want you to meet my aunt and uncle. I'm also going to show

you around Los Angeles because it's a very interesting city.

Then, we're going to go surfing at Zuma Beach because it's very exciting. Then we can sunbathe on the beach to relax.

I'm sure we'll have a great time. See you soon!

Bye for now,

Matthew

Values

Ss try to explain the quotation in their mother tongue. If Ss have difficulty, explain the quotation. Ask Ss to memorise this quotation and check in the next lesson.

The saying means that doing something different from your normal daily routine can be as refreshing and relaxing as a break.

Culture 11

Listening & Reading

1 **Aim** To introduce the topic

- Read out the title of the text and elicit what Ss think the Arbor Day Foundation does.
- Play the recording.
- Ss listen and read the text. Then elicit what the Arbor Day Foundation does from Ss.

Answer Key

The Arbor Day Foundation is a charity and education organisation in the USA that raises money, works hard to plant trees in the towns and cities, looks after national forests, replants trees after natural disasters and helps young people learn about trees and connect with the natural world.

2 **Aim** To read for author's purpose

Ss read the text. Elicit Ss' ideas about the author's purpose.

Answer Key

I think the author's purpose is to inform the reader about the Arbor Day Foundation because the text gives a lot of information. The text also asks for support, so they either want donations or volunteers.

3 **Aim** To read for specific information (T/F/DS statements)

- Ask Ss to read the statements 1-3 and then give them time to read the text again and mark the statements according to the text.
- Check Ss' answers.

Answer Key

1 T	2 DS	3 F

- Play the video for Ss and elicit their comments.
- Refer Ss to the Word List to look up the meanings of the words in the **Check these words** box.

4 **Aim** To consolidate new vocabulary

- Ask Ss to read the text again and elicit explanations for the words in bold.
- Check Ss' answers.

Answer Key

care for: *look after*
amazing: *fantastic*
volunteer: *give time/work for free*

5 **Aim** **THINK** To develop critical thinking skills; to express an opinion

Read out the question and give Ss time to consider their answer. Then elicit answers from Ss around the class with reasons.

Suggested Answer Key

Yes, I would like to join the Arbor Day Foundation because I want to help the environment and I think they do amazing work.

Speaking & Writing

6 **Aim** ICT To develop research skills; to make notes; to give a presentation

- Explain the task and ask Ss to work in small groups. They research online to find out about a charity in their country and make notes under the headings provided.
- Give Ss time to use the information to prepare a presentation.
- Then ask various Ss to present their information to the class.
- Alternatively, assign the task as HW and ask Ss to present their information in the next lesson.

Suggested Answer Key

Name of organisation: *ARCHELON*
History of organisation: *in 1977, couple Dimitris & Anna saw sea turtle nests in Zakynthos, Greece and studied them, nesting sites became protected, in 1983 Sea Turtle Protection Society (STPS) was founded, later became known as ARCHELON*
Activities: *to study and protect the sea turtles, volunteers protect nests, work with fishermen to protect turtles in water, work with government to make*

105

laws to protect sea turtles, tag and monitor sea turtles, run educational programmes for students and tourists

Hi, I'm Georgia Callis. Have you ever wanted to volunteer to work with animals? Well, in my country, Greece, there's an organisation called ARCHELON that helps sea turtles. Let me tell you about it.

In 1977, a couple named Dimitris and Anna saw sea turtle nests on the island of Zakynthos and studied them. They sent their findings to the government and the nesting sites became protected. In 1983, the Sea Turtle Protection Society (STPS) was founded and it later became ARCHELON.

There are lots of ways to help ARCHELON. They study and protect sea turtles. Volunteers help by protecting nests. They also work with fishermen to protect sea turtles in the water and the government to make laws that protect sea turtles. They tag and monitor sea turtles and run educational programmes for students and tourists, too!

ARCHELON is a great organisation that helps protect sea turtles. Why don't you spend a summer volunteering for them? It'll be great fun!

Thank you for listening.

Review 11

Vocabulary

1 **Aim** To practise vocabulary relating to the environment

- Explain the task.
- Give Ss time to complete it.
- Check Ss' answers.

Answer Key

1	e	3	a	5	b	7	h
2	c	4	f	6	d	8	g

2 **Aim** To practise vocabulary relating to helping the environment

- Explain the task.
- Give Ss time to complete it.
- Check Ss' answers.

Answer Key

1	have	5	save	9	plant
2	join	6	work	10	give
3	recycle	7	go		
4	move	8	volunteer		

3 **Aim** To practise vocabulary from the unit

- Explain the task.
- Give Ss time to complete it.
- Check Ss' answers.

Answer Key

1	animal	4	plastic
2	cloth	5	environmental
3	computer	6	summer

Grammar

4 **Aim** To practise *should/shouldn't*

- Explain the task.
- Give Ss time to complete it.
- Check Ss' answers.

Answer Key

1 We should recycle.
2 You shouldn't throw cans into the bin.
3 Sally shouldn't leave her job.
4 You should turn the heating down.
5 You shouldn't go out without a coat.

5 **Aim** To practise *will/won't, be going to*, the present continuous and *it/there*

- Explain the task.
- Give Ss time to complete it.
- Check Ss' answers.

Answer Key

1	is going to wash	5	will you order
2	is coming	6	is going to work
3	'll be	7	It
4	is going to study	8	There

Everyday English

6 **Aim** To practise functional language

- Explain the task.
- Give Ss time to complete it.
- Check Ss' answers.

Answer Key

1 D	2 B	3 A	4 C	5 E

Competences

Ask Ss to assess their own performance in the module by ticking the items according to how competent they feel for each of the listed activities.

Take a break  12

Topic

In this unit, Ss will explore the topics of holiday activities and travel experiences.

12a Reading & Vocabulary   98-99

Lesson objectives: To learn vocabulary for holiday activities, to read for gist, to listen and read for specific information (T/F statements), to talk about a person's trip, to write about Morocco
Vocabulary: Holiday activities (*see ancient temples, buy handmade souvenirs, visit a market, try traditional dishes, buy spices, ride a camel, take photos, go sightseeing*), Adjectives (*disgusting, cold, quiet, horrible, empty, modern, wonderful, noisy, crowded, traditional, delicious, hot*); Nouns (*spices, palace, exhibit*); Verb (*try*)

12b Grammar in Use   100-101

Lesson objectives: To learn the present perfect, to learn the present perfect with *ever/never*, to learn the present perfect with *yet/already*, to learn the present perfect with *just*, to learn the present perfect with *for/since*, to practise the present perfect vs the past simple, to learn the definite article *the*

12c Skills in Action   102-103

Lesson objectives: To learn vocabulary for travel experiences, to listen for specific information (multiple choice), to act out a dialogue and practise everyday English expressions for describing a holiday experience, to pronounce /h/ pronounced or silent, to listen and read for gist, to read for specific information (take notes), to write a blog comment about a holiday experience
Vocabulary: Travel experiences (*go on a helicopter tour, go ice skating, go camping, go snorkelling, go canoeing, swim with dolphins*)

Culture 12   104

Lesson objectives: To listen and read for specific information (multiple matching), to talk about a dream destination, to design a travel brochure for tourist destinations in your country
Vocabulary: Nouns (*package holiday, trip*); Adjective (*frozen*); Phrase (*nature lover*)

Review 12   105

Lesson objectives: To test/consolidate vocabulary and grammar learnt throughout the unit; to practise everyday English

Go through the objectives box and tell Ss that these are the topics, skills and activities this unit will cover.

12a

Vocabulary

1 Aim To present vocabulary for holiday activities

- Ask Ss to look at the pictures and explain/elicit the meanings of any unknown words.
- Read out the list of verbs and give Ss time to complete the phrases.
- Play the recording for Ss to listen and check their answers.

Answer Key

1 ride	*3 see*	*5 visit*	*7 buy*
2 take	*4 buy*	*6 try*	*8 go*

2 Aim To talk about holiday activities

Ask Ss to discuss in pairs what they did when they last went on holiday using the activities in Ex. 1 and their own ideas following the example.

Suggested Answer Key

Last July I went to Italy. I visited a market and bought souvenirs. I tried some traditional dishes. I saw some ancient buildings and I took lots of photos. I went to the beach and swam in the sea.

Reading & Listening

3 Aim To read for gist

- Ask Ss to read the text quickly and then choose the most appropriate title for the text.
- Elicit Ss' answers.

Answer Key

Exotic Morocco

4 Aim To listen and read for specific information (T/F statements)

- Ask Ss to read the statements (1-4).
- Play the recording. Ss listen, read and mark the statements according to the text.
- Check Ss' answers.

Answer Key

1 T	*2 T*	*3 F*	*4 F*

- Play the video for Ss and elicit their comments.

107

12

Background Information

Morocco is a country in North Africa. It has a long coastline and large areas of desert. The capital city is Rabat and the population is almost 36 million people.

Marrakech is a large city in Morocco. It is an old city and its nickname is 'the Red City' because of the red sandstone buildings and city walls. It is famous for having the largest traditional market (souk) in Morocco.

Casablanca is the largest city in Morocco. It is also one of the most important cities. It is the main port and the main financial centre in the country. 3.5 million people live there.

5 **Aim** To consolidate information in a text

- Explain the task and read out the example exchange.
- Ask Ss to work in pairs and take turns to say three false statements based on the text for their partner to correct.
- Monitor the activity around the class.

Suggested Answer Key

A: *Jack visited the market on Monday.*
B: *No, he didn't visit the market on Monday. He visited it on Tuesday.*
A: *Tagine is a dish with fish.*
B: *No, it isn't a dish with fish. It's a dish with chicken, fruit, vegetables and spices.*
A: *Jack has visited the museum.*
B: *No, he hasn't visited the museum yet.*

6 **Aim** To consolidate new vocabulary through antonyms

- Read out the adjectives in the list and explain/elicit the meanings of any unknown ones.
- Give Ss time to match the adjectives in bold to their opposites and then check Ss' answers.

Answer Key

1 *wonderful ≠ horrible*
2 *noisy ≠ quiet, crowded ≠ empty*
3 *traditional ≠ modern*
4 *delicious ≠ disgusting*
5 *hot ≠ cold*

7 **Aim** To practise prepositional phrases from a text

- Read out the prepositions in the list and give Ss time to use them to complete the phrases.
- Check Ss' answers and then give Ss time to use the competed phrases to write sentences based on the text.

Answer Key

1 *with*   2 *in*   3 *for*   4 *on*   5 *on*   6 *to*

Suggested Answer Key

Jack went to Morocco on Monday and he is staying with his friend, Mohammed.
Mohammed lives in Marrakesh.
Marrakech is famous for its beautiful buildings, palaces and markets.
On Tuesday, Jack visited the market.
Jack is going on a day trip to Casablanca tomorrow.
Jack is returning to England on Sunday.

Speaking

8 **Aim** To identify key information; to make notes; to summarise a text using notes

- Ask Ss to read the email again and then copy the table into their notebooks and complete it with information from the text.
- Then ask Ss to ask and answer questions in pairs using the information in the table and following the example.

Suggested Answer Key

ACTIVITIES HE DID	WHEN	WHAT HE DID THERE	WHAT IT WAS LIKE
went to the desert	yesterday	rode a camel	fun
went to a traditional restaurant	last night	tried a Moroccan dish – tagine	place – fantastic, food – delicious

A: *Did Jack go to the desert?*
B: *Yes, he did.*
A: *When did he go there?*
B: *Yesterday.*
A: *What did he do there?*
B: *He rode a camel.*
A: *What was it like?*
B: *It was fun.*

A: *Did Jack go to a traditional restaurant?*
B: *Yes, he did.*
A: *When did he go?*
B: *Last night.*
A: *What did he do there?*
B: *He tried a Moroccan dish – tagine.*
A: *What was it like?*
B: *The place was fantastic and the food was delicious.*

Writing

9 **Aim** **THINK** **To develop critical thinking skills; to give reasons**

- Give Ss time to think of three reasons they would like to visit Morocco and write them down.
- Ask various Ss to read their sentences to the class and elicit how many Ss agree.

Suggested Answer Key

I would like to visit Morocco because I want to try tagine, I want to ride a camel and I like visiting markets.

12b Grammar in Use

1 **Aim** **To present the present perfect**

- Present the present perfect.
- Say, then write on the board: *I have visited Paris. Tom hasn't visited Paris.* Underline: *have visited* and *hasn't visited.*
- Explain that this verb is in the present perfect and that we form it in the affirmative with **have/has** + past participle and in the negative with **haven't/ hasn't** + past participle.
- Explain that we use the present perfect to talk about *actions that started in the past and continue to the present and personal experiences.*
- Explain that we form questions in the present perfect with **have/has** + personal pronoun + past participle.
- Explain/Elicit that we form short answers with **Yes/No** + personal pronoun + **have/has/haven't/hasn't**.
- Ask Ss to read the table and the dialogue in their books. Then, elicit examples from the dialogue.

Answer Key

Examples in the text: *Have you stayed in our hotel before? Yes, we have. Have you visited Walt Disney World? We've also seen Universal Studios, but we haven't been to Discovery Cove yet. Have you ever swum with dolphins? I haven't tried anything like that before! Have you booked tickets? No, we haven't. We've driven down from New York and we're tired.*

Background Information

Orlando is a city in Florida in the USA. It is known as 'the theme park capital of the world'. Around 60 million people visit it every year. It is home to Walt Disney World Resort, Lake Buena Vista, Universal Orlando Resort, Sea World and more.

2 **Aim** **To practise past participles**

- Explain that the past participles of regular verbs are formed by adding **-ed** to the end of the verb and that irregular verbs have their own forms.
- Explain the task and give Ss time to complete it.
- Check Ss' answers around the class.

Answer Key

1 swum	4 been	7 booked
2 stayed	5 seen	8 driven
3 visited	6 tried	

3 **Aim** **To practise the present perfect (affirmative/negative)**

- Explain the task and read out the example.
- Give Ss time to complete the task.
- Check Ss' answers.

Answer Key

2 hasn't been	6 hasn't stayed
3 haven't swum	7 have driven
4 has visited	8 haven't booked
5 have tried	

4 **Aim** **To practise the present perfect (interrogative and short answers)**

- Explain the task and read out the example.
- Give Ss time to complete the task.
- Check Ss' answers.

Answer Key

2 *Have they flown, they haven't*
3 *Have you been, I haven't*
4 *Have they lived, they haven't*
5 *Has Bob told, he has*
6 *Has Paula slept, she has*

5 **Aim** **To present and practise the present perfect + *ever/never***

- Explain that we use **ever** with the present perfect in questions and statements and **never** in statements.
- Ask Ss to read the theory box and ask three Ss to read the example aloud.
  Then explain the task and read out the example exchange.
- Have Ss work in pairs and ask and answer questions using **ever/never** and the prompts following the example.

Suggested Answer Key

A: Italy is the best country I've ever visited. Have you ever been there?
B: No, I've never been there.
A: Egypt is the best country I've ever visited. Have you ever been there?
B: No, I've never been there.
A: Spain is the best country I've ever visited. Have you ever been there?
B: No, I've never been there.
A: Australia is the best country I've ever visited. Have you ever been there?
B: No, I've never been there.
A: Poland is the best country I've ever visited. Have you ever been there?
B: No, I've never been there.
A: Brazil is the best country I've ever visited. Have you ever been there?
B: No, I've never been there.
A: Vietnam is the best country I have ever been to. Have you ever been there?
B: No, I've never been there.

6 **Aim** To present and practise the present perfect + *yet/already*

- Explain that we use **already** with the present perfect in questions and statements and **yet** in questions and negatives.
- Ask Ss to read the theory box and ask two Ss to read the example exchange.
- Then explain the task and read out the example.
- Play the recording and have Ss tick the activities they have done.
- Then have Ss work in pairs and ask and answer questions using **yet/already** following the example.

Answer Key

3 ✓   4 ✓   6 ✓

A: Have they been shopping yet?
B: Yes, they have already been shopping. Have they seen the Arc de Triomphe yet?
A: Yes, they have already seen the Arc de Triomphe. Have they been on a boat on the Seine yet?
B: No, they haven't been on a boat on the Seine yet. Have they visited the Louvre yet?
A: Yes, they have already visited the Louvre. Have they seen Notre Dame yet?
B: No, they haven't seen Notre Dame yet.

7 **Aim** To present and practise the present perfect + *just*

- Explain that we use **just** with the present perfect to show that an action only finished a short time before.
- Ask Ss to read the theory box.
- Explain the task and ask two Ss to read the example exchange aloud.
- Then have Ss work in pairs and ask and answer questions using **just** and the prompts following the example.

Suggested Answer Key

2 A: Have you ordered lunch yet?
   B: Yes, I've just ordered it.
3 A: Have you spoken to the receptionist?
   B: Yes, I've just spoken to the receptionist.
4 A: Have you met the guide?
   B: Yes, I've just met the guide.

8 **Aim** To present and practise the present perfect + *for/since*

- Explain that we use **for** with the present perfect to talk about duration and we use **since** to talk about when an action started.
- Ask Ss to read the theory box. Then explain the task and read out the example.
- Have Ss complete the task using **for/since** and following the example.

Answer Key

2 He has lived in Rome for three years.
3 I haven't seen Jane for ten years.
4 I haven't travelled by train since 2015.
5 They have been on holiday since last Monday.

9 **Aim** To practise the present perfect and the past simple

- Explain the task and give Ss time to read the text and complete the gaps with the correct verb forms.
- Check Ss' answers around the class.

Answer Key

1 haven't written	7 have tried
2 arrived	8 was
3 have been	9 haven't bought
4 have ever visited	10 went
5 have cycled	11 have never seen
6 have already swum	

Background Information

San Juan is the capital city of Puerto Rico. It has a population of around 400,000 people. It is an important seaport and the financial, cultural and tourism centre of the country.

Puerto Rico is an island territory in the Caribbean Sea. Around 3.4 million people live there. It is a popular tourist destination because of its history, tropical climate and beautiful scenery.

10 **Aim** To present the definite article *the*

- Present the definite article ***the***.
- Explain that we use ***the*** with nouns when talking about something specific or something that has already been mentioned. *(I caught a bus home. The bus broke down.)*; with the names of rivers *(the River Nile)*, groups of islands *(the Channel Islands)*, mountain ranges *(the Alps)*, deserts *(the Sahara Desert)*, oceans *(the Pacific Ocean)*, seas *(the Baltic Sea)*, unique landmarks *(the Eiffel Tower)*; hotels *(the Royal)* and museums *(the British museum)*.
- Explain that we do not use ***the*** with uncountable and plural nouns when talking about something in general. *(Computers are everywhere.)*; with the names of countries *(Spain)*, streets *(New Street)*, parks *(Hyde Park)*, cities *(London)*, single mountains *(Everest)*, single islands *(Kos)*, lakes *(Lake Como)* and continents *(Africa)*.
- Ask Ss to read the theory box and then explain the task and give Ss time to complete it.
- Check Ss' answers around the class.

Answer Key

1	–, the	3	–	5	the	7	The, –
2	the	4	–	6	The	8	–, –

11 **Aim** THINK To develop critical thinking skills; to practise the present perfect

- Explain the task and read out the example exchange.
- Ask Ss to take turns and ask and answer questions in pairs using the present perfect.
- Monitor the activity around the class and then ask some pairs to ask and answer in front of the class.
- Check Ss' answers.

Suggested Answer Key

A: *Have you ever been to Spain?*
B: *Yes, I have already been to Spain.*
A: *Have you ever visited Madrid?*
B: *No, I haven't. Not yet. etc*

12c Skills in Action

Vocabulary

1 **Aim** To present vocabulary for travel experiences

- Ask Ss to look at the pictures and read the phrases underneath them.
- Explain the task and ask two Ss to read out the example exchange.
- Then give Ss time to complete the task in pairs. Explain/Elicit the meanings of any unknown words.
- Monitor the activity around the class and then ask some pairs to ask and answer in front of the class.

Suggested Answer Key

2 A: *Have you ever been ice skating?*
   B: *Yes, I have. It was difficult./No, I haven't.*
3 A: *Have you ever been camping?*
   B: *Yes, I have. It was terrible./No, I haven't.*
4 A: *Have you ever been snorkelling?*
   B: *Yes, I have. It was fantastic./No, I haven't.*
5 A: *Have you ever been canoeing?*
   B: *Yes, I have. It was great./No, I haven't.*
6 A: *Have you ever swum with dolphins?*
   B: *Yes, I have. It was exciting./No, I haven't.*

Listening

2 **Aim** To listen for specific information (multiple choice)

- Ask Ss to read the questions and the answer choices.
- Play the recording. Ss listen and choose their answers.
- Check Ss' answers.

Answer Key

1	B	2	A	3	B

Everyday English

3 a) **Aim** To read for cohesion and coherence

Ask Ss to read the dialogue and complete the gaps with the phrases (A-E).

b) **Aim** To listen for confirmation

Play the recording. Ss listen and check their answers.

Answer Key

1 C   2 D   3 A   4 E   5 B

Background Information

Grenada is a sovereign state in the Caribbean Sea that is made up of the islands of Grenada and six smaller islands. It is also known as the 'Island of Spice' because nutmeg and mace are grown here and exported to the rest of the world. The capital city is St George's.

---

4 **Aim** To act out a dialogue describing a holiday experience

- Explain the task and ask Ss to act out a similar dialogue to the one in Ex. 3a in pairs using the Useful Language box.
- Write this diagram on the board for Ss to follow.

A	B
Greet B. *Hey ... , how ...?*	Reply. Say where've you just got back from. *Great! I've just ... .*
Express surprise. Ask when B went. *Really? When ...?*	Say when you went there. *We went ... .*
Ask what it was like. *What ...?*	Express feelings. *Oh, it ... ! I had ... .*
Ask what you did there. *Nice. Was there ...?*	Say what you did. *Yes, we went ... .*
Ask what else you did there. *Wow! Did you ...?*	Say what else you did. *We ... .*
Comment. *It sounds ... .*	Reply. *It was. I can't ... !*

- Monitor the activity around the class and offer assistance as necessary.
- Then ask some pairs to act out their dialogues in front of the rest of the class.

Suggested Answer Key

A: *Hey Rachel, how are you?*
B: *Great! I've just got back from a family holiday in Cuba.*
A: *Really? When did you go?*

B: *We went three weeks ago and got back yesterday.*
A: *What was it like there?*
B: *Oh, it was terrific! I had a fantastic time!*
A: *Nice. Was there much to do there?*
B: *Yes, we went snorkelling in the sea and we swam with dolphins.*
A: *Wow! Did you do anything else?*
B: *We went to some traditional restaurants and tried some local dishes.*
A: *It sounds amazing!*
B: *It was. I can't wait to go again!*

Pronunciation

5 **Aim** To practise pronunciation of /h/ pronounced or silent

- Play the recording and have Ss circle the words in which the /h/ is silent.
- Play the recording again with pauses for Ss to repeat chorally and/or individually.
- Check Ss' pronunciation and intonation.

Answer Key

hour, rhyme, while, John, school

Reading & Writing

6 **Aim** To listen and read for gist

- Ask Ss to look at the blog entry and the comments and read out the question.
- Play the recording. Ss listen and read to find out.
- Check Ss' answers.

Answer Key

The topic of the blog post is recommending places for a group of people to visit in the summer.

Background Information

Chile is a country that runs along the southwest coast of South America. The capital city is Santiago and the population is 18,140,804 million people. The people speak Spanish. Chile's neighbours are Peru, Bolivia, and Argentina. Chile has a varied climate and has the world's driest desert, the Atacama, as well as forests and volcanoes and lakes.

Japan is an island country in East Asia in the Pacific Ocean. It is also known as the 'Land of the Rising Sun'. The capital city is Tokyo and the population is around 127 million people.

7 **Aim** To read for specific information

- Give Ss time to read the blog comments again and then ask Ss to copy and complete the table in their notebooks.
- Check Ss' answers on the board.

Suggested Answer Key

	Place	*Activities*	*Feelings*
Charlotte	*Chile*	*camping, canoeing, sandboarding*	*a bit difficult and hot but fun/had a great time*
Jamie	*Japan*	*windsurfing, visited a medieval castle, went hiking in the forests*	*had an amazing time/ time of his life*

8 **Aim** To analyse structure of a blog comment; to practise language used in blogs

- Read out the **Writing Tip** box and explain that this information will help Ss complete the writing task successfully.
- Give Ss time to substitute the underlined phrases in the blog comments with suitable alternatives from the list.
- Check Ss' answers.

Answer Key

Love your blog: *Great blog!*
Can't wait for your next post!: *Post again soon!*
By the way, great blog William.: *I really enjoy reading your blog.*
Looking forward to your next post!: *Can't wait to read your next post!*

Writing

9 **Aim** To brainstorm and make notes

- Ask Ss to copy the headings into their notebooks and make notes under them about a place they have been to.
- Then ask various Ss around the class to share their answers with the class.

Suggested Answer Key

Name: *Zakynthos, Greece*
Activities: *swimming with turtles, snorkelling, buy handmade souvenirs, try local dishes at a traditional restaurant*
Feelings: *had a terrific time, was amazing, delicious food*

10 **Aim** To write a blog comment about a holiday experience

- Explain the task. Then give Ss time to write their blog comment using their notes from Ex. 9 and the plan to help them.
- Check Ss' answers.
- Alternatively, assign the task as HW and check Ss' answers in the next lesson.

Suggested Answer key

Hey William! Anna here. Great blog!
For me, Zakynthos in Greece is the perfect place to go. I've visited it twice and I had a terrific time. I swam with turtles and went snorkelling. I also bought some handmade souvenirs and tried local dishes at a traditional restaurant. It was amazing! Go there – I'm sure you'll love it. Can't wait for your next post!

Values

Ss try to explain the quotation in their mother tongue. If Ss have difficulty, explain the quotation. Ask Ss to memorise this quotation and check in the next lesson.
The quotation means that if you visit another culture and learn about people's way of life and values then you will understand those people better because you have learnt how they live and what they think is important.

Culture 12

Listening & Reading

1 **Aim** To listen and read for specific information

- Ask Ss to read through the text quickly and try to answer the questions in the rubric.
- Check Ss' answers.

Answer Key

The text is about places to go on holiday in Canada. You can go camping in British Columbia and you can see Niagara Falls by boat.

- Play the video for Ss and elicit their comments.
- Refer Ss to the Word List to look up the meanings of the words in the **Check these words** box.

2 **Aim** To listen and read for specific information (multiple matching)

- Ask Ss to read the questions and then play the recording. Ss listen, read the text and complete the task.
- Check Ss' answers.

Answer Key

1 B	2 A	3 A	4 B

Background Information

British Columbia is a province in the far west of Canada. The capital city is Victoria and the largest city is Vancouver. Its coastline stretches for more than 27,000 kilometres and has deep, mountainous fjords and about 6,000 islands.

Ontario is a province in the southeast of Canada. The capital and largest city is Toronto. It is the home of Niagara Falls and the Great Lakes.

3 **Aim** **THINK** **To develop thinking skills**

Ask Ss to discuss the questions in pairs and then ask some pairs to share their answers with the class.

Suggested Answer Key

Have you ever wanted to visit a city that has no roads and you can only access it by water over the many canals? Venice is the place to go.

4 **Aim** **ICT** **To develop research skills; to select information; to design a travel brochure**

- Explain the task and ask Ss to work in small groups and research online to find out about tourist destinations in their country.
- Give Ss time to use the information and prepare a travel brochure.
- Then ask various Ss to present their brochures to the class.
- Alternatively, assign the task as HW and ask Ss to present their brochures in the next lesson.

Suggested Answer Key

ITALIAN HOLIDAYS

VENICE

Have you ever wanted to travel around a city by boat? Then Venice is the place to go! History lovers can go on a boat trip around the city and see lots of beautiful buildings. You can also take photos in the famous St Mark's Square and try Italian dishes in a traditional restaurant.

LIVIGNO

Imagine camping in the Alps and canoeing across Gallo Lake. Book one of our Livigno package holidays and make your dream come true. We also offer ski resort holidays where you can go skiing or snowboarding and see breathtaking views.

Review 12

Vocabulary

1 **Aim** **To practise vocabulary for holiday activities**

- Explain the task.
- Give Ss time to complete it.
- Check Ss' answers.

Answer Key

1 buy	3 take	5 go	7 ride
2 visit	4 try	6 see	8 go

2 **Aim** **To practise vocabulary for holiday activities**

- Explain the task.
- Give Ss time to complete it.
- Check Ss' answers.

Answer Key

1 D	3 E	5 C	7 F
2 G	4 A	6 B	

Grammar

3 **Aim** **To practise the present perfect**

- Explain the task.
- Give Ss time to complete it.
- Check Ss' answers.

Answer Key

1 hasn't	3 gone	5 have
2 haven't	4 has	6 been

4 **Aim** **To practise *just, yet, since, for, never, ever, already* and the present perfect**

- Explain the task.
- Give Ss time to complete it.
- Check Ss' answers.

Answer Key

1 already	4 never	7 yet
2 just	5 for	
3 since	6 ever	

5 **Aim** To practise the present perfect and the past simple

- Explain the task.
- Give Ss time to complete it.
- Check Ss' answers.

Answer Key

1 *have already visited*
2 *went*
3 *took*
4 *didn't buy*
5 *haven't done*

6 *haven't been*
7 *haven't ridden*
8 *Have you had*

Everyday English

6 **Aim** To practise functional language

- Explain the task.
- Give Ss time to complete it.
- Check Ss' answers.

Answer Key

1 *C*   2 *E*   3 *D*   4 *A*   5 *B*

Competences

Ask Ss to assess their own performance in the unit by ticking the items according to how competent they feel for each of the listed activities.

D Values: Environmental awareness

1 **Aim** To listen and read for specific information

- Elicit how a city can go green from various Ss around the class.
- Play the recording. Ss listen and read the text to find out.

Answer Key

A city can go green by building parks, creating public spaces, encouraging public transport, setting up recycling programmes and using clean energy.

- Play the video for Ss and elicit their comments.

2 **Aim** **THINK** To read for specific information

- Ask Ss to copy the table into their notebooks.
- Give Ss time to read the text again and then ask them to complete the table.
- Check Ss' answers on the board.

Suggested Answer Key

Suggestions	Benefits
Parks	clean air, relaxing place for people
Public spaces e.g. pedestrian-only streets	people get around on foot, less pollution from cars
Public transport, e.g. buses & trains	move around quickly, less traffic
Recycling programmes for waste like cans, bottles & electronics	less rubbish
Clean Energy, e.g. solar power & wind power	clean air, save money

3 **Aim** **THINK** To develop thinking skills; to identify similarities

- Ask Ss to work in pairs and describe how green it is where they live.
- Monitor the activity around the class and then ask some pairs to tell the class.

Suggested Answer Key

Where I live is very green. There are lots of parks and pedestrian-only streets. The public transport is excellent and most people recycle their cans, bottles and electronics. One way that my city can improve is to use more clean energy like solar and wind power.

4 **Aim** ICT To research characteristics of a green city

- Ask Ss to work in small groups and research online to collect information about more characteristics of a green city.
- Then give Ss time to use this information to prepare a leaflet.
- Ask various groups of Ss to present their leaflets to the class.
- Alternatively, assign the task as HW and ask Ss to present their leaflets in the next lesson.

Suggested Answer Key

Green Cities

*There are many ways to make cities greener. Encourage people to use **bicycles** to get around. Cities with **cycle lanes** mean less traffic and less pollution from cars.*

*Encourage people to use **electric cars**. Electric cars don't cause a lot of pollution. They are better for getting around in cities.*

*Cities can have **drinking fountains** for people to use. This means they can drink water and they can stop buying plastic bottles of water. Plastic bottles cause a lot of pollution.*

***Spread the word!** Tell other people how they can make the city greener. Then more people can do their part.*

1 a) **Aim** To analyse a public speaking task

- Read out the **Study Skills** box and tell Ss that this tip will help Ss with their digital presentations.
- Ask Ss to read the task. Elicit who the speaker is (an environmental club's rep), who the audience is (people at a local Earth Day event), what the presentation will be about (a green city).

b) **Aim** To analyse a model and assess slides for a digital presentation

- Play the recording. Ss listen and read the model.
- Then ask Ss to look at the slides and order them according to the order of the information in the presentation.
- Elicit which slide is not appropriate and why.

Answer Key

1 D   2 C   3 A   4 B   5 E

Suggested Answer Key

Slide D is not very effective because the writing is not clear and there is a multi-coloured background.

2 a) **Aim** ICT To develop research skills; to collect information; to prepare for a digital presentation

Ask Ss to research online and collect information about a green city in their country or another country. Give Ss time to make notes under the headings.

Suggested Answer Key

Name/Location of city: *Curitiba, Brazil*
Characteristics: *1,908,360 people live there, capital city of the Brazilian state Parana, name means 'Many pines'*
How people help the environment: *70% of waste is recycled in the city, started recycling in the 1980s, excellent public transport system, government works hard to make city greener, planting trees around roads and making more parks*

b) **Aim** To give a digital presentation

- Ask Ss to use their notes from Ex. 2a to help them prepare slides for their digital presentation.
- Then ask Ss to use their notes and the model to help them prepare a presentation about a green city.
- Ask various Ss to give their presentation to the class.
- Alternatively, assign the whole of Ex. 2 as HW and have Ss give their presentations in the next lesson.

Suggested Answer Key

Hi. I'm Maria Silva. James G. Watt once said, "They kill good trees to put out bad newspapers." Well, the city of Curitiba in my country, Brazil, is trying to change things. Curitiba is the capital city of the Brazilian state Parana. The name means 'Many pines' and 1,800,000 people live there. They help the environment in many ways. For one, 70% of the waste of the city is recycled. Also, the city started recycling in the 1980s. This is earlier than many other cities in the world. Thirdly, the city has an excellent public transport system. This means that there is less pollution than other cities. Finally, the government in Curitiba works hard to make the city greener. They plant trees around roads and make more parks. This makes the air clean and gives people a place to enjoy their free time.
Curitiba is a green city and I think it's an example for other cities to follow. What if every city is green one day? Are there any questions? ... Thank you for listening.

Slide 1

Slide 2

Slide 3

Slide 4

Slide 5

A CLIL: Citizenship

Listening & Reading

1 **Aim** **To listen and read for specific information**

- Ask Ss to look at the leaflet.
- Elicit how we can be good citizens of the world today.
- Play the recording. Ss listen and read the text to find out.

Answer Key

We can be good citizens of the world by helping other people, by being polite and not a bully, by being creative, by listening to everyone's opinion, by caring for nature and keep learning about the world around us.

2 **Aim** **To read for specific information**

- Ask Ss to match the examples (A-F) to the tips (1-6) in the text.
- Check Ss' answers.

Answer Key

A 2   B 1   C 6   D 5   E 3   F 4

Speaking & Writing

3 **Aim** **THINK** **To develop thinking skills; to expand on the topic**

Elicit ideas from Ss around the class as to what else they can do to be a good citizen.

Suggested Answer Key

We can care for animals, volunteer for a charity, recycle, buy things from charity shops, work hard, read/watch the news, pick up litter, save water/energy, use public transport, etc.

4 **Aim** **PROJECT** **To design a poster**

- Ask Ss to work in small groups and discuss being a good citizen. Ask them to bring photos based on their answers to Ex. 3.
- Then give Ss time to design a poster.
- Ask various groups of Ss to present their posters to the class.
- Alternatively, assign the task as HW and ask Ss to present their posters in the next lesson.

Suggested Answer Key

How to be a good citizen

care for animals

public transport

volunteer for a charity

recycle

CLIL: Geography

Listening & Reading

1 **Aim** **To listen and read for specific information**

- Elicit how many climate zones there are and how many seasons each one has got.
- Play the recording. Ss listen and read the text and find out.

Answer Key

There are 3 main climate zones. The polar climate has two seasons (a long winter and a short summer), the temperate climate has four seasons (spring, summer, autumn and winter) and the tropical climate has one or two seasons (a wet season/a wet season and a dry season).

Speaking & Writing

2 **Aim** **To read for specific information**

- Ask Ss to read the text again and copy and complete the table in their notebooks.
- Check Ss' answers on the board and then ask various Ss to compare the different types of climates.

Suggested Answer Key

Climate	Polar	Temperate	Tropical
Weather/ Seasons	*very cold, long winters and short summers*	*four seasons, spring, summer, autumn, winter*	*a wet season/a wet season and a dry season*
Temperatures	*-89°C to 17°C*	*-30°C to 30°C*	*20°C to 34°C*
Countries	*Greenland, Finland, Iceland*	*the USA, the UK, France*	*Brazil, Indonesia and the Philippines*
Animals	*polar bears, Arctic foxes*	*brown bears, deer*	*parrots, monkeys*

The polar climate has got two seasons, the tropical climate one or two, and the temperate climate four seasons – spring, summer, autumn and winter. The temperatures are much lower in areas with the polar climate than in areas with the tropical climate. Temperate areas have got both cold and warm weather. Different animals live in different climates. Polar bears and Arctic foxes need the cold polar climate, but parrots and monkeys need the hot, wet tropical climate to survive.

3 **Aim** **ICT** **To develop research skills; to make notes; to compare and contrast two climates**

- Ask Ss to research online and collect information about the climate in their country and in another country.
- Then have Ss compare and contrast the climates in the two countries.
- Ask various Ss to tell the class.
- Alternatively, assign the task as HW and check their answers in the next lesson.

Suggested Answer Key

In Italy there is a temperate climate, but in Cuba there is a tropical climate. There are four seasons in Italy; spring, summer, autumn and winter. Cuba has got two seasons; a wet season and a dry season. In Italy in the summer it is hot and dry and in the winter it is cold and wet. Both countries can get hot, but Italy is colder in the winter than Cuba. The weather is rainier in Cuba and drier in Italy.

CLIL: History

Listening & Reading

1 (Aim) **To predict the content of the text and listen and read for specific information**

- Ask Ss to look at the pictures and elicit Ss' guesses as to what they expect to read in the text.
- Play the recording. Ss listen and read the text and find out if their guesses were correct.

Suggested Answer Key

I think I am going to read about how people lived in ancient Egypt. I think the text will mention work, homes and education.

2 (Aim) **To read for specific information (T/F statements)**

- Ask Ss to read the statements (1-5) and then give Ss time to read the text again and mark the statements according to what they read.
- Check Ss' answers and then elicit explanations for the words in bold.

Answer Key

1 F   2 F   3 F   4 F   5 T

Suggested Answer Key

important: *having great significance*
diet: *the kinds of food that a person eats*
education: *the process of receiving knowledge in a school*
cool: *not hot, almost cold*
flat: *having a level surface*
sunset: *the time of day when the sun goes down and it starts to get dark*
passenger: *a person on a means of transport who is not the driver*

Speaking & Writing

3 (Aim) (THINK) **To develop thinking skills; to make comparisons**

Elicit answers from Ss around the class as to ways life in ancient Egypt is the same/different to their life today.

Suggested Answer Key

Some things in ancient Egypt are similar to my life. For example, the food the ancient Egyptians had is similar to the food I eat. I eat a lot of bread, vegetables, fruit, milk, cheese, eggs and fish. Also, today, rich people live in big houses with lots of rooms and poor people live in small houses just like the ancient Egyptians.

The ancient Egyptians are different because most children didn't go to school. Today, most children in my country go to school to learn about lots of different subjects. Also, most of the ancient Egyptians were farmers, but people today do lots of different jobs and not many are farmers.

4 (Aim) **ICT** **To develop research skills; to identify information and make notes; to give a presentation on life in the past in your country**

Ask Ss to work in small groups and research online to find out about life during a time between 3000 BC and 30 BC in their country. Ss should collect information and make notes under the headings provided.
Then give Ss time to prepare a presentation.
Ask various groups of Ss to give their presentations to the class.
Alternatively, assign the task as HW and ask Ss to make their presentations in the next lesson.

Suggested Answer Key

LIFE IN ANCIENT GREECE

Jobs

In ancient Greece, the men were farmers or skilled workers such as potters, builders and sculptors. The women often stayed at home and looked after children, cleaned the house, prepared meals and wove cloth.

Food

They had lots of bread and they ate olives, lentils, figs and other fruits. They also had chickens for eggs and cows for milk and cheese. Rich people sometimes ate fish and meat.

Education

Some young boys went to school from age seven and others learnt skills from their fathers. Young girls didn't go to school. They stayed at home with their mothers and learnt how to prepare food, raise children and weave cloth.

Homes

People lived in small houses made from dried mud. They had clay tiles on the roof and a small garden. The houses had small windows with wooden shutters to keep out the hot sun.

Travel

Many people travelled on foot, even for long distances, but some people used donkeys and horses, too. They moved goods across the sea using boats.

CLIL: Literature

Listening & Reading

1 **Aim** To read for specific information

- Read out the questions in the rubric and then give Ss time to read the biography and find out the answers.
- Check Ss' answers around the class.

Suggested Answer Key

H G Wells was a British writer. He wrote science-fiction stories.

2 **Aim** To listen and read for specific information

- Ask Ss to look at the picture and elicit Ss' guesses as to who the people are and where they are.
- Play the recording. Ss listen and read the text and find out if their guesses were correct.

Suggested Answer Key

The picture shows a man and his friend Weena, the Eloi and the Morlocks.
The man and his friend Weena are in a garden and the Morlocks are underground.

3 **Aim** To read for specific information (multiple choice)

- Ask Ss to read the questions 1-3 and the answer choices and then give Ss time to read the text again and choose their answers according to what they read.
- Check Ss' answers.

Answer Key

1 B	2 C	3 A

- Give Ss time to look up the meanings of the words in the **Check these words** box in the Word List.

Speaking & Writing

4 **Aim** THINK To develop thinking skills; to express a feeling

Elicit answers from Ss around the class as to whether or not they feel sorry for the Morlocks and why.

Suggested Answer Key

Yes, I do feel sorry for the Morlocks because the Eloi made them live underground and work for them.

5 **Aim** ICT To research information; to make notes; to present a story from notes

- Ask Ss to research online and find another story by H. G. Wells and collect information about it under the headings.
- Ask various Ss to present the story to the class covering all the points in the rubric.
- Alternatively, assign the task as HW and have Ss present their stories in the next lesson.

Suggested Answer Key

Another story by H G Wells is 'The War of the Worlds'. The main character is the Narrator. The other characters include the Narrator's wife, the Narrator's cousin, the Curate, the Artilleryman and the Martians. The Martians are big ugly aliens from Mars.
The story takes place in England in the 1890s. In the story, Martians land on Earth and take over the cities with their Death-Ray. Many people die and the others run away. The Narrator tries to find his wife. The army fights the Martians, but they lose. In the end, the Martians become ill because of bacteria and they all die.

121

Student's Book Audioscripts

UNIT 1 – Hi!

1c – Exercise 2b (p. 8)

Carlos: Hola! Oh I'm sorry, hello. My name's Carlos and this is Diego.
Diego: Hello! We are students here. What's your name?
Elsa: Hi, I'm Elsa. Are you both from Spain?
Carlos: No. We're from Mexico. Where are you from, Elsa?
Elsa: I'm from Sweden. How old are you Diego?
Diego: I'm 18 years old and Carlos is 20. How old are you?
Elsa: I'm 21 years old. Carlos, are you in Year 3 of college like me?
Carlos: No. I'm in Year 2 and Diego is in Year 1.
Elsa: Are you a Geography student?
Diego: No. I'm an Art student. And you?
Elsa: English! I'm not really crazy about subjects like Chemistry or Biology. What about you, Carlos?
Carlos: I'm a Chemistry student. It's a cool subject!
Elsa: Oops! Sorry, I'm sure it is. Well, see you guys around college!
Carlos: Bye! See you later!
Diego: Great to meet you.

UNIT 2 – Families

2c – Exercises 2a & 2b (p. 16)

Bob: Hey Tom. Is that your brother over there; the one with short black hair?
Tom: Yes, he is my clever brother Alex. He's with one of my cousins, and her mum.
Bob: Oh yes, he's got short hair now. Is that your cousin, Margaret?
Tom: No, Margaret is my aunt. She's really funny.
Bob: Oh! I'm sorry. So, what's your cousin's name? We're at the same school, but I can't remember her name.
Tom: It's Martha. She's OK but she can be silly at times.
Bob: And who's David? Is he your dad or your uncle?
Tom: He's my uncle and he's very kind. David is my dad's brother.
Bob: And who is she?
Tom: That's Claire, my sister. She is a bit shy.
Bob: Oh really? I have an idea! Let's go and talk to her.
Tom: OK. But let's take Michelle with us.
Bob: Oh, is Michelle your mum?
Tom: No, she is my grandma. She is in the kitchen again.
Bob: Now I remember Michelle, your grandma. She can cook great food!
Tom: Yes, everyone in my family is crazy about her dishes! She's very friendly. Come on let's go!

UNIT 3 – Home sweet home!

3c – Exercise 2 (p. 24)

A: Good afternoon, this is Robert at Lion Estates. How can I help?
B: Hello, my name's Catherine Barnes; I'm interested in renting my flat out.
A: Sure. Can you tell us a little about your flat?
B: OK. It's at 12 Greenbank Park.
A: Good. That's really near the city centre. Can you tell me how many rooms it's got?
B: There are five rooms: a spacious living room, a kitchen, a small bathroom and two large bedrooms.
A: Is there a garden?
B: Yes. There's a small garden and a double garage.
A: How much is the rent?
B: £800 per month.
A: Great, well that's everything. Thank you for your call.
B: Bye.

UNIT 4 – Busy days

4a – Exercise 6 (p. 31)

Hi, I'm Tony and on weekdays I have a really busy daily routine! I always get up at 7:30 in the morning. Then, I have a shower and I get dressed. After, I eat breakfast with my family and catch the bus to college at 8:15. At noon, I have a break for lunch. I usually finish college at 4 pm in the afternoon. Then, I go to my part-time job in a café. I work there from 5 pm to 8 pm. In the evening, at 9 pm, I do my homework and then I watch TV. I go to bed at around 11 pm and I sleep straightaway.

4c – Exercise 2 (p. 34)

Holly: Hey, Ann. How are you?
Ann: Hi, Holly! I'm fine. I'm at home. Do you know Halen and the Queens? Their music is great! I love listening to them. What about you?
Holly: I'm off to the park to read a book. I like reading there because the park is very quiet. Hey, Isabel and I want to go to the mall later. Do you want to come with us?
Ann: Aww, I don't like going there; there are too many people. Can't we do something else?
Holly: Sure. Why don't we visit that new museum of natural history – The Nussbaum Museum? I like visiting museums and I think it's open now.
Ann: Great. I like doing that, too! What time do you want to meet, then?
Holly: Let's meet there at two o'clock. I need to talk to Isabel first to see if she wants to come as well.
Ann: OK. See you there.

Student's Book Audioscripts

UNIT 5 – Birds of a feather

5b – Exercise 2 (p. 40)

Good morning, everyone, and welcome to your first day at work. Before we go near the shark tank, you need to know the rules. First, you mustn't work alone – ever! It's really dangerous! You need another diver with you and someone watching from the top of the tank. Remember, you must enter a tank full of sharks – that's the job! We can't take them out for you to go in! So you need someone at your back. And you must clean tanks after meals, not before. A hungry shark is a naughty shark!

Now, about the job. You need to stay fit, because you must do 1,000 or more dives a year. The dives are quite short, though. We have a rule – that divers mustn't stay in the water very long.

Finally, what do you need to clean a tank? It's pretty basic – a brush or a sponge, that's all. You see, you mustn't use strong soap – it's bad for the sharks…

5c – Exercise 2 (p. 42)

Rosie: Hey Matt, your farm's great. Thanks for inviting me.
Matt: My pleasure. Do you want to see some of the animals?
Rosie: Sure. Are those your horses? They're really beautiful.
Matt: Yes. Their names are Misty, Rocky and Blaze.
Rosie: How old are they?
Matt: Misty is two years old, but Rocky and Blaze are both one year old.
Rosie: Wow! They're quite big for that age. What do they eat?
Matt: They eat lots of apples and carrots, but their favourite food is hay. That's dried glass.
Rosie: How often do you feed them?
Matt: I usually feed them once in the morning and again in the afternoon.
Rosie: I see. Do you keep them in this stable all day?
Matt: No, we usually take them out into the fields in the morning. Then, in the evening, we bring them back in. They like being outside.
Rosie: So, how often do you clean their stable?
Matt: Every morning.
Rosie: It sounds like a lot of work to look after a few horses.
Matt: Yes, but it's worth it. They're really fun to ride.
Rosie: Yeah, I can see that!

UNIT 6 – Come rain or shine

6c – Exercise 2a p. 50

Judy: Good morning. Today, I have a special guest with me. He is a new name in fashion. He comes from Manchester and he has some of his latest designs to show us. Welcome, Victor Green.
Victor: Thank you, Judy. I'm happy to be here.
Judy: Let's bring out the first model.
Victor: This is Steve. He's wearing a grey T-shirt, shorts, white trainers and a cap. This is a casual look for summer.
Judy: Thank you, Steve.
Victor: This is Mary. She's wearing a colourful blouse with a green jacket, a black skirt and black shoes. This is perfect for a working woman. With her is Jenny. Jenny is wearing clothes for the evening. She is wearing a blue dress with a blue scarf and black sandals.
Judy: Thank you, Mary and Jenny. You both look great.
Victor: Now, this is Paul. He's wearing a dark suit and black shoes, with a green shirt and a grey tie.
Judy: Thank you, Paul. That's a very nice suit.
Victor: Here is Diana. She's wearing a black top with a long cardigan on top, white trousers and red sandals.
Judy: Doesn't she look lovely? Thank you, Diana.
Victor: The final outfit is for everyday wear. John is wearing a shirt and jeans with brown boots and a black jacket.
Judy: Thank you so much for coming in and showing us your latest designs.

UNIT 7 – Taste the world

7b – Exercise 7 p. 59

A: Let's check what I need for the dinner party tonight. Would you look in the fridge please, Tom?
B: Okay. There's not much here. Would you like me to make a shopping list?
A: Yes. Is there any meat in the fridge?
B: No. How much do you need?
A: I need two kilos of meat.
B: Alright. Do you need any eggs?
A: No, I think we have enough eggs, but I do need a kilo of cheese.
B: What about ham and bread?
A: Yes, I need some ham and some bread.
B: How much do you need?
A: Get me twenty slices of ham and two loaves of bread, please.
B: Do you need any tomatoes?
A: No, I think there are enough tomatoes.
B: Is there anything else you need?
A: Yes, I need some flour.
B: How much?

Student's Book Audioscripts

A: I think two bags of flour will be fine. And some cola, please.
B: How many bottles do you want?
A: Three bottles will be okay.
B: Shall I buy some orange juice?
A: No, we don't need any — and we don't need any bananas, either.
B: Okay, then. I'll be back with everything you need in half an hour.

7c – Exercise 2b p. 60

The Blue Lagoon is the new Hawaiian restaurant on Long Street and it's open for lunch and dinner every day.

The food is very well cooked. Come and try our fresh fish dishes or our delicious Hawaiian burgers with pineapple. For dessert, treat yourself to creamy coconut ice cream.

A meal for two people costs about £30. The service is excellent with very helpful and friendly waiters. The restaurant is open from two in the afternoon to twelve midnight.

The Blue Lagoon is a very nice restaurant for the whole family. Don't forget to book a table now. Tel: 6620102

UNIT 8 – New places, new faces

8b – Exercise 6 p. 67

Host: Welcome to Teen Quiz. Tonight, we have Ray Mitchell and Anne Winter. Nice to have you with us, and good luck to both of you. Ready?
Anne: Yes.
Ray: I'm ready.
Host: Good, then let's begin … The first question is for you, Ray. Tell me, which is the largest desert in the world?
Ray: I think it's the Sahara Desert …
Host: That's right! Well done! Now, Anne, which is the highest mountain in the world?
Anne: That's easy — Mount Everest is the world's highest mountain.
Host: Correct. Ray, do you know which is the longest river in the world?
Ray: The Mississippi, isn't it?
Host: Sorry — that's the longest river in the USA, but the longest river in the world is —
Ray: Oh, the Amazon!
Host: Yes, the Amazon, but I can't give you a point, I'm afraid. Now, Anne, where is the driest place in the world?
Anne: Is it somewhere in Australia?
Host: Bad luck — the driest place in the world is the Atacama Desert in Chile. Ray, your turn — which is the smallest country in the world?
Ray: I'm not sure … Luxembourg?
Host: Well, Luxembourg is small, but the State of the Vatican City is much smaller. Never mind. Okay, Anne, back to you — which is the tallest building in the USA?

Anne: I know the Sears Tower in Chicago was the tallest, but it isn't now … now it's the One World Trade Center in New York, I think.
Host: That's right! The One World Trade Center in New York is the tallest building in the USA. So, the score is one point for Ray, and two points for Anne — but we still have more questions. The next question for you, Ray, is this — which is …

8b – Exercise 8 p. 67

Tim: Hello?
Sean: Hi, Tim, it's Sean. How are you?
Tim: Sean! I'm fine, thanks. How are things in London?
Sean: Busy as usual. How are you getting along in Edinburgh?
Tim: It's still the best city in the world!
Sean: There you go again. Don't you realise that London is better? I mean, London is bigger, and there are so many different things to see and do here.
Tim: Yes, Edinburgh is smaller than London, but it's a lot safer.
Sean: It's too quiet there. I'm glad London is noisier. It means the city is alive.
Tim: What about the pollution?
Sean: I know London is more polluted than Edinburgh, but it's not that bad!
Tim: But can you afford to go anywhere? London is far more expensive than Edinburgh.
Sean: So, you aren't planning to move to London, are you?
Tim: I don't think so. I'm quite happy here. Edinburgh is the perfect city for me.
Sean: That's how I feel about London.
Tim: We'll just have to visit each other, then.
Sean: I agree. Take care, Tim.
Tim: You too, Sean. Bye.
Sean: Bye.

8c – Exercise 2 p. 68

Sue: Hello, Liam. Are you enjoying the exhibition?
Liam: Yes thanks. They've got some great pictures on show. It's a pity the others from the class can't be here.
Sue: Where is everyone? Sally's busy, I know.
Liam: Yes, she's at the theatre rehearsing for a new play she's in.
Sue: Oh, isn't she playing football at that new stadium today?
Liam: No, that's tomorrow. But Ralph's there at the moment. He's practising for the match.
Sue: Right. And what about Helen? Why isn't she here?
Liam: She doesn't like art! She's having fun at the theme park!
Sue: Hmm … I think theme parks are a bit silly … And I suppose Ronny's busy at the gift shop of the zoo. That's where he works on Saturday, isn't it?

Student's Book Audioscripts

Liam: Yes, but he has the day off. He's got a history project to finish so he's at the museum.

Sue: Oh, that's right! Maybe Mary's at the museum too. Isn't she doing the same project?

Liam: She is, but Saturday is her day to work in the restaurant. She is a waitress there every weekend and she doesn't have a day off.

Sue: Then it's just you and me! Let's go and check out the statues!

UNIT 9 – Times change

9b – Exercise 1 p. 74

Host: Welcome to Teen Quiz. Tonight we have David Rawlings and Lynn Summerton. Nice to have you with us, and the best of luck to you both. Are you ready?

David: Yes!

Lynn: I'm ready!

Host: Great. Let's begin… The first question is for you, David. Tell me, in which year did London buses become red?

David: Hmmm, I know it was in the early 1900s. I think it was 1907.

Host: Correct! Well done! Now, Lynn, which was the first city where people could use an underground train?

Lynn: I know that! It's London.

Host: That's right! David, what didn't the first cars have?

David: Hmmm, lights, right?

Host: Sorry – that's not right! The first cars didn't have doors. Now, Lynn, The Wright Brothers were the first people to fly in a powered and controlled aeroplane on the 17th of December in which year?

Lynn: Hmmm, It was either in the late 1800s or the early 1900s. …Oh yes, it's 1903.

Host: Well done! So, the score is one point for David and two points for Lynn. But, don't worry, David, you can catch up with Lynn in round two…

9b – Exercise 10a p. 75

Doug: Paul, what were you like when you were little?

Paul: Oh, I was quite clever in some ways. For example, I could talk when I was one, and I could count when I was two. I could read when I was two, as well.

Doug: Really? That's very impressive! I don't know anyone who could do those things at such an early age.

Paul: Thank you – but that's not all.

Doug: What do you mean?

Paul: Well, I could walk when I was two, and I could ride a bicycle when I was three. But the best thing was that I could swim when I was four.

Doug: Wow! You were a genius! I wasn't like that when I was young. I couldn't talk until I was two, and I couldn't count until I was three. And reading … well, I couldn't read until I was five.

Paul: So? That's completely normal.

Doug: Yes, but I couldn't walk until I was three, and I couldn't ride a bicycle until I was about ten! I couldn't swim until I was ten, too.

Paul: That's normal, too. And look at all the other things you could do when you were young. You could play the piano when you were very young, your mother says, and I still can't play the piano! You could [fade] speak French, too …

9b – Exercise 12a p. 75

Life for ancient Inca children was exciting. They had wooden toys. They didn't have any paper books. By the age of eight they could cook, farm and fish. Inca children couldn't read or write because the Inca didn't have an alphabet. The Incas could grow crops of potatoes, quinoa and corn. They didn't have meat because they didn't have any animals. The children's favourite food was potatoes and corn. There were lots of games for children. A popular ball game was something like football and basketball, called Tlachtli. But all children were crazy about board games and they had a lot of them!

9c – Exercise 2 p. 76

Welcome to Map App. Please choose your destination. *(beep)* Destination: the Grand Hotel, Hill Street. Please press 'start' to begin your journey. *(beep)* Go up King Street. … In 400 metres, turn right onto Hill Street. … Continue straight for 100 metres. … Your destination is on your left. … You are at your destination. Thank you for using Map App.

UNIT 10 – Their stories live on

10c – Exercise 2b p. 86

One sunny day last summer, Claire and Greg went to a wildlife park. Soon after they drove in, they saw some lions. Greg was very happy because he loved lions. Greg stopped the car and started taking pictures of them. The lions walked around the car and made Claire feel a little frightened. 'Let's go and see the gorillas now,' she said. Greg tried to start the car, but nothing happened. He tried twice more, and was turning the key a third time when they noticed there was smoke coming out of the engine! A few moments later, the car was on fire! 'We can't get out – the lions want to attack us!' said Claire. 'We can't stay in the car either!' said Greg. He pressed the horn and Claire opened her window a little and shouted for help. Just as it started getting uncomfortably hot in the car, the rangers arrived in two trucks. One ranger chased away the lions by beeping and flashing the lights of his truck, while the other truck stopped right next to Claire's window. Claire opened it fully and climbed straight into the ranger's truck. Greg followed, and the ranger drove off. Greg and Claire felt shocked at how quickly their lovely day out

Student's Book Audioscripts

had turned into a nightmare. They were happy to be safe, and they thanked the rangers warmly for their help.

10c – Exercise 9b p. 87

That cold winter afternoon, I decided to take my dog, Rex, for a walk on the beach. Suddenly, Rex began to bark loudly. There was a woman a little way down the beach. She looked terribly frightened and she kept shouting, "Help! Help!" I ran towards her, with Rex just behind. As I got close, I heard her shout, "The sea! He's in the sea!" I quickly looked out over the water and saw the head of a child. "A wave took him, but I can't swim," cried the woman. I didn't wait a moment longer. I took off my jacket and dived into the water. It was freezing cold, but I swam out to the boy fast and brought him back to shore.

We brought the boy back home. He was soon warm and felt better. The woman, who was the boy's nanny, felt so happy that the boy was all right. She kept thanking me, and I felt proud that I saved him.

UNIT 11 – Time will tell

11b – Exercise 4a p. 92

A: Good afternoon. I'm from Channel 7 and we're conducting a survey to find out what the public thinks the world will be like in 30 years' time. Would you like to tell us your opinions?

B/C: Yes, of course.

A: What do you think, madam?

B: Ooh, I think people will travel in flying cars ... like in that film – what was it? Oh, never mind, anyway, people will probably live in underwater cities, too – that will be fun! People will go on holiday to the Moon – I'm sure about that because there was something about it on the news the other day.

A: Thank you, madam. Sir? What do you think?

C: Hmm ... Well, I think the pollution will be worse in 30 years' time and people will use oxygen masks to breathe. I think they already do in some big cities today. Yeah, and there won't be enough water for everyone, either.

A: Oh, dear. That does sound bad! Well, thanks very much for your time.

B: You're welcome.

C: No problem.

11c – Exercise 2 p. 94

Ken: The summer's here at last! Any plans, Tim? Making money like last year?

Tim: No, Ken. This summer I want to make a difference. I'm volunteering for an environmental group. We're going to plant trees and clean up rubbish and so on.

Ken: Good for you, Tim! And what else?

Tim: Mandy and I are taking a computer course. She wants to learn how to start a blog about cooking, but I'm just interested in figuring out my new laptop. How about you?

Ken: I'm tired from all the studying, Tim. I'm going to enjoy myself a bit. First, I'm going windsurfing – every day, if possible!

Tim: Are you going on holiday at all?

Ken: Yes! I'm going to stay at a luxury hotel with my two cousins. They won five nights there in a competition, starting on the 6th of August!

Tim: You're so lucky!

UNIT 12 – New places, new faces

12b – Exercise 6 p. 101

A: Hi, Mum. It's me, Ann. How are you?

B: Oooh, hello, dear. I'm fine. How are you? How's Kate? Are you having a good time?

A: Whoa, Mum! One question at a time. Yes, I'm fine, Kate's fine and we are having a lovely time.

B: Sorry. I'm just very pleased to hear from you. So, have you visited the Eiffel Tower yet?

A: Yes, we went there yesterday. The view from the top was fantastic.

B: Oh, lovely. Have you been to Versailles as well?

A: No, not yet. We're planning to go to Versailles on Tuesday.

B: Have you been shopping at all?

A: Yes, we went shopping yesterday and I've bought you a really lovely gift. I hope you'll like it.

B: Oh, I'm sure I will. Where did you go shopping?

A: We went to the Galleries Lafayette. There were some beautiful shops but they were quite expensive.

B: Don't spend all your money on gifts. Have you been to see the Arc de Triomphe? What's it like?

A: Oh yes, we've already seen the Arc de Triomphe. It's quite an impressive monument.

B: Lovely. Have you been on a boat trip on the Seine yet?

A: No, we haven't. We're hoping to do that on Thursday.

B: What about the Louvre? Have you been there yet? I've heard it's a wonderful place to visit.

A: Yes, we've already visited the Louvre. We spent a whole day there. It was amazing.

B: Have you seen Notre Dame? What's it like inside?

Student's Book Audioscripts

A: I don't know – we haven't seen it yet. We're planning to go there on Wednesday. I'll have to go now, Mum. I'm running out of units.

B: Okay, dear. I'll see you when you get home. Bye.

12c – Exercise 2 p. 102

1 *Sally:* Hey, Luke. How're you? How's your holiday in Canada going?

Luke: Oh, it's going great, Sally. There are so many exciting things to do here. I've just been canoeing, in fact. What about you?

Sally: My trip's going well. I love the cold weather here in Norway.

Luke: Did you go ice skating, like you said?

Sally: Not yet, I'm going to go tomorrow … I hope! But that's outside the city. I've been here in Oslo for three days now. I've taken some fantastic photos and I also went on a helicopter tour yesterday. I've never done that before!

Luke: Wow! That sounds amazing!

Sally: It was! Well, have a great time. See you when we get back.

Luke: Bye Sally!

2 *Grace:* Hi, John. How's New Zealand?

John: Hello, Grace! It's fantastic! We're staying in Auckland at the moment and yesterday I went snorkelling! What an experience! How's your trip to Brazil going?

Grace: Brazil's amazing. Since last week, we've been in the Amazon Rainforest. I've been on a helicopter tour and I've even swum with dolphins in the river. But when did you first arrive in New Zealand?

John: Well, it's Tuesday now and we've been in the country for three days. We're going to stay for a week. Isn't that great?

Grace: Lucky you! Don't forget to buy souvenirs!

John: I won't! Bye!

3 *Ben:* Hello, Kevin. It's Ben.

Kevin: Hi, Ben. How are you?

Ben: Great! I've just come back from a two-week holiday in Egypt.

Kevin: Really?

Ben: Yeah, it was fantastic. Why don't you come around to my place this evening? Then I can tell you all about it.

Kevin: Sure! And I'll show you photos from my holiday in Turkey.

Ben: OK! I'd love that! See you later!

Formative Evaluation Chart

Name of game/activity: ....

Aim of game/activity: ....

Unit: .... Course: ....

	Students' names:	Mark and comments
1		
2		
3		
4		
5		
6		
7		
8		
9		
10		
11		
12		
13		
14		
15		
16		
17		
18		
19		
20		
21		
22		
23		
24		
25		

Cumulative Evaluation

Student's Self Assessment Forms

CODE			
**** Excellent	*** Very Good	** OK	* Not Very Good

Student's Self Assessment Form — UNIT 1

Go through Unit 1 and find examples of the following. Use the code to evaluate yourself.

• use words related to numbers, countries & nationalities, jobs, abilities, colours	
• understand short texts related to people	
• read for specific information – get an idea of the content of simple informational material & short simple descriptions about people	
• listen and produce simple sentences about people (numbers, names, nationalities, etc)	
• greet & introduce yourself/others	
• give personal information	
• understand everyday expressions, describe myself/others	
• ask questions	

Go through the corrected writing tasks. Use the code to evaluate yourself.

• write simple sentences about people	
• write a social media profile (write numbers and dates, own name, nationality etc)	
• link words/groups of words with basic connectors (and, but)	

CODE			
**** Excellent	***** Very Good**	**** OK**	*** Not Very Good**

Student's Self Assessment Form UNIT 2

Go through Unit 2 and find examples of the following. Use the code to evaluate yourself.	
• use words/phrases related to people's appearance, character	
• understand information in short texts about family members, understand short descriptions with visual support	
• listen and understand relations	
• identify and describe people – describe myself & others	
• understand everyday expressions in a conversation	
• pronounce words with the sounds /iː/, /ɪ/	

Go through the corrected writing tasks. Use the code to evaluate yourself.	
• write simple sentences about a famous TV/film family	
• punctuate sentences	
• write a blog entry about my favourite famous person	
• write short text about famous siblings	

CODE			
**** **Excellent**	*** **Very Good**	** **OK**	* **Not Very Good**

Student's Self Assessment Form

UNIT 3

Go through Unit 3 and find examples of the following. Use the code to evaluate yourself.

• use words/phrases related to rooms, furniture & appliances; ordinal numbers; types of houses	
• read for specific information – understand short texts related to houses	
• understand descriptions of houses with visual support	
• listen and understand dialogues about renting a house	
• understand everyday expressions and ask people for information about renting a house	
• describe location	
• pronounce words with the sounds /ɒː/, /æ/	

Go through the corrected writing tasks. Use the code to evaluate yourself.

• write a short advert for a house	
• write an email describing my new flat	
• write a short text about a special building	

CODE			
**** Excellent	***** Very Good**	**** OK**	*** Not Very Good**

Student's Self Assessment Form   UNIT 4

Go through Unit 4 and find examples of the following. Use the code to evaluate yourself.

• understand words/phrases related to daily routines; free-time activities; days of the week; sports	
• ask for/tell the time	
• understand texts related to daily routines & free-time activities	
• understand the main idea of a paragraph in a text about daily routines	
• listen and understand interaction between friends talking about their free-time activities	
• make arrangements indicating the time	
• pronounce words with the sounds /s/, /z/, /ɪz/	

Go through the corrected writing tasks. Use the code to evaluate yourself.

• write an email about my daily routine using informal language	
• write a blog entry about my typical Sunday	
• write a short text about popular sports in my country	

CODE			
**** Excellent	***** Very Good**	**** OK**	*** Not Very Good**

Student's Self Assessment Form

UNIT 5

Go through Unit 5 and find examples of the following. Use the code to evaluate yourself.

• understand words/phrases related to wild animals, farm animals	
• describe animals	
• understand texts about animals & rules	
• listen and understand dialogues about farm animals & routines	
• understand short texts with visual support related to animals	
• ask for/refuse-grant permission	
• listen for specific information	
• ask people for information, give information	
• reply in an interview	
• pronounce words with the sounds /e/, /ɜː/	

Go through the corrected writing tasks. Use the code to evaluate yourself.

• write a fact file about an animal	
• fill in a volunteer application form	
• write a short text about unique animals in my country	

CODE			
**** Excellent	*** Very Good	** OK	* Not Very Good

Student's Self Assessment Form UNIT 6

Go through Unit 6 and find examples of the following. Use the code to evaluate yourself.

• understand words/phrases related to the weather; seasons; months; seasonal activities, clothes	
• describe a person's clothes	
• describe actions happening now	
• understand short texts with visual support related to the weather	
• understand short texts related to the weather	
• listen and identify people & their clothes	
• shop for clothes	
• pronounce words with the sounds /n/, /y/	

Go through the corrected writing tasks. Use the code to evaluate yourself.

• write a blog post reporting the weather	
• write a short postcard, write addresses	
• create a calendar showing the weather	

Student's Self Assessment Form

Go through Unit 7 and find examples of the following. Use the code to evaluate yourself.

• understand words/phrases related to types of food/drinks; meals; ways to cook	
• understand short texts related to food/drinks	
• understand simple instructions about making a dish	
• decide on a shopping list	
• listen to an advert and extract key details about a restaurant	
• order food at a restaurant	
• pronounce words with the sounds /g/, /dʒ/	

Go through the corrected writing tasks. Use the code to evaluate yourself.

• write a short text about a typical dish and drink in my country	
• write a short restaurant review using adjectives	
• write a recipe	

Student's Self Assessment Form

UNIT 8

Go through Unit 8 and find examples of the following. Use the code to evaluate yourself.

• understand words/phrases related to places in a city; tourist attractions	
• understand information/advertising texts about places & tourist attractions	
• understand texts with visual support about places	
• compare places	
• identify author's purpose	
• listen and identify people and places	
• make suggestions	
• pronounce words with the sounds /s/, /ʃ/	

Go through the corrected writing tasks. Use the code to evaluate yourself.

• write sentences comparing places	
• write an article describing a place	
• write short texts about places of natural beauty	

Student's Self Assessment Form

UNIT 9

Go through Unit 9 and find examples of the following. Use the code to evaluate yourself.	
• understand words/phrases related to features in a place; places/buildings in a town/ city; transport	
• understand texts about places then & now	
• understand directions	
• reply in an interview	
• describe past abilities	
• listen to and understand simple directions	
• ask for/give directions	
• pronounce words with /ℓ/ pronounced or silent	

Go through the corrected writing tasks. Use the code to evaluate yourself.	
• write a short text comparing two places	
• write an article about a place then and now	
• create my own city and street names	

Student's Self Assessment Form UNIT 10

Go through Unit 10 and find examples of the following. Use the code to evaluate yourself.

• understand words/phrases related to famous people and their achievements; jobs; feelings/reactions	
• understand texts related to famous people	
• describe past activities/events	
• listen to and understand main events in a narration	
• narrate past events	
• react to news	

Go through the corrected writing tasks. Use the code to evaluate yourself.

• write a short story using linkers (and, but, because, so, then, when, etc)	
• write a short biography	

Student's Self Assessment Form

UNIT 11

Go through Unit 11 and find examples of the following. Use the code to evaluate yourself.	
• understand words/phrases related to the environment; summer plans	
• understand short texts related to summer activities	
• understand texts with visual support about the environment	
• listen to a dialogue and identify speakers' summer plans	
• express reason, result or purpose	
• invite-accept/refuse invitations	
• discuss future plans & arrangements	
• pronounce *'ll - won't*	

Go through the corrected writing tasks. Use the code to evaluate yourself.	
• write a leaflet	
• write an email about my summer plans	
• join sentences using connectors (*because, so*)	

Student's Self Assessment Form

UNIT 12

Go through Unit 12 and find examples of the following. Use the code to evaluate yourself.	
• understand words/phrases related to holiday activities; travel experiences	
• understand emails about travel experiences	
• understand texts about holiday activities with visual support	
• listen and identify content of conversations about travel experiences	
• describe a holiday experience	
• pronounce words with /h/ pronounced or silent	

Go through the corrected writing tasks. Use the code to evaluate yourself.	
• write a blog comment about a holiday experience	
• design a travel brochure for tourist destinations	

Progress Report Cards

Progress Report Card

.... (name) can:

Unit 1

	very well	OK	not very well
use words related to numbers, countries & nationalities, jobs, abilities, colours			
understand short texts related to people			
read for specific information – get an idea of the content of simple informational material & short simple descriptions about people			
listen and produce simple sentences about people (numbers, names, nationalities, etc)			
greet & introduce themselves/others			
give personal information			
understand everyday expressions, describe themselves/others			
ask questions			
write simple sentences about people			
write a social media profile (write numbers and dates, own name, nationality etc)			
link words/groups of words with basic connectors (and, but)			

Progress Report Card

.... (name) can:

Unit 2

	very well	OK	not very well
use words/phrases related to people's appearance, character			
understand information in short texts about family members, understand short descriptions with visual support			
listen and understand relations			
identify and describe people – describe themselves & others			
understand everyday expressions in a conversation			
pronounce words with the sounds /iː/, /ɪ/			
write simple sentences about a famous TV/film family			
punctuate sentences			
write a blog entry about my favourite famous person			
write short text about famous siblings			

Progress Report Card

.... (name) can:			Unit 3
	very well	**OK**	**not very well**
use words/phrases related to rooms, furniture & appliances; ordinal numbers; types of houses			
read for specific information – understand short texts related to houses			
understand descriptions of houses with visual support			
listen and understand dialogues about renting a house			
understand everyday expressions and ask people for information about renting a house			
describe location			
pronounce words with the sounds /ɒː/, /æ/			
write a short advert for a house			
write an email describing their new flat			
write a short text about a special building			

Progress Report Card

.... (name) can:			Unit 4
	very well	**OK**	**not very well**
understand words/phrases related to daily routines; free-time activities; days of the week; sports			
ask for/tell the time			
understand texts related to daily routines & free-time activities			
understand the main idea of a paragraph in a text about daily routines			
listen and understand interaction between friends talking about their free-time activities			
make arrangements indicating the time			
pronounce words with the sounds /s/, /z/, /ɪz/			
write an email about their daily routine using informal language			
write a blog entry about their typical Sunday			
write a short text about popular sports in their country			

Progress Report Card

<table>
<tr><td>.. (name) can:</td><td colspan="3">Unit 5</td></tr>
<tr><td></td><td>very well</td><td>OK</td><td>not very well</td></tr>
<tr><td>understand words/phrases related to wild animals, farm animals</td><td></td><td></td><td></td></tr>
<tr><td>describe animals</td><td></td><td></td><td></td></tr>
<tr><td>understand texts about animals & rules</td><td></td><td></td><td></td></tr>
<tr><td>listen and understand dialogues about farm animals & routines</td><td></td><td></td><td></td></tr>
<tr><td>understand short texts with visual support related to animals</td><td></td><td></td><td></td></tr>
<tr><td>ask for/refuse-grant permission</td><td></td><td></td><td></td></tr>
<tr><td>listen for specific information</td><td></td><td></td><td></td></tr>
<tr><td>ask people for information, give information</td><td></td><td></td><td></td></tr>
<tr><td>reply in an interview</td><td></td><td></td><td></td></tr>
<tr><td>pronounce words with the sounds /e/, /ɜː/</td><td></td><td></td><td></td></tr>
<tr><td>write a fact file about an animal</td><td></td><td></td><td></td></tr>
<tr><td>fill in a volunteer application form</td><td></td><td></td><td></td></tr>
<tr><td>write a short text about unique animals in their country</td><td></td><td></td><td></td></tr>
</table>

Progress Report Card

<table>
<tr><td>.. (name) can:</td><td colspan="3">Unit 6</td></tr>
<tr><td></td><td>very well</td><td>OK</td><td>not very well</td></tr>
<tr><td>understand words/phrases related to the weather; seasons; months; seasonal activities, clothes</td><td></td><td></td><td></td></tr>
<tr><td>describe a person's clothes</td><td></td><td></td><td></td></tr>
<tr><td>describe actions happening now</td><td></td><td></td><td></td></tr>
<tr><td>understand short texts with visual support related to the weather</td><td></td><td></td><td></td></tr>
<tr><td>understand short texts related to the weather</td><td></td><td></td><td></td></tr>
<tr><td>listen and identify people & their clothes</td><td></td><td></td><td></td></tr>
<tr><td>shop for clothes</td><td></td><td></td><td></td></tr>
<tr><td>pronounce words with the sounds /n/, /y/</td><td></td><td></td><td></td></tr>
<tr><td>write a blog post reporting the weather</td><td></td><td></td><td></td></tr>
<tr><td>write a short postcard, write addresses</td><td></td><td></td><td></td></tr>
<tr><td>create a calendar showing the weather</td><td></td><td></td><td></td></tr>
</table>

Progress Report Card

.... (name) can: **Unit 7**

	very well	OK	not very well
understand words/phrases related to types of food/drinks; meals; ways to cook			
understand short texts related to food/drinks			
understand simple instructions about making a dish			
decide on a shopping list			
listen to an advert and extract key details about a restaurant			
order food at a restaurant			
pronounce words with the sounds /g/, /dʒ/			
write a short text about a typical dish and drink in their country			
write a short restaurant review using adjectives			
write a recipe			

Progress Report Card

.... (name) can: **Unit 8**

	very well	OK	not very well
understand words/phrases related to places in a city; tourist attractions			
understand information/advertising texts about places & tourist attractions			
understand texts with visual support about places			
compare places			
identify author's purpose			
listen and identify people and places			
make suggestions			
pronounce words with the sounds /s/, /ʃ/			
write sentences comparing places			
write an article describing a place			
write short texts about places of natural beauty			

Progress Report Card

.... (name) can: **Unit 9**

	very well	OK	not very well
understand words/phrases related to features in a place; places/buildings in a town/city; transport			
understand texts about places then & now			
understand directions			
reply in an interview			
describe past abilities			
listen to and understand simple directions			
ask for/give directions			
pronounce words with /ℓ/ pronounced or silent			
write a short text comparing two places			
write an article about a place then and now			
create their own city and street names			

Progress Report Card

.... (name) can: **Unit 10**

	very well	OK	not very well
understand words/phrases related to famous people and their achievements; jobs; feelings/reactions			
understand texts related to famous people			
describe past activities/events			
listen to and understand main events in a narration			
narrate past events			
react to news			
write a short story using linkers (and, but, because, so, then, when, etc)			
write a short biography			

Progress Report Card

.... (name) can:	very well	OK	not very well
understand words/phrases related to the environment; summer plans			
understand short texts related to summer activities			
understand texts with visual support about the environment			
listen to a dialogue and identify speakers' summer plans			
express reason, result or purpose			
invite-accept/refuse invitations			
discuss future plans & arrangements			
pronounce 'll - won't			
write a leaflet			
write an email about their summer plans			
join sentences using connectors (because, so)			

Unit 11

Progress Report Card

.... (name) can:	very well	OK	not very well
understand words/phrases related to holiday activities; travel experiences;			
understand emails about travel experiences			
understand texts about holiday activities with visual support			
listen and identify content of conversations about travel experiences			
describe a holiday experience			
pronounce words with /h/ pronounced or silent			
write a blog comment about a holiday experience			
design a travel brochure for tourist destinations			

Unit 12

Workbook Key

Unit 1

1a – Vocabulary

1   11 – eleven   50 – fifty
        7 – seven   68 – sixty-eight
        25 – twenty-five

2   2 54   3 92   4 16   5 29

3   2 eighteen years old.
        3 He's forty-five years old.
        4 She's seventy-five years old.
        5 She's twenty-six years old.
        6 She's thirty-nine years old.

4   Brazil – Brazilian   Turkey – Turkish
        Spain – Spanish   Poland – Polish
        Greece – Greek

5   2 Japanese   4 Finnish
        3 American   5 Argentinian

6   2 twenty-five, Greek   4 twenty-nine, Brazilian
        3 forty-five, Canadian

1b – Grammar

1   1 'm not   3 Are   5 're
        2 aren't   4 Is

2   1 B: isn't, is/'s   4 A: Is
        2 A: is/'s   B: isn't, is/'s
           B: is/'s   5 A: are
        3 A: Are   B: am/'m
           B: aren't, are/'re

3   2 Are you Spanish?   4 Are they from Spain?
        3 Is she an actress?   5 Is he a doctor?

4   1 an   2 an   3 a   4 a

5   1 He   2 We   3 She   4 They   5 I

6   1 can   3 Can   5 can
        2 can't   4 can't

7   1 can   3 can't, can   5 can, can't
        2 can, can't   4 can

8   2 'm   5 is   8 are   11 can't
        3 a   6 He's   9 an   12 We
        4 can   7 a   10 can

1c – Vocabulary

1   Geography   Maths
        English Language   Physics
        Chemistry   History

        Ss' own answers

2   1 Chemistry   4 Music, Art
        2 Maths   5 English Language
        3 Computer Science

3   1 I'm OK.
        2 Not bad.
        3 Nice to meet you, too!

4   1 b   2 a   3 a   4 b   5 b

5   1 What's your name   4 What's your job
        2 How old are you   5 How old are you
        3 Where are you from

6   1 Buenos Aires in Argentina
        2 18/eighteen
        3 Physics and Maths
        4 type very fast

7   1 Chemistry   3 a scientist
        2 problems   4 Fernandez

8   1 Buenos Aires is in Argentina.
        2 Pablo is a student at Columbia College.
        3 Pablo isn't good at Chemistry.
        4 Stephen Hawking is his favourite scientist.

Unit 2

2a – Vocabulary

1   1 uncle   3 parents   5 wife
        2 daughter   4 brother

2   1 granddad   3 son   5 nephew
        2 aunt   4 husband

3   1 hair   3 teeth   5 nose
        2 lips   4 eyes

4   1 dark   5 well-built   8 bald
        2 straight   6 thin   9 moustache
        3 blue   7 beard   10 long
        4 curly

Workbook Key

2b — Grammar

1
1 have
2 Have
3 haven't
4 hasn't
5 has
6 Has

2
2 hasn't
3 've
4 's
5 haven't
6 hasn't
7 hasn't
8 's

3
1 haven't, have/'ve
2 Has, hasn't, has/'s
3 Has, has
4 Have, haven't, have/'ve
5 Have, haven't, have/'ve
6 Has, has, has/'s

4
1 My, Hers
2 our, theirs
3 him, He
4 her, mine
5 my, yours
6 them, They

5
2 Whose sister is that, Emma and Sally's
3 Whose parents are they, Mark and Tom's
4 Who is Jane, boys'

6
2 wives
3 feet
4 countries
5 sheep
6 tomatoes

7
1 have
2 friend
3 Her
4 has
5 eyes
6 has
7 dog
8 Its
9 lessons
10 my
11 your

2c — Vocabulary

1
1 hard-working
2 quiet
3 serious
4 shy

2
1 kind
2 noisy
3 clever
4 quiet

3
1 funny
2 outgoing
3 hard-working
4 serious

4 1 c 2 d 3 b 4 a

5 1 b 2 a 3 b 4 a

6
1 Who's that
2 That's our new professor
3 How old is he
4 What's he like
5 What's his name

7 1 California 2 young 3 products

8
1 Mary-Kate and Ashley are the same age.
2 Mary-Kate and Ashley are actresses.
3 They have got a clothing company.

9
1 Mary-Kate's nickname is M.K.
2 The Olsen sisters' eyes are green.
3 Ashley is serious and shy.
4 Mary-Kate is outgoing and funny.

Unit 3

3a — Vocabulary

1 1 A 2 B 3 B 4 A 5 A 6 A

2
1 bed
2 desk
3 chair
4 bedside cabinet
5 lamp
6 bookcase
7 curtains

3
1 wonderful
2 huge
3 modern, spacious
4 lovely
5 cosy
6 large

4
1 walls
2 door
3 cupboards
4 sofa
5 table
6 carpet
7 chairs
8 bath
9 pictures

3b — Grammar

1
1 There isn't a
2 There is a
3 There aren't any
4 There are some

2
2 That is, those are
3 This is, those are
4 This is, these are

3
1 eighteenth
2 second
3 thirteenth
4 twelfth
5 ninth
6 first
7 twentieth
8 third

4
1 in front of
2 on
3 behind
4 under

5
1 This
2 is
3 some
4 Opposite
5 a
6 on
7 between
8 There
9 near
10 some
11 are
12 any

6
1 B
2 A
3 C
4 A
5 C
6 B
7 A
8 A
9 C
10 A
11 B

Workbook Key

3c – Vocabulary

1
A terraced
B detached
C block of flats
D semi-detached

2
1 block of flats
2 semi-detached
3 detached
4 terraced

3 1 a 2 b 3 a 4 a

4
1 How much is the rent?
2 What's the address?
3 How many rooms has it got?

5
1 Where is it?
2 How many rooms has it got?
3 And which floor is it on?
4 How much is the rent?
5 When can I see it?

6
1 Prague
2 over 20 years
3 the ground floor
4 close to the Dancing House

7 1 F 2 F 3 F 4 T

8
1 The other name of the building is "Fred and Ginger".
2 The hotel has got 21 rooms.
3 The Dancing House is in the centre of Prague.

Skills Practice (Units 1-3)

Reading

1
A Sunspot
B Cannonball
C Wolfsbane
D Mirage

2
1 a wolf
2 Kentucky (in the) USA
3 the sun
4 people's fears

3 1 T 2 F 3 T 4 F 5 T

4
1 c 3 f 5 g 7 b
2 d 4 a 6 h 8 e

5
1 a 3 a 5 b 7 b
2 b 4 a 6 b 8 a

6 a) 1 D 2 C 3 B 4 A

b) The dialogue is about girl A.

7 1 C 2 A 3 B 4 A 5 C

8
1 semi-detached 4 bedrooms
2 Green 5 garage
3 bathroom

9 1 C 2 G 3 B 4 H 5 A

10
Name: Emilia Clarke
Nationality: British
Appearance: short, slim, long dark hair, green eyes
Character: outgoing, hard-working, kind
Job: actress
Famous role: Daenerys Targaryen, Game of Thrones

11
Emilia Clarke is British.
She is short and slim.
She has got long dark hair and blue eyes.
She is outgoing, hard-working and kind.
She is an actress.
She is famous for the role of Daenerys Targaryen in Game of Thrones.

12
1 (big) garage
2 (small) garden
3 a kitchen, a living room and a dining room
4 spacious
5 a cooker, a fridge and some beautiful cupboards
6 a bathroom and two (big) bedrooms
7 a carpet/a (large) wardrobe
8 a (large) wardrobe/a carpet

Revision (Units 1-3)

Vocabulary

1

1	B	6	A	11	B	16	B	21	C
2	B	7	A	12	C	17	C	22	B
3	B	8	A	13	B	18	B	23	B
4	A	9	C	14	B	19	A	24	A
5	C	10	A	15	C	20	B	25	B

Grammar

1

1	C	6	A	11	C	16	A	21	C
2	B	7	A	12	B	17	C	22	A
3	C	8	A	13	A	18	C	23	B
4	A	9	B	14	C	19	A	24	C
5	B	10	A	15	C	20	B	25	B

Workbook Key

Unit 4

4a – Vocabulary

1
1	wake	3	catch	5	have
2	get	4	chat	6	go

2   1 past   2 half   3 to   4 past

3
3 (a) quarter past eleven/eleven fifteen in the evening
4 half past eight/eight thirty in the morning
5 (a) quarter to five/four forty-five in the afternoon
6 (a) quarter past nine/nine fifteen in the morning
7 two o'clock in the morning
8 twenty past seven/seven twenty in the evening

4
1 seven-thirty/half past seven
2 have/take
3 get
4 catch
5 nine o'clock
6 chat
7 At
8 In
9 go
10 a quarter past four/four fifteen
11 do
12 evening
13 bed
14 go
15 work

4b – Grammar

1
-s	swims, plays, lives, likes, says, laughs, walks, bites
-es	washes, relaxes, does, kisses, goes
-ies	carries, cries, studies

2
1	don't	3	go	5	Does
2	Do	4	doesn't		

3
1	doesn't go	5	don't get
2	Does Tony swim	6	drive
3	Do you walk	7	Do they play
4	closes	8	tidies

4
1 Jenny and Chris hate watching horror films.
2 She doesn't like going fishing.
3 Janet loves listening to jazz music.
4 They like camping.

5
1	rarely, in	4	always, on
2	sometimes, at	5	usually, at
3	never, in	6	often, on

6
At Sundays = On Sundays
on 10 o'clock = at 10 o'clock
at the morning = in the morning
We often goes = We often go
I watches TV = I watch TV
I doesn't help = I don't help
hate cook = hate cooking
I does the = I do the
in Sundays = on Sundays

4c – Vocabulary

1   1 c   2 e   3 a   4 b   5 f   6 d

2
1	do yoga	4	visit museums
2	listen to music	5	go on a picnic
3	read a book	6	meet friends

3
1	listens	3	does	5	goes
2	reads	4	visits	6	watches

4   1 c   2 a   3 b

5   1 a   2 b   3 a

6
1 I think so.
2 What time do you want to meet?
3 I'm afraid I can't.
4 Sure.
5 Make sure you're on time.

7   1 c   2 a   3 b

8   1 T   2 F   3 T

9
1 Bonja's birthday is on 21st August.
2 The K-9 Corps is a group of dogs with special skills.
3 Bonja plays with Jason's children in the garden.
4 Jason watches TV with his wife in the evenings.

Unit 5

5a – Vocabulary

1
1	eagle	4	penguin	7	snake
2	dolphin	5	flamingo	8	bear
3	crocodile	6	monkey		

2
1	tail	3	neck	5	feathers
2	wing	4	beak		

Workbook Key

3
1	fins	5	claws	9	whiskers
2	a mane	6	neck	10	stripes
3	trunk	7	mouth		
4	skin	8	fur		

4
1	large	5	body/tail	9	live
2	sharp	6	tail/body	10	dangerous
3	fur	7	hunt		
4	spots	8	weigh		

5b – Grammar

1
1	must	3	mustn't	5	mustn't
2	mustn't	4	must		

2
1	Can	3	Could	5	can't
2	can't	4	mustn't		

3
2 You can bring your own food.
3 Could/Can we bring our cameras with us?
4 You mustn't feed the animals.
5 We can't go near the animals.

4
1	Where	3	How much	5	How long
2	What	4	How long	6	How many

5
1 How much does the African elephant weigh?
2 How long does it live?
3 What does it eat?
4 How long is its trunk?

6 1 A 2 B 3 C 4 A 5 C

5c – Vocabulary

1
DOWN		ACROSS	
1	duck	3	donkey
2	rooster	4	goat
5	sheep	6	hen
		7	horse

2 1 duck 2 sheep 3 horse 4 rooster

3
2 Anna's dog has got very long ears.
3 Anna's dog has got quite big eyes.
4 Anna's dog has got quite a long tail.
5 Anna's dog has got short fur.

4 1 c 2 b 3 a

5 1 a 2 b 3 b 4 a

6
1	how	3	When	5	Can	7	When
2	What	4	free	6	can	8	Perfect

7 1 F 2 T 3 T

8
1 Scottish wildcats have got light brown fur and black stripes.
2 Brown hares have got a short black and white tail.
3 Brown hares eat wild grasses and herbs.

9

Kind of animal:	Scottish wildcat
They live:	in Scotland
They have got:	light brown fur, black stripes, beautiful thick tail
They weigh:	5-9 kg but some of them can grow up to 14 kg
They eat:	rabbits and small mammals

Kind of animal:	Brown hare
They live:	In the UK
They have got:	long body, very long legs, very long ears, brown and white fur, short tail (black on top and white underneath)
They weigh:	3-4 kg
They eat:	wild grasses and herbs

Unit 6

6a – Vocabulary

1
1	October	3	summer	5	winter
2	December	4	March		

2
1	sunny	3	snowy	5	windy
2	rainy	4	foggy	6	cloudy

3
1 sun, shining, sunny   3 clouds, blowing
2 raining, rainy

4
1	winter	5	Skiing	9	rains
2	January	6	autumn	10	waterproof
3	cold	7	warm	11	sightseeing
4	snowy	8	weather		

6b – Grammar

1 1 are 2 is 3 am 4 are 5 are

2
1 Thomas isn't skiing down the slope.
  Is Thomas skiing down the slope?
2 The boys aren't doing their homework.
  Are the boys doing their homework?
3 It isn't raining today.
  Is it raining today?

Workbook Key

4 We aren't having a barbecue.
Are we having a barbecue?

3 2 Is Sylvia making a cake at the moment?
No, she is cooking dinner.
3 Is your friend reading a magazine now?
No, he is reading a book.
4 Are Samantha and Paul flying to Paris at the moment?
No, they are going to the airport.
5 Is she tidying her room now?
Yes, she is.

4 2 a   3 b   4 a   5 a

5 1 works   4 Are they playing
   2 snows   5 drive
   3 isn't listening

6 1 am writing   7 aren't going
   2 are staying   8 is raining
   3 visit   9 don't like
   4 takes   10 are having
   5 eat   11 is shopping
   6 walk   12 are you spending

6c – Vocabulary

1 1 high-heeled shoes   5 trainers
   2 cap   6 jacket
   3 socks   7 shirt
   4 dress   8 T-shirt

2 1 gloves   2 jacket   3 sandals   4 tie

3 Jeff is wearing a T-shirt, jeans and shoes.
Laura is wearing boots, trousers, a top, a jacket and a scarf.

4 1 c   2 d   3 a   4 b

5 1 a   2 b   3 b

6 1 how can I help you   5 Let me check
   2 I'd like   6 medium
   3 I'm afraid   7 Can I try
   4 give you a refund   8 Of course

7 1 c   2 b   3 a

8 1 F   2 T   3 DS

9 1 Bora Bora, Tahiti
   2 hot and sunny with rainy days
   3 snorkelling, fishing, sitting on the beach
   4 €350
   5 have breakfast, tour the island by helicopter

Skills Practice (Units 4-6)

Reading

1 B

2 1 F   2 DS   3 F   4 T   5 F   6 F

3 1 Terry plans to go skiing.
   2 You can see dolphins, sea eagles and moose around the Lofoten Islands.
   3 Stacy is checking her emails (in a café) right now.
   4 Tony usually sees the sights on holiday.

4 1 c   2 e   3 a   4 d   5 b

5 1 b   2 b   3 a   4 a   5 a

6 1 G Can I help you?
   2 E I'd like to return these trousers, please.
   3 A What's wrong with them?
   4 F Do you have it in a smaller size?
   5 B What size are you?
   6 D Can I try the brown one, please?

Listening

7 1 F   2 F   3 F   4 T

8 1 cows   3 groups of kids   5 gates
   2 eggs   4 doors

9 1 Sunday   3 basketball   5 tablet
   2 Kim   4 cinema

Writing

10 All you need to know about the donkey!
What does it eat? straw and grass
When does it sleep? at night
Why do farms have donkeys? they are very strong
How much does it weight? up to 480 kg
How long does it live? 30-50 years
How many donkeys are there in the world? 41 million

Workbook Key

11 Suggested answer

Title: Mr
Name: Jeffery Dale
Address: 56 Hopkin Road, Devizes, Wiltshire
Postcode: SN00 5AA
Telephone: 01380 626263
Email: jdwilt@email.com
Age: 20
Days & times available: Saturdays 9 am to 5 pm
Skills: I can use a computer and I can operate farm machinery.
Can you drive a car? Yes.

12 Suggested answer

Hi Sam,
Greetings from Chelmer City Farm! The weather is sunny and warm here. In the mornings, I feed the donkeys. In the afternoons, I clean out the hen houses. Right now, I'm digging up some fresh vegetables for dinner. I'm wearing rubber boots and heavy gloves to protect my hands. It's great here and I'm really having an interesting time!
See you,
Alvin

Revision (Units 4-6)

Vocabulary

1

1	A	6	A	11	A	16	C	21	A
2	A	7	B	12	A	17	A	22	B
3	B	8	C	13	C	18	B	23	A
4	C	9	C	14	C	19	B	24	A
5	C	10	A	15	B	20	B	25	B

Grammar

1

1	C	6	B	11	C	16	C	21	C
2	A	7	B	12	B	17	A	22	B
3	C	8	A	13	A	18	B	23	C
4	A	9	A	14	C	19	B	24	C
5	C	10	B	15	B	20	A	25	A

Unit 7

7a – Vocabulary

1

1	strawberries	10	ice cream
2	orange juice	11	lamb
3	beef	12	rice
4	butter	13	grapes
5	biscuits	14	lettuce
6	pancakes	15	prawns
7	cereal	16	salt & pepper
8	garlic	17	coffee
9	cabbage	18	fish

2

Fruit	strawberries, grapes
Vegetables	garlic, cabbage, lettuce
Meat & Poultry	beef, lamb
Sweets	biscuits, ice cream, pancakes
Grains	cereal, rice
Dairy & Eggs	butter
Seafood	prawns, fish
Drinks	coffee, orange juice
Other	salt & pepper

3

1	teaspoon	4	knife	7	fork
2	glass	5	bowl		
3	tablespoon	6	plate		

4

1	eat	5	cereal	9	egg
2	drink	6	milk	10	meal
3	fresh	7	fruit		
4	refreshing	8	hungry		

7b – Grammar

1

Countable	Uncountable
bottle	milk
peach	butter
cabbage	cheese
pineapple	sugar
carrot	lamb
onion	water

1

1	any	3	some	5	an	7	any
2	some	4	any	6	some	8	a

3

2 a cup of tea
3 a carton of milk
4 a glass of orange juice
5 a packet of pasta

4

1	B	2	C	3	A	4	C	5	A

5

2 **much** – many   5 **much** – many
3 **a little** – a few   6 **a** – some
4 **many** – much

6

1 much, much   4 some, a little
2 many, many, some, any   5 a lot of
3 many, a few   6 any, a little, much

Workbook Key

7c – Vocabulary

1
1 grill 3 roast 5 bake
2 boil 4 fry

2
1 boil 3 fry 5 grill
2 bake 4 roast

3 grill – fry, fry – boil, roast – bake, boil – roast

4 1 c 2 d 3 a 4 b

5
6 A: Here you are.
2 B: Good evening. Have you got a table for three?
4 A: Would you like to see the menu?
1 A: Good evening, madam.
5 B: Yes, please.
3 A: Yes, of course. This way, near the fireplace.

6
1 Table 5 start 9 drink
2 way 6 want 10 dessert
3 look 7 main
4 order 8 Excellent

7 1 F 2 T 3 DS

8
1 You need 8 soft tacos in your taco recipe.
2 You need to fry beef for your tacos.
3 You need 2 cloves of garlic for your nachos.
4 You need 2 cups of cheese for the sauce.

9 1 B 2 B 3 A 4 C

Unit 8

8a – Vocabulary

1
1 heavy 3 delicious 5 crowded
2 outdoor 4 polluted

2 1 B 2 C 3 A 4 C 5 C 6 A

3
1 b 3 h 5 g 7 c
2 a 4 f 6 d 8 e

4
1 unforgettable 4 bright 7 exciting
2 fascinating 5 fashionable 8 boring
3 tasty 6 near

5
1 noisy 3 old 5 exciting
2 clean 4 expensive 6 small

8b – Grammar

1

adjective	comparative	superlative
large	larger	the largest
safe	safer	the safest
sunny	sunnier	the sunniest
fashionable	more fashionable	the most fashionable
bad	worse	the worst
noisy	noisier	the noisiest
much	more	the most
expensive	more expensive	the most expensive
little	less	the least

2
1 than 3 in 5 as, as
2 of 4 the 6 in

3
1 cheapest 3 more 5 quieter
2 tastier 4 most 6 oldest

4 1 quite 2 too 3 enough 4 very

5
1 the oldest 4 the most fashionable
2 worse 5 the best
3 more polluted 6 the most crowded

6
2 Big cities are usually more polluted than small towns.
3 The first course of a meal is always less expensive than the second one.
4 Isn't this the most boring place of all? Let's leave!
5 New York is noisier than York.
6 The driest place in the world is in Chile.

8c – Vocabulary

1
1 theatre 5 museum
2 sports stadium 6 park
3 restaurant 7 art gallery
4 gift shop 8 theme park

2
1 theatre 5 sports stadium
2 museum 6 park
3 restaurants 7 theme park
4 gift shop 8 art gallery

3
1 sports stadium 3 theatre
2 art gallery 4 restaurant

4 1 c 2 d 3 a 4 b

5 1 a 2 b 3 a

6
1 first 4 rather 7 about
2 let's 5 fancy 8 idea
3 gift 6 sound 9 why

Workbook Key

7 1 Germany.
2 boutiques, clothing stores and cool cafés.
3 the Alster Lakes.
4 statues of the members of the famous band (The Beatles)

8 1 F   2 DS   3 T

9 1 You can have lunch outdoors on the square near Schulterblatt.
2 They exercise by jogging or cycling (around the lakes, through beautiful parks and neighbourhoods).
3 You can see the world's largest model railway and a replica of Hamburg Airport at Miniatur Wunderland.

Unit 9

9a – Vocabulary

1 1 f   2 c   3 a   4 e   5 b   6 d

2 1 a guest house
2 a ferry boat
3 fishing boats
4 souvenir shops
5 a stone cottage
6 green fields

3 1 fishing boats
2 stone cottages
3 green fields
4 a ferry boat
5 guest houses
6 souvenir shops

4 a) 1 b   2 d   3 a   4 c

b) 1 busy
2 difficult
3 quiet
4 the same

5 1 Back
2 In
3 running
4 get
5 work

6 3 get around
4 Back then
5 running water
6 difficult
7 busy
8 the same
9 work hard

9b – Grammar

1 1 wasn't   2 Was   3 was   4 weren't

2 1 wasn't
2 weren't
3 Was, was
4 Were, weren't
5 weren't
6 was

3 Yesterday
2 Yes, he was.
3 They were at the cinema.
4 No, he wasn't.

Last Saturday
1 She was
2 No, she wasn't.
3 Yes, they were.
4 Yes, she was.

4 1 have
2 couldn't
3 Have
4 Could
5 didn't have

5 1 had, have
2 didn't have, had
3 had, have
4 didn't have, had

6 1 Could, could
2 Could, couldn't, can
3 Could, couldn't, can't, can
4 Can, could

7 1 Tim can't – Tim couldn't
2 Did he has – Did he have
3 We are – We were
4 He can – He could
5 There isn't – There wasn't
6 was Presidents – were Presidents
7 Can you – Could you
8 There is – There was

9c – Vocabulary

1 1 hospital
2 train station
3 restaurant
4 petrol station
5 department store
6 cinema
7 museum
8 school
9 supermarket
10 park
11 café
12 bank
13 police station
14 bus stop
15 fire station

2 1 on
2 between
3 next to
4 in front of
5 opposite

3 1 café
2 police station
3 department store
4 petrol station

4 1 where's   2 left   3 Walk   4 left

5 3 A: Can you please tell me the way there?
5 A: Thank you.
2 B: Yes, it's on Broad Street.
1 A: Excuse me, is there a petrol station near here?
4 A: Of course. Go down High Street, turn right onto Market Street, then right again onto Broad Street. It's on your right, next to the museum.

6 **Suggested answers**
- A: Excuse me. Is there a department store near here?
  B: Yes, it's on High Street.
  A: Can you please tell me the way there?
  B: Of course. Walk up Market Street and turn left onto High Street. Walk past the supermarket. The department store is on your left, opposite the cinema.
  A: Thank you.
- A: Excuse me. Is there a cinema near here?
  B: Yes, it's on High Street.
  A: Can you please tell me the way there?
  B: Of course. Go down Cannon Street and turn left onto Broad Street. Walk past the school and the supermarket and turn left again onto High Street. The cinema is on your right opposite the department store.
  A: Thank you.

7 1 DS   2 F   3 T

8 1 Rich Londoners had big houses in the 19th century.
2 The streets of London were very dirty back then.
3 Today all houses in London have got running water.

9 **THEN**
1 big houses
2 small houses
3 carriages
4 horses
5 ice-skating
6 parties
NOW
1 tall skyscrapers
2 flats
3 buses
4 department stores

Skills Practice (Units 7-9)

Reading

1 True sentences: 1, 4, 5

2 1 Gansu
2 sunny
3 bus
4 time of year to visit
5 a hot air balloon

3 1 The Zhangye Danxia National Park is 322 square kilometres.
2 You can see red, blue, gold, orange, purple and green colours on the mountains.
3 You can take photographs from four different places.

4 In summer, the weather there is warm and sunny.
5 Julie was at the park in early October.

4 1 Excuse   4 going   7 corner
2 would   5 Walk   8 way
3 next   6 Let's

5 1 a   2 b   3 a   4 a   5 a   6 a

6 1 How about
2 I don't think so
3 Shall we
4 That doesn't sound like fun
5 That sounds great

7 1 T   2 F   3 T   4 F   5 T

8 1 souvenirs   3 burgers   5 3/three
2 Indian   4 8/eight

9 1 C   2 E   3 F   4 A   5 B

10

Location	20 Parkside Road
Food	big choice of starters, tasty main courses with garden-fresh vegetables, delicious desserts
Service	friendly and polite
Cost	£10-15 per person
Opening hours	1 pm to 1 am
Recommendation	great place for both friends and families

11 The Park Restaurant at 20 Parkside Road is very popular. There are some excellent dishes to choose from. There is a big choice of starters and some tasty main courses with garden-fresh vegetables. For those who like sweets, there are also some delicious desserts. The service is friendly and polite and meals cost £10-15 per person. The restaurant is open from 1 pm to 1 am. The Park Restaurant is a great place for both friends and families.

12 **Suggested answer**
My town is Bray on the east coast of Ireland. It's very different to how it was fifty years ago.
Then, there were only a few shops. People lived in small, old houses because they didn't have a lot of money. They had to get around by bicycle or by bus because there were not many cars. There were only one or two cafés so people couldn't really eat out.

Workbook Key

Now, Bray has a lot more shops and new buildings like blocks of flats for people to live in. People can get to work by car. They have more money so they can eat out at expensive restaurants.

Bray is a much more modern place today!

Revision (Units 7-9)

Vocabulary

1

1	B	6	A	11	B	16	B	21	A
2	C	7	B	12	A	17	C	22	B
3	B	8	C	13	C	18	B	23	B
4	C	9	A	14	A	19	A	24	C
5	A	10	C	15	A	20	C	25	C

Grammar

1

1	B	6	C	11	C	16	C	21	A
2	B	7	A	12	A	17	B	22	B
3	A	8	C	13	C	18	C	23	A
4	C	9	B	14	B	19	B	24	B
5	B	10	B	15	B	20	C	25	C

Unit 10

10a – Vocabulary

1
1	director	3	lawyer	5	physicist
2	politician	4	engineer	6	writer

2 1 writer 2 actress 3 painter 4 engineer

3 1 B 2 A 3 C 4 A

4 1 job 2 work 3 job 4 work

5
1	in	3	into	5	of	7	into
2	on	4	up	6	along	8	on

6
1	sculptor	4	wanted	7	won
2	born	5	studied	8	died
3	teacher	6	famous		

10b – Grammar

1
1	directed	7	finished	12	came
2	lost	8	moved	13	stopped
3	produced	9	bought	14	won
4	appeared	10	travelled	15	studied
5	wrote	11	married	16	starred
6	sang				

2
1	Did Spielberg direct	6	composed
2	became	7	didn't win
3	received	8	wrote
4	didn't invent	9	walked
5	sang	10	Did the Titanic sink

3
1 didn't, stayed, watched
2 Did you take part, did, baked, won
3 Did Peter enjoy, did, saw
4 Did you go, didn't, was

4
1	under	3	towards, through
2	into	4	over

5
1	up	3	over	5	across
2	past	4	through	6	into

6
1	visited	8	saw	14	carried
2	went	9	parked	15	down
3	didn't know	10	up	16	into
4	drove	11	across	17	spent
5	along	12	found	18	didn't leave
6	over	13	showed	19	was
7	through				

10c – Vocabulary

1
1	happy	3	shocked
2	worried	4	proud

2

POSITIVE
happy, excited
NEGATIVE
frightened, shocked, upset, worried

3
1	worried	3	confused	5	upset
2	proud	4	frightened		

4 1 c 2 a 3 b

5 1 a 2 b 3 b 4 a

6
1	like	4	Really	7	asked
2	amazing	5	across	8	lucky
3	happened	6	do		

7
1. 7th February 1812
2. clerk in the navy
3. Catherine Hogarth
4. 9th June 1870

8
1	T	2	F	3	T	4	DS

9
1. Charles Dickens left school and started work because his family didn't have much money.
2. The three years he spent in the factory gave him ideas for many of his stories.
3. Dickens wrote novels and plays.
4. He was full of energy and loved travelling abroad.
5. His classic stories, such as *Great Expectations*, *Oliver Twist* and *David Copperfield* make him one of the greatest English writers of all time.

Unit 11

11a – Vocabulary

1
1	planting	3	turning
2	recycling	4	walking

2
1	c	2	d	3	a	4	b	5	f	6	e

3
1	pollution	3	water	5	animals
2	rainforests	4	rubbish		

4
1	should turn off	3	should give
2	shouldn't use	4	shouldn't drive

5
1	C	3	B	5	B	7	B
2	A	4	A	6	C	8	A

11b – Grammar

1
1	It	2	There	3	It	4	There

2
1	will	4	're going to
2	'm not going to	5	Will we
3	Are you going to		

3
2	'll turn off	4	'm going to buy
3	'm not going to cook		

4
1	aren't going	4	is meeting
2	'm leaving	5	aren't flying
3	Are you driving		

5
1	are you doing	7	'm watching
2	'm waiting	8	'll live
3	'm going to go	9	there
4	it's	10	won't have
5	'll come	11	'm not going to use
6	are you doing	12	'll try

11c – Vocabulary

1
1	d	2	e	3	a	4	f	5	b	6	c

2
1. work in an animal sanctuary
2. start a computer course
3. move house
4. go windsurfing
5. volunteer for a green charity
6. join a gym

3
1	have	3	volunteer	5	join
2	go	4	part-		

4
1	b	2	c	3	d	4	a

5
1	a	2	b	3	a	4	b

6
1	busy	5	pity	9	arrange
2	Would	6	back	10	sounds
3	afraid	7	meet		
4	Sorry	8	love		

7
1. Friends of the Earth International began in 1969.
2. Anyone can volunteer for Friends of the Earth (EWNI).
3. The group stops companies building roads through forests.
4. The 'Bee Saver Kit' has seeds inside (which grow into wildflowers).

8
1	T	2	DS	3	F	4	F

9
1. England, Wales and Northern Ireland are in Friends of the Earth (EWNI).
2. Volunteers for the group send emails to important businesspeople and politicians.
3. Friends of the Earth (EWNI) wants companies to start using renewable energy (like solar and wind power).
4. The seeds from the 'Bee Saver Kit' grow into wildflowers.

Workbook Key

Unit 12

12a – Vocabulary

1 1 f   2 e   3 d   4 b   5 c   6 a

2
1 ride a camel
2 take photos
3 try traditional dishes
4 go sightseeing
5 visit a market
6 buy handmade souvenirs

3
1 with
2 to, on
3 in
4 on
5 for

4
1 ancient
2 fascinating
3 traditional
4 exhibits
5 spices

5
1 hot
2 wonderful
3 noisy
4 crowded
5 traditional
6 delicious

6
1 fascinating
2 traditional
3 with
4 sightseeing
5 for
6 crowded
7 On
8 on
9 trip
10 ancient

12b – Grammar

1
1 have travelled
2 has not/hasn't visited
3 Have you met
4 have/'ve tried
5 Have they left
6 have not/haven't spoken

2
1 ever
2 since
3 ever
4 for
5 never
6 yet
7 just
8 already

3
1 been
2 been
3 gone
4 been
5 gone

4
1 has never flown
2 left
3 hasn't booked
4 has worked
5 went

5
1 has not/hasn't played
2 has read
3 have not/haven't ridden
4 have tried
5 have not/haven't visited
6 has/'s bought
7 have not/haven't travelled
8 have lived

6
1 The, -
2 The, -, the
3 The, -
4 -, the, the
5 The, the
6 -, -

7
1 Have you ever visited
2 –
3 –
4 have/'ve just returned
5 loved
6 went
7 took
8 the
9 enjoyed
10 have/'ve already bought
11 –

12c – Vocabulary

1
A snorkelling
B canoeing
C camping
D helicopter
E ice skating
F dolphins

2 1 A   2 D   3 C   4 F   5 E   6 B

3
1 amazing
2 difficult
3 fantastic
4 terrible
5 great
6 exciting

4 1 d   2 a   3 b   4 c

5 1 a   2 b   3 a   4 b

6
1 returned
2 go
3 back
4 amazing
5 time
6 much
7 anything
8 also
9 sounds
10 wait

7 1 F   2 T   3 T   4 DS

8
1 the Valley Isle
2 the sunrise and sunset
3 snorkelling, windsurfing or swimming
4 helicopter tour

9 1 A   2 C   3 B

Skills Practice (Units 10-12)

Reading

1 B

2 1 AF   2 MG   3 NT   4 MG

3
1 Gandhi wasn't good at Geography.
2 Fleming worked in an office before going to university.
3 Fleming managed to study Medicine when an uncle of his died and left him a small amount of money.
4 Tesla's father promised to send him to university when he got well.
5 Tesla didn't complete his studies because he had money problems.

Workbook Key

4   1 d   2 c   3 a   4 b

5   1 a   2 a   3 b   4 a   5 b

6
1   E   Would you like to
2   H   I'd love to but
3   C   That's all
4   A   Why don't we
5   D   Sure, why
6   F   have to go

7   1 D   2 B   3 A   4 C

8   1 B   2 A   3 B

9
1 tour   3 national   5 900/nine hundred
2 sights   4 snowboarding   6 online

10
1 market   3 camel   5 dishes
2 souvenirs   4 snorkelling   6 temple

11   **Suggested answer**

Hi Amber,

How are you? I'm so excited that I'm flying to Cairo next month. It's all planned!

I'm flying out from London on Monday, 18th April. On Tuesday, I'm going to visit a street market where I can buy handmade souvenirs. On Wednesday, I'm going to see the Pyramids. I'm also going to ride a camel because it sounds like fun. Thursday is very exciting. I'm going to go snorkelling in the Red Sea and stop at a local restaurant so I can try traditional Egyptian food. They say it's really delicious! The big highlight is on Friday. I'm going to visit Karnak to see the ancient temple. I'm flying back to London on Saturday, 23rd April.

It's going to be an amazing experience. I'll take lots of photos so you can see them when I get back. See you soon!

Yours,
Wendy

12   Suggested answer

It was a bright sunny day in summer. Holly and her friends were in the woods camping because they volunteered to plant trees there.

It was hot so Holly went to her tent to drink water. When she opened her tent, there was a poisonous snake inside! Holly was terrified. Very slowly, she backed away. Her friend Lisa came over and saw the snake sliding away through the grass.

The girls checked the tent carefully but there were no other snakes. Holly felt glad to be alive!

Revision (Units 10-12)

Vocabulary

1

1 C	6 A	11 C	16 C	21 A
2 A	7 C	12 A	17 B	22 C
3 A	8 A	13 B	18 C	23 C
4 B	9 B	14 C	19 B	24 B
5 B	10 B	15 A	20 A	25 C

Grammar

1

1 A	6 C	11 B	16 A	21 A
2 B	7 B	12 C	17 C	22 B
3 A	8 A	13 A	18 B	23 B
4 A	9 C	14 C	19 B	24 C
5 B	10 B	15 B	20 A	25 B

Workbook Audioscripts

Skills Practice A

Exercise 7 p. 18

Jean: Hi! My name's Jean and this is Dino.
Dino: Hello! We are students here. What's your name?
Ana: Hi, I'm Ana. Are you both from Italy?
Jean: No. I'm from France and Dino is from Italy. Where are you from, Ana?
Ana: I'm from Spain. How old are you, Dino?
Dino: I'm 19 years old and Jean is 18. How old are you?
Ana: I'm 20 years old. Dino, are you in Year 3 of college like me?
Dino: No. I'm in Year 2 and Jean is in Year 1.
Ana: Are you a history student?
Dino: No. I'm an art student. And you?
Ana: Biology! I'm really crazy about science subjects. What about you, Jean?
Jean: I'm a maths student. It's a cool subject!
Ana: I'm sure it is. Well, see you guys around college!
Jean: Bye! See you later!
Dino: Great to meet you.

Exercise 8 p. 18

This lovely semi-detached house has got lots of room for a growing family. It's on Green Avenue in the area of Pooltown, near to schools and shops.
Downstairs there is a large kitchen, a big living room, a small bathroom as well as a dining room and study. Upstairs there are two bathrooms and three bedrooms. There is a lot of outside space too with a small front garden and a large back garden as well as a spacious garage. Come and see it today! Call: 01253 854369

Exercise 9 p. 18

Tim: Hey Molly. Is that your brother over there; the one with short blond hair?
Molly: Yes, he is my noisy brother Arthur. He's with one of my cousins, and her dad.
Tim: Oh yes. What's your cousin's name – Maggie?
Molly: No, Maggie is my aunt. She's really kind.
Tim: Oh! I'm sorry. So, what's your cousin's name? We're at the same gym, but I can't remember her name.
Molly: It's Rose. She's got the same name as my grandma and she's very clever.
Tim: And her dad is your uncle, right?
Molly: Yes, that's my Uncle Andrew. He's my dad's brother and he's a very funny guy.
Tim: And who is that next to your mum?
Molly: That's Jackie, my sister. She's quiet and not very outgoing.
Tim: Oh, really? Let's go and talk to her.
Molly: OK. Come on, let's go!

Skills Practice B

Exercise 7 p. 36

Good morning, everyone. First, thanks for getting here on time. It's really important that you arrive at 8:45 am each morning so that we are ready to open the shop at 9. Now, before we open the shop today, I want to go over a few things with you. As for breaks, you get fifteen minutes at around 11, and half an hour for lunch at around 1. Please remember that everyone can't take their break at the same time – there must always be at least four people in the shop. You can organise the breaks yourselves. OK, what else? Well, sometimes there aren't a lot of customers in the shop, but that doesn't mean you can relax. There are always jobs to do. Make sure that all the clothes are folded and in their correct place in the shop. Also, check the changing rooms for clothes, too, and put them back on the shelves. Another thing is how to deal with customers. My advice is to offer customers help once and only once. When they just want to browse, it's best to leave them alone. We don't want to be pushy! Finally, the shop closes at 5 pm, but don't run out the door straight away. We always need to tidy up a little after 5 – but usually it only takes ten minutes. OK, I think that's everything. Good luck today, everyone!

Exercise 8 p. 36

Paula: So, Steve, are you enjoying your summer job at the farm?
Steve: I love it, Paula! I'm learning a lot there, and, of course, I'm earning some money, too!
Paula: So, what do you do every day?
Steve: Well, there are five of us working there during the summer and we each have different jobs. I arrive there at 8 am and the first thing I do is feed the cows. The farmer milks them at 6 am, and they're really hungry when I arrive.
Paula: OK, that's interesting. When do you have your first break?
Steve: At around 12: 15. I collect the eggs in the hen house at 12 and it usually takes me a quarter of an hour. There are thirty hens there now, so they lay a lot of eggs!
Paula: And isn't the farm open to visitors? Do you do anything with them?
Steve: Yes, most visitors arrive in the afternoon. I usually show groups of kids around, while the adults have coffee in our café. I answer any questions they have about the animals. It's a lot of fun!
Paula: It sounds like you have a long day!
Steve: Yes, when the visitors leave at 5 pm, I'm usually exhausted – but my day isn't finished yet! Before I leave at 5:30, I have to lock all the doors and gates around the farm, so that the animals don't get out.
Paula: Oh, yes. I guess that's very important!

Workbook Audioscripts

Exercise 9 p. 36

I guess that everyone likes the weekend – and I'm no different – but I much prefer Sundays to Saturdays. Why? Well, Sundays are a really relaxing day for me. I usually get up late and have breakfast with my flatmate Kim. Then, I finish any homework I have for college and do my household chores so I can have the rest of the day free! At noon, I always play basketball with some friends in the park. I'm in a team, but we don't practise seriously on Sundays – it's just for fun. After that, I visit my parents and we usually go for a walk in the forest near their house. Or, when the weather's bad we go to the cinema. In the evening, I return home and usually just surf the Net on my tablet. I never go out on Sunday evenings because I have to get up early for college on Mondays. I really enjoy Sundays, but then – who doesn't?

Skills Practice C

Exercise 7 p. 54

Emma: Hello?
Paul: Hi, Emma, it's Paul.
Emma: Oh, hi Paul! Are you on that business trip in Manchester?
Paul: Yes, I am, but I need your help!
Emma: Why, what's the matter?
Paul: I don't know where my hotel is! My phone's got a problem and all the hotel details are on it. Can you check for me on your computer?
Emma: No problem. Where are you exactly?
Paul: I'm in a café on the corner of Maple Avenue and Cedar Road.
Emma: I think I see where you are. Is it the Golden Grill Café?
Paul: Yes, that's right. I'm having a cup of tea here.
Emma: And can you remember the name of your hotel?
Paul: It's the Royal Hotel.
Emma: Oh, then that's easy. You just walk down Maple Avenue and turn right onto Queen Street. The hotel is on your left opposite a park.
Paul: Thank you so much, Emma!
Emma: Glad to be of help, Paul!

Exercise 8 p. 54

Good morning, shoppers, and welcome to Westside Shopping Mall. All you need is here on the ground floor, from shoes and jewellery to electricals and computers. We've got the cheapest prices for designer clothes, and unique gifts and souvenirs are on sale in the smaller shops. When it comes to food, why not treat yourself to lunch at one of the ten restaurants on the first floor? There's a choice of Italian, Mexican or Indian dishes. For a quicker snack, the tasty burgers at Monty's Place are the best value in town! Fancy watching a film in the evening? The 8-screen cinema complex on the second floor has three evening performances after the shops close. After the show, Romano's late night café is open for coffee! Thank you for shopping at Westside. Have a great day!

Exercise 9 p. 54

Jane: I had a great night last night, Mum! We were at Brad's house to celebrate the end of the exams. He had a big dinner ready for us!
Kate: That's nice, Jane. Was the food good?
Jane: Oh, yes! Brad's a great cook. The first course was Brad's favourite – prawn salad.
Kate: Lovely! I do like prawns. And what was there for main course?
Jane: Well, most of us had roast lamb, but not Sarah. She doesn't eat lamb.
Kate: So what did she have instead?
Jane: Brad had some fish in the freezer so she had it grilled. And Mike couldn't eat the lamb either. He doesn't eat meat at all, not even chicken. There was a nice big salad for him!
Kate: Wow! That was a lot of work for Brad!
Jane: Yes, but he doesn't mind – he really likes cooking! There was a noodle dish too for Lily. She's from Japan and Brad knows she loves them!
Kate: What was the best bit of the meal?
Jane: Oh, for me it was the chocolate cake for dessert! Yum!
Kate: Well, I know how much you like sweets!

Workbook Audioscripts

Skills Practice D

Exercise 7 p. 72

It was a bright sunny day in June. Holly and her friends were at a campsite in the woods because they volunteered to plant some trees there. It was hot and Holly stopped for a drink of water. The bottle was in her tent so she made her way there.

She opened the tent and then screamed loudly. "Help! There's a snake on my sleeping bag!" The long black poisonous snake lifted its head and looked at her. For a moment Holly was too terrified to move. She didn't want to frighten the snake as that can make them dangerous. So, very very slowly, she stepped back away from the tent. Just then, her friend Lisa came over quickly to see what the matter was. She was just in time to see the snake slide away smoothly through the grass!

The girls checked the tent but there were no more snakes. Then Holly gave a sigh of relief. "I knew what to do because I read the camping safety leaflet they gave us," she said. "I think it saved my life!"

Exercise 8 p. 72

1 *John:* Hey, Liam. How're you? How's your holiday in New Zealand going?
Liam: Oh, it's going great, John. There are so many exciting things to do here. I've just been canoeing, in fact. What about you?
John: My trip's going well. I love the hot weather here in Spain.
Liam: Did you go snorkelling, like you said?
John: Not yet, I'm going to go tomorrow .... I hope! I've been here in Barcelona for three days now. I've taken some fantastic photos and I also went sightseeing yesterday. It was fantastic!
Liam: Wow! That sounds amazing!
John: It was! Well, have a great time. See you when we get back.
Liam: Bye John!

2 *Sue:* Hi, James. It's Sue. How's Mexico?
James: Oh, hello, Sue! Well, it's just amazing! We're staying in Cancun at the moment and yesterday I swam with dolphins! What an experience! How's your trip to Moscow going?
Sue: Moscow's fantastic. Since last week, we've been sightseeing, I've visited a market and I've even been ice skating on a river. When did you arrive in Mexico?
James: Well, it's Wednesday now and we've been here for two days. We're going to stay for a week. I'm so excited!
Sue: Lucky you! Don't forget to take lots of photos!
James: I won't! Bye!
Sue: Bye!

3 *Linda:* Hello, Katy. It's Linda.
Katy: Hi, Linda. How are you?
Linda: Great! I've just come back from my holiday in Italy.
Katy: Really?
Linda: Yeah, it was amazing. Why don't you come round tonight? Then I can show you my photos.
Katy: OK! I'd love that! See you later!

Exercise 9 p. 72

Queenstown, New Zealand

Have you ever wanted to go on a helicopter tour over mountains and lakes? Then Queenstown, New Zealand with its amazing natural sights is the place to go! Nature lovers can go trekking in the national parks. In winter, you can also go skiing and snowboarding at the many resorts around Queenstown. From $900 per person for 5 nights.
Book online now or call 00220 5789 64321!

Grammar Book Key

Unit 1

1 2 they   5 it   8 they   11 they
    3 she   6 it   9 they   12 they
    4 he   7 he   10 they

2 1 a   3 a   5 an   7 a   9 an   11 a
    2 an   4 an   6 a   8 an 10 a   12 a

3 2 is – 's   7 is – 's
    3 is – isn't   8 are – 're
    4 is– 's   9 am – 'm not
    5 are – aren't   10 is – 's
    6 are – aren't

4 2 isn't   5 's   8 aren't
    3 aren't   6 'm   9 's
    4 'm not   7 's   10 'm not

5 1 B: isn't, 's/is   7 A: Is
    2 A: Are   B: isn't, 's/is
       B: 'm, 'm   8 A: are
    3 A: 's/is   B: 're/are
       B: is   9 A: Is
    4 A: Are   B: isn't, 's/is
       B: aren't, 're/are   10 A: 's/is
    5 A: Is   B: 's/is
       B: is
    6 A: Are
       B: 'm, 'm

6 1 is   4 Are   7 Are   10 're/are
    2 's/is   5 'm/am   8 am   11 are
    3 is   6 'm/am   9 's/is 12 'm/am

7 2 Are you from Canada? No, I'm not. I'm from Australia.
    3 Is he a vet? No, he isn't. He's a pilot.
    4 Is she 17? No, she isn't. She's 15.
    5 Is Bob a waiter? No, he isn't. He's an actor.
    6 Are they from Italy? No, they aren't. They're from Japan.

8 2 Munich is in Germany.
    3 I am not Dutch.
    4 What is your favourite subject?
    5 We are twenty-two years old.
    6 What are the colours of Denmark's flag?
    7 Where are you from?
    8 Are they from New Zealand?
    9 We are not from Spain.
    10 He is good at drawing.

9 a) 1 can, can't   3 can, can't   5 can, can't
      2 can't, can   4 can't, can

b) (Suggested Answer)
    A: Can Jack and Karen speak French?
    B: No, they can't.
    A: Can Jack and Chris drive?
    B: Yes, they can. etc

10 2 A: What can she do?
      B: She can paint.
    3 A: What can he do?
      B: He can play the guitar.
    4 A: What can it do?
      B: It can fly.
    5 A: What can he do?
      B: He can fly a plane.
    6 A: What can they do?
      B: They can play basketball.

11 a) (Suggested Answers)
    1 Yes, I can.   5 Yes, I can.
    2 Yes, I can.   6 No, I can't.
    3 No, I can't.   7 Yes, I can.
    4 No, I can't.   8 No, I can't.

b) (Suggested Answer)
    She can speak English, ride a bicycle and dance, but she can't drive, paint or roller-skate.

Unit 2

1 2 have   7 has
    3 has   8 haven't, have
    4 Have, haven't   9 has
    5 Has, hasn't   10 have
    6 has

2 1 has, hasn't   5 hasn't, has
    2 hasn't, has   6 has, hasn't
    3 has, hasn't   7 have, haven't
    4 haven't, have

3 2 Has he got a basketball? Yes, he has.
    3 Has she got short hair? No, she hasn't. She's/has got long hair.
    4 Have they got books? Yes, they have.
    5 Has he got a guitar? No, he hasn't. He's/has got a piano.
    6 Has he got a beard? Yes, he has.
    7 Has he got a hat? Yes, he has.
    8 Has she got a magazine? No, she hasn't. She's/has got a newspaper.
    9 Has she got a computer? Yes, she has.

Grammar Book Key

4
2 hers, Claire's
3 his, his
4 theirs, Joanne's
5 his, Jessica's
6 his, his
7 hers, Bill and Laura's

8 theirs, their
9 yours, Paul's
10 hers, her
11 mine, Mary's
12 hers, her

5
1 His	5 my	9 her	13 your
2 our	6 his	10 your	14 My
3 her	7 Its	11 our	15 Their
4 Their	8 their	12 Its/His	

6
2 That's my son. His name is Tom.
3 That's my wife. Her name is Carol.
4 That's my brother. His name is Jim.
5 That's my dog. Its/His name is Spike.

7
1 yours, mine
2 Alex and Rachel's
3 Whose, theirs
4 Paul's, yours
5 Who's, my
6 yours, ours

7 Whose, theirs
8 Who's, Sally's
9 ours, Mark's and Amanda's
10 your, my

8
1 carpets	4 shops	7 benches
2 bedrooms	5 buses	8 plants
3 brushes	6 glasses	

9
1 cherries	5 radios	9 photos
2 cliffs	6 bananas	10 cities
3 butterflies	7 toys	
4 tomatoes	8 loaves	

10
1 They are buses.
2 Are they lamps?
3 They are watches.
4 Where are the torches?
5 Are they oxen?

11
2 They are police officers.
3 They are cats.
4 We are singers.
5 They are girls.
6 They are armchairs.
7 We are men.
8 They are pilots.
9 You are farmers.
10 They are mice.
11 We are surgeons.
12 They are foxes.
13 They are fish.
14 You are actresses.
15 They are astronauts.

Unit 3

1
3 That is , those are
4 That is, these are
5 This is , those are

2
2 This is a table and that is a lamp.
3 That is a bed and this is a fireplace.

4 This is a bookcase and those are towels.
5 That is a cushion and these are armchairs.

3
1 is , on	4 is, under	7 is, next to
2 is, in	5 are, on	8 are, on
3 is, opposite	6 is, in front of	

4
2 Where are my books? They're on the table.
3 Where are the girls? They're in the kitchen.
4 Where are my clothes? They're in the wardrobe.
5 Where are the posters? They're on the wall.
6 Where's Jeff? He's in the/his bedroom.
7 Where's the carpet? It's on the floor.
8 Where are the flowers? They're in the vase.
9 Where's Sara? She's in the bathroom.
10 Where are the pillows? They're on the bed.

5
1 some	3 a	5 some	7 an	9 some
2 any	4 a	6 any	8 a	10 any

6
1 are, some	5 are, some	9 are, some
2 Are, any	6 isn't, a	10 isn't, an
3 are, some	7 Are, any	
4 aren't, any	8 aren't, any	

7
1 on	3 on	5 in
2 next to	4 in	6 in front of

8
1 between	5 any	9 This
2 any	6 aren't	10 any
3 opposite	7 Those	11 on
4 an	8 a	12 some

9
2 any → some / are → aren't
3 That → Those
4 some → any
5 in → on
6 some → an
7 is → are
8 some → any

Revision A – (Units 1-3)

1
2 hasn't → haven't
3 has → is
4 Can't → Can
5 Are → Is
6 have → has
7 is → are
8 hasn't → haven't/ neighbours → neighbour
9 a → an
10 Have → Has
11 is → are
12 have → has
13 Has → Have
14 are → is
15 Has → Is
16 can → can't
17 Has → Have
18 that → those

Grammar Book Key

2
2	an	7	a	12	a, a
3	a	8	a	13	a, an
4	a, a	9	a	14	an
5	an, an	10	an	15	a
6	an	11	an, an	16	a, a

3
2	she	4	They	6	you
3	he	5	it		

4
2	No, he isn't.	7	No, he hasn't.
3	No, he isn't.	8	Yes, he has.
4	Yes, he has.	9	Yes, he can.
5	No, he hasn't.	10	Yes, he can.
6	No, he isn't.		

5

-s:	students, chairs, beds, koalas, penguins, dolphins, tigers
-es:	actresses, buses, pouches, brushes, addresses, benches
irregular:	teeth, mice, sheep, children, men, deer, feet, fish, women, geese

6
2	They are smartphones.	9	They are mice.
3	We are teachers.	10	You are astronauts.
4	You are surgeons.	11	We are women.
5	They are boys.	12	They are singers.
6	They are torches.	13	They are knives.
7	You are children.	14	We are ladies.
8	They are oxen.	15	They are sheep.

7
3 There are (some) pictures on the walls, but there aren't any posters.
4 Is there a post office in your area?
5 There is/There's a fireplace in the living room, but there isn't a bed.
6 Are there any books in your bag?
7 There are four boys in my family, but there aren't any girls.
8 Is there a mirror in your room?
9 There is/There's a dishwasher in the kitchen, but there isn't an armchair.
10 Are there any flats for rent?

8
1	Daniel's	6	mother's
2	John and Lisa's	7	sister's
3	Tommy's	8	parents'
4	girls'	9	Robyn and Tim's
5	Steven's	10	Sean's

Unit 4

1
1	is	5	listens	9	helps
2	lives	6	watches	10	walks
3	plays	7	reads	11	gives
4	has	8	uses	12	hates

2

-s:	cooks, starts, runs, writes, enjoys
-es:	watches, finishes, washes, does, catches
-ies:	cries, tries

3
2 Ann has a shower after breakfast.
3 Mary and Laura have lunch at 12 o'clock.
4 Kate surfs the Net at the weekend.
5 Dad goes shopping in the afternoon.
6 Jenny goes to the gym in the evening.
7 Sam cooks dinner with his dad.
8 Bob watches TV after dinner.

4
2 They don't watch TV in the evenings.
Do they watch TV in the evenings?
3 Jane doesn't go to school every day.
Does Jane go to school every day?
4 You don't play games on your computer.
Do you play games on your computer?
5 Their father isn't a firefighter.
Is their father a firefighter?

5
2	A: Does	7	A: Do
	B: doesn't		B: don't
3	A: does	8	A: does
4	A: Do	9	A: Does
	B: do		B: doesn't
5	B: doesn't		
6	A: Does		
	B: does		

6
1	is	6	wants
2	has	7	likes
3	lives	8	goes
4	doesn't have	9	plays
5	loves	10	watches

7
2 Terry hates listening to classical music.
3 We love going to the cinema.
4 Adam and Kelly don't like exercising.
5 She likes going on picnics.
6 They hate cleaning the house.
7 I love travelling.
8 George likes playing computer games.
9 I hate doing the washing-up.

Grammar Book Key

10 Rebecca doesn't like fishing.
11 He likes walking in the park.
12 David and Anna hate waking up early.

8 2 Bob often washes the car.
3 Jane is sometimes late for school.
4 I rarely have breakfast in the morning.
5 Do you usually chat on the phone?
6 She never goes to bed early.

9 **(Suggested Answers)**

I never clean my room on Mondays.
I sometimes play football on Mondays.
I rarely go for a walk on Mondays.
I always go to school on Mondays.
I often watch TV on Mondays.
I usually play computer games on Mondays.
I rarely go out with friends on Mondays.

10 1 at   3 on   5 at   7 in   9 at
2 in   4 on   6 in   8 in   10 in

11 1 at, in   5 in   9 in
2 on   6 at   10 on
3 at   7 on, in
4 on   8 in

12 1 at   3 on   5 at   7 In   9 On
2 in   4 at   6 at   8 at   10 on

Unit 5

1 1 mustn't   5 mustn't   9 mustn't
2 must   6 must   10 must
3 must   7 must
4 mustn't   8 must

2 1 must   4 mustn't/can't
2 mustn't/can't   5 must
3 mustn't/can't   6 mustn't/can't

3 2 mustn't stay up late/must do your homework
3 must tidy it
4 must go to the supermarket
5 mustn't play loud music
6 must do my homework/mustn't stay up late

4 1 must   6 can
2 mustn't   7 mustn't/can't
3 Can   8 Can
4 can't   9 must
5 Can

5 1 Could   3 Could   5 can
2 can   4 can't   6 Could

6 2 mustn't/can't   5 mustn't/can't
3 mustn't/can't   6 must
4 mustn't/can't

7 1 What   8 How much
2 Where   9 What
3 When   10 Why
4 How often   11 How
5 Who   12 How long
6 Why   13 Who
7 How many   14 What

8 1 Where – d   4 How many – b
2 What – e   5 How long – c
3 How much – a

Unit 6

1 1 shining   6 listening
2 throwing   7 going
3 making   8 reading
4 swimming   9 watching
5 playing   10 wearing

2 2 Dad and the boys are riding their bikes now.
3 Wendy is swimming at the pool now.
4 Bob is walking the dog at the moment.
5 Helen is studying hard these days.
6 We are having a great time at the party.

3 2 They aren't wearing heavy jackets. Are they wearing heavy jackets?
3 You aren't making a sandcastle. Are you making a sandcastle?
4 She isn't decorating the Christmas tree. Is she decorating the Christmas tree?
5 It isn't raining today. Is it raining today?
6 I'm not going on a picnic. Am I going on a picnic?
7 He isn't sunbathing. Is he sunbathing?
8 They aren't listening to music. Are they listening to music?
9 We aren't swimming. Are we swimming?

4 2 they are   7 I'm not/we aren't
3 she isn't   8 he is
4 I am/we are   9 they/you aren't
5 we/you aren't   10 we are
6 it is

5
1   B: is chatting
2   A: Is Nina reading
    B: isn't reading, is watching
3   A: Is it snowing
    B: are building
4   A: Is Sally going
    B: is going, are waiting

6
1   is relaxing   5   am wearing
2   is reading   6   am sunbathing
3   isn't swimming   7   is having
4   is having   8   are enjoying

7
1   wakes up   9   are decorating
2   am playing   10   watches
3   listens   11   are sleeping
4   shines   12   drives
5   are making   13   is working
6   are swimming   14   wears
7   goes   15   is snowing
8   is having

8
1   am writing   6   are
2   am   7   are trying
3   are visiting   8   is shopping
4   snows   9   am planning
5   is shining   10   are having

9
2   a   ✓   5   a   ✓   8   a   ✓
3   a   ✓   6   b   ✓   9   b   ✓
4   b   ✓   7   a   ✓   10   a   ✓

10
2   am watching   5   go
3   Do you want   6   is raining
4   go

11 a)
2   are visiting   7   am sitting
3   are staying   8   are eating
4   is   9   wants
5   is it   10   loves
6   Is it raining   11   don't like

b)
2   Who is Moira visiting?
    She is visiting her friend, Crystal.
3   Where are they staying?
    They are staying at a B&B.
4   What is the weather like?
    The weather is amazing.
5   Where is Rachel?
    She is in New York.
6   What are Moira and Crystal doing right now?
    They are sitting in a café.
7   What are they eating?
    They are eating ice cream.

8   What does Moira's sister want to do in the afternoon?
    She wants to go see a football match.

Revision B – (Units 1-6)

1
1   Does, does   6   Are, are
2   Are, am   7   Are, aren't
3   Do, don't, do   8   is, isn't, doesn't
4   Do, don't   9   Are, aren't
5   Does, doesn't, doesn't   10   am, am, am not

2
2   Does Karl love going dancing at weekends, too?
3   Do Joe and Ian play computer games in their free time, too?
4   Does Pam hate camping, too?
5   Do your parents wake up early on Sundays, too?

3 a)
1   is   9   finishes
2   gets up   10   has
3   has   11   goes
4   has   12   reads
5   goes   13   watches
6   finishes   14   enjoys
7   goes   15   am
8   starts

b)
1   Jack Warren gets up late in the morning. (at about midday)
2   Jack has lunch at about 1 pm.
3   Rehearsal finishes at about 4 pm.
4   The show starts at 8 pm and finishes at about 10 pm.
5   Jack goes to bed at about 1 am.
6   Jack reads books and watches TV in his free time.
7   Jack is very satisfied with his career.

4 a)
1   works   8   takes
2   goes   9   finishes
3   opens   10   meets
4   sets   11   gets
5   arrive   12   listens
6   tidy   13   is
7   come   14   get

b)
3   SA: Do the first customers come in at 7:30?
    SB: Yes, they do.
4   SA: Do you take a break at 11 o'clock?
    SB: No, I don't. I take a break at 10 o'clock.
5   SA: Do you finish work at 2 o'clock?
    SB: Yes, I do.

Grammar Book Key

6   SA: Do you get home at 4 o'clock?
      SB: No, I don't. I (usually) get home at about 3 o'clock.
7   SA: Do you listen to music in your free time?
      SB: Yes, I do.

5   2   Does Susan like the theatre?
     3   Do your parents like reading?
     4   Does he like rock music?
     5   Do you like exercising?

6   2   Does she, does   4   Do they, don't
     3   are, They are   5   Does, doesn't

7   1   are you going   6   visit
     2   'm/am going   7   live
     3   'm/am   8   do you spend
     4   go   9   swim
     5   do you do   10   play

Unit 7

1   1   a, (C)   9   an, (C)
     2   some, (U)   10   an, (C)
     3   a, (C)   11   some, (C)
     4   some, (C)   12   an, (C)
     5   some, (U)   13   a, (C)
     6   some, (C)   14   a, (C)
     7   some, (U)   15   some, (U)
     8   some, (C)

2   2   U   4   C   6   U   8   U   10   U   12   U
     3   C   5   U   7   C   9   C   11   C

3   1   A: some   4   A: any
          B: any   B: a
     2   A: a   5   A: an
          B: some   B: any
     3   A: some   6   A: some
          B: a   B: an

4   **a)**   1   kilo   5   bottle
          2   slice   6   glass
          3   piece   7   carton
          4   cup   8   packet

     b)   1   piece/kilo   5   glass/bottle
          2   slice   6   cup
          3   glass/bottle   7   kilo
          4   packet   8   glass/carton

5   1   much   3   many   5   a little
     2   much   4   a lot of   6   much

6   1   How many   4   How many
     2   How much   5   How much
     3   How much

7   1   A: How many   6   A: How much
          B: a few   B: a little
     2   A: some   7   A: some
          B: any   B: some
     3   A: How much   8   A: any
          B: a little   B: some
     4   A: How many   9   A: How much
          B: a few/some, any   B: a little
     5   A: How many   10   A: any
          B: any   B: a few/some, any

8   2   many → much   10   many → much
     3   a → some   11   some → any
     4   much → many   12   any → some
     5   a → any   13   little → some
     6   many → much   14   some → any
     7   much → many   15   any → some
     8   hams → ham   16   cheeses → cheese
     9   any → some

9   2   a   3   e   4   b   5   f   6   c

10   1   Don't beat the eggs.
      2   Mix the vegetables in a bowl.
      3   Don't cut the carrots into small pieces.
      4   Put the mixture in a frying pan.
      5   Give me some cake please.

Unit 8

1   1   expensive   9   much/many
     2   the most expensive   10   the most
     3   bad   11   tiny
     4   worse   12   tinier
     5   older   13   high
     6   the oldest   14   the highest
     7   smaller   15   hotter
     8   the smallest   16   the hottest

2   1   than   4   of   7   in
     2   the, in   5   in   8   as, as
     3   as, as   6   than

3   2   The tickets for the museum are cheaper than the tickets for the aquarium.
     3   Milan is more expensive than Rome.
     4   York is colder than Bath.
     5   London is busier than Edinburgh.
     6   The Eiffel Tower is taller than the Statue of Liberty.

4
1. the most beautiful
2. the largest
3. the most impressive
4. the biggest
5. the most crowded
6. the driest

5
1. drier
2. more interesting
3. highest
4. longest
5. largest
6. better
7. the most beautiful

6
1. more expensive
2. more crowded
3. high
4. the oldest
5. the largest
6. cheaper
7. the tallest
8. more polluted
9. the best
10. smaller

7
2. smaller than
3. as friendly as
4. the heaviest
5. the most dangerous
6. as fast as

8
2. noisy
3. more, than
4. the fastest, of
5. expensive
6. the best
7. the driest, in
8. bigger than
9. famous
10. the tallest, of
11. the largest, in
12. prettier than
13. more dangerous than
14. safer, than
15. more crowded than
16. tall
17. the kindest

9 **(Suggested Answers)**
My father is the oldest in our family.
My mother is more patient than my father.
My sister is the shortest in our family.
My brother is the funniest person in our family.
My sister is kinder than my brother.

10
1. too cold
2. warm enough
3. tall enough
4. too busy
5. too heavy

11
1. B   3. A   5. A   7. A
2. C   4. B   6. C   8. B

12
1. the busiest
2. much
3. bigger
4. cheaper
5. tastier
6. high
7. the most beautiful

Unit 9

1
1. Were
2. wasn't
3. was
4. were
5. was
6. was
7. was
8. were
9. was
10. Were
11. wasn't
12. was

2
1. weren't
2. Was, wasn't
3. were, were
4. weren't
5. wasn't
6. were, was
7. were
8. was, was
9. Was
10. Were

3
1. Were   3. is   5. are   7. am   9. are
2. was   4. am   6. were   8. was   10. is

4
2. Was the performance good? No, it wasn't.
3. Were you at the theatre with your friend?/Were you with your friend at the theatre? Yes, I was.
4. Were there many people at the theatre? No, there weren't.
5. Was the performance very long? Yes, it was.

5
1. didn't   3. Did   5. had   7. have
2. had   4. have   6. Did   8. didn't

6
2. Mario had a big breakfast yesterday morning.
3. Mary didn't have football practice yesterday.
4. They had a barbecue last Saturday evening.

7 a)
2. Did you have a car when you were four years old? No, I didn't.
3. Did you have a watch when you were four years old? No, I didn't.
4. Did you have a ball when you were four years old? Yes, I did.
5. Did you have a doll when you were four years old? No, I didn't.
6. Did you have a bike when you were four years old? Yes, I did.
7. Did you have a smartphone when you were four years old? No, I didn't.
8. Did you have a guitar when you were four years old? No, I didn't.
9. Did you have an umbrella when you were four years old? Yes, I did.

b) **(Suggested Answer)**
I had a ball, a doll, a bike and an umbrella, but I didn't have a dog, a car, a watch, a smartphone or a guitar.

8 a)
3. Laura couldn't use a computer when she was five years old, but she can use a computer now.
4. Laura couldn't ride a horse when she was five years old, but she can ride a horse now.
5. Laura couldn't paint when she was five years old, but she can paint now.
6. Laura couldn't play the piano when she was five years old and she still can't play the piano.

Grammar Book Key

b) (Suggested Answers)

I couldn't ride a bike when I was five years old, but I can ride a bike now.

I couldn't cook when I was five years old, but I can cook now.

I couldn't use a computer when I was five years old, but I can use a computer now.

9
1	Can	8	weren't	15	Can, can't
2	have	9	have, had	16	were
3	Was, wasn't	10	Could	17	wasn't
4	were	11	weren't	18	didn't have
5	had, couldn't	12	Was	19	was
6	Were	13	wasn't	20	weren't
7	couldn't	14	had		

Revision C – (Units 1-9)

1
1. Are, 'm/am not, 'm/am
2. Could, can
3. Was, wasn't, is
4. were, aren't, weren't
5. had, didn't have

2
1. couldn't, could, have got, can
2. was, had, is, hasn't got
3. Can, can't, Could, were, couldn't
4. have got, haven't got, had
5. has got, didn't have, had, aren't
6. Are, aren't, haven't got
7. Were, wasn't, was

3
2	is → was	7	are → was
3	had → have	8	have → had
4	was → is	9	are → were
5	could → can	10	isn't → wasn't
6	had → have		

4
1	more beautiful	6	cleverer/more clever
2	noisier	7	bigger
3	older, the oldest	8	taller, the tallest
4	the largest	9	the most luxurious
5	more expensive	10	quieter

5 (Suggested Answers)

- Flats are expensive.
  Houses are more expensive than flats.
  Castles are the most expensive of all.

- Flats are spacious.
  Houses are more spacious than flats.
  Castles are the most spacious of all.

- Castles are comfortable.
  Houses are more comfortable than castles.
  Flats are the most comfortable of all.

6
2	have → are having	7	some → any
3	speaks → speak	8	many → much
4	any → some	9	any → some
5	live → lives	10	mine → my
6	are → is		

7
2. Where is Karen?
3. How old is he?
4. Is he a doctor?
5. Where is the Eiffel Tower?
6. Are you married?

8
1	B	5	B	9	B	13	B
2	B	6	A	10	B	14	C
3	C	7	B	11	B	15	C
4	B	8	C	12	B	16	A

Unit 10

1
1	did	7	listened	13	discovered
2	loved	8	cared	14	completed
3	called	9	went	15	started
4	admired	10	invited	16	became
5	visited	11	appeared		
6	made	12	bought		

2
-ed	worked, watched, looked, played, returned
-d	died, continued, smiled, received, divorced
-ied	married, buried, studied, tidied
irregular	wrote, said, got, was/were, had, came

3
1	was	5	took	9	made
2	went	6	enjoyed	10	divorced
3	worked	7	married	11	died
4	went	8	wrote	12	buried

Irregular verbs: be, go, take, write, make

4
1	was	4	lectured	7	married
2	began	5	opened	8	died
3	moved	6	invented		

5
2	did she go, **g**	6	did Brian work, **e**
3	did he leave, **b**	7	did Margaret buy, **d**
4	did you borrow, **h**	8	did you see, **f**
5	did you have, **c**		

6
2. I went on a picnic with Steve.
3. He studied Maths (at university).
4. She called Ben last Monday.
5. They cooked soup (for dinner).

Grammar Book Key

6   I invited my best friend (to my house).

7 2   What did she wear to the meeting?
3   Where did he go last night?
4   When did you tidy your room?
5   Who did you visit last week?
6   When did you wash the car?
7   Where did she go for a walk?
8   What did Andrew buy at the weekend?
9   When did you leave for work?
10 What did he do at the weekend?

8 2   A: When did you buy those trousers?
   B: I bought them on Tuesday.
3   A: Where did she go on holiday?
   B: She went to Portugal.
4   A: Who did they invite for dinner?
   B: They invited Jason and Marie.
5   A: What did he study at university?
   B: He studied Physics.

9 1   Did you go   8   did you buy
2   made   9   didn't find
3   Did Bill play   10 painted
4   cut   11 was
5   composed   12 Did you enjoy
6   went   13 did
7   studied

10 1   was   5   taught   9   travelled
2   believed   6   continued   10 left
3   graduated 7   opened   11 went
4   began   8   wrote   12 died

2   She didn't graduate from Oxford University. She graduated from the University of Rome.
3   She didn't continue her studies in Maths and History. She continued her studies in Philosophy, Psychology and Education.
4   She didn't open her first school in 1900. She opened her first school in 1907.
5   She didn't leave Canada in 1934. She left Italy in 1934.
6   She didn't go to England. She went to the Netherlands.
7   She didn't die in America in 1952. She died in the Netherlands in 1952.

11 2   "Did Sue play tennis?" "No, she didn't."
3   "Did Sue listen to music?" "No, she didn't."
4   "Did Sue hang out with her friends?" "Yes, she did."
5   "Did Sue chat online?" "No, she didn't."
6   "Did she go to bed late? "Yes, she did."

12 1   B: didn't, stayed, uploaded
2   A: Did Steve enjoy
   B: did, saw
3   A: Did Ann spend
   B: didn't, went
4   A: Did you take
   B: did, won
5   A: Did you have
   B: did, ordered, played
6   A: Did John fly
   B: didn't, travelled

13 2   went   7   left   12 bought
3   arrived   8   did   13 took
4   stayed   9   went   14 was
5   wanted   10 loved
6   spent   11 tried

14 1   A: Does your brother like
   B: likes
2   A: are you doing
   B: are watching
3   A: Did you go
   B: was, went
4   A: did Bob work
   B: worked
5   A: is she doing
   B: is playing, plays

15 1   because   4   when   7   when
2   and   5   so   8   but
3   but   6   because

16 2   a   3   f   4   e   5   g   6   c   7   b

17 1   so   5   and   9   but
2   when   6   so   10 because
3   and   7   and
4   but   8   when

18 1   because   3   so   5   when
2   then   4   and   6   but

19 1   interesting   3   strange   5   happy
2   careful   4   gorgeous

20 1   easily   3   happily   5   closely
2   proudly   4   well   6   sleepily

21 1   tightly   5   quickly   9   carefully
2   loudly   6   nervously   10 hard
3   suddenly   7   immediately
4   desperately   8   fast

Grammar Book Key

22
1 quickly   4 desperately   7 loudly
2 Suddenly   5 lucky   8 careless
3 well   6 proud

23
1 up   4 towards   7 down
2 through   5 into   8 under
3 along   6 over

Unit 11

1
1 should   5 shouldn't   9 should
2 should   6 shouldn't   10 shouldn't
3 shouldn't   7 should
4 should   8 shouldn't

2
2 You shouldn't leave your cat outside for a long time.
3 You should take your cat to the vet every six months.
4 You shouldn't forget to fill the water bowl.
5 You should empty the litter tray once a week.

3
1 must   5 Can   9 should
2 mustn't   6 should   10 can't
3 shouldn't   7 shouldn't
4 can't   8 mustn't

4
1 I think it's a good idea   3 you should
2 you shouldn't   4 Why don't you

5
They're visiting Heather's parents on Tuesday.
They're taking the car to a mechanic on Wednesday.
They're buying a computer on Thursday.
They're cleaning the house on Friday.
They're having a dinner party on Saturday.
They're going on a picnic on Sunday.

6
1 'll/will   6 won't/will not
2 won't/will not   7 'll/will
3 'll/will   8 'll/will
4 'll/will   9 won't/will not
5 'll/will   10 'll/will

7
1 will   7 will   13 am going to
2 am going to   8 will   14 will
3 am going to   9 am going to   15 am going to
4 will   10 will   16 are going to
5 am going to   11 is going to
6 will   12 is going to

8
2 will have   7 is going to stay
3 is going to rain   8 are going to spend
4 will phone   9 will clean
5 am going to paint   10 will cook
6 will answer

9
2 is going to fix it
3 am going to make a cake
4 is going to lose weight
5 is going to be late for school

10
2 will let   7 is/'s meeting
3 is/'s going to fall   8 am/'m flying
4 are having   9 will call
5 am/'m visiting   10 am/'m taking
6 will/'ll put on

11
2 f   3 a   4 e   5 c   6 b

2 Amanda likes music, so she is going to take piano lessons.
3 Chris wants to go on holiday, so he is going to save money.
4 Lisa needs to relax, so she is going to stay in tonight.
5 Dave wants to have a party, so he is going to send invitations to his friends.
6 Jill likes taking photos, so she is going to buy a camera.

12
1 There   3 There   5 There   7 It
2 It   4 It   6 There   8 There

Unit 12

1
2 He has been ill for three days.
3 They haven't visited their grandparents since last month.
4 I have been a policeman for twenty years.
5 Karen hasn't been home since October.
6 He hasn't travelled by boat since last summer.
7 I haven't visited Paris for six years.
8 Jack has worked in Canada for ten years.
9 She hasn't been abroad for two years.
10 Jeff hasn't called since Monday.

2 (Suggested Answers)
- … has swum with dolphins, but she hasn't eaten Mexican food. She hasn't also gone canoeing, but she has ridden a camel.
- … have swum with dolphins, but they haven't eaten Mexican food. They have also gone canoeing, but they haven't ridden a camel.

3
3 A: Has Bill done the shopping yet?
   B: No, he hasn't done the shopping yet.
4 A: Has Laura finished her homework yet?
   B: Yes, she has already finished her homework.
5 A: Have they bought their tickets yet?
   B: Yes, they have already bought their tickets.

Grammar Book Key

6   A: Has Bill done the ironing yet?
     B: No, he hasn't done the ironing yet.

7   A: Has Mike visited the Louvre yet?
     B: Yes, he has already visited the Louvre.

8   A: Have you tidied your room yet?
     B: No, I haven't tidied my room yet.

4
1   A: Have   5   A: Has
    B: have   B: hasn't

2   A: Have   6   A: Have
    B: have   B: haven't

3   A: Have   7   A: Has
    B: haven't   B: hasn't

4   A: Has   8   A: Have
    B: has   B: have

5
2   has already started
3   has just passed, hasn't bought
4   have already sent
5   hasn't found
6   has just left

6
2   since   6   for   10   since
3   since   7   for   11   since
4   for   8   since   12   for
5   since   9   for

7
1   already   6   yet   11   for
2   for   7   since   12   yet
3   just   8   already   13   since
4   never   9   never   14   just
5   ever   10   ever   15   never

8
2   never   7   just   12   How long
3   just   8   never   13   yet
4   since   9   ever   14   for
5   yet   10   since   15   ever
6   How long   11   for

9
1   B: went
    A: Did you have
    B: had

2   A: Did you go
    B: saw
    A: did you see

3   A: Have you done
    B: did
    A: Have you washed
    B: have already washed

4   A: Have you ever eaten
    B: ate
    A: Did you like
    B: tasted

5   A: Have you ever worked
    B: worked
    A: Did you enjoy
    B: enjoyed

6   A: Have they been
    B: were
    A: did they go

10
1   –, –   11   –, –   21   The, the
2   a   12   the   22   –
3   an   13   a, an   23   a
4   The, –   14   –, an   24   the
5   a, the   15   –   25   the
6   –, a   16   a   26   –, –
7   an, the   17   the, –   27   the
8   The, –   18   a   28   The
9   an, –   19   a   29   the
10   a   20   –, the   30   –

Revision D – (Units 1-12)

1
1   C   3   B   5   A   7   A   9   A
2   A   4   B   6   C   8   C   10   B

2
2   comes   8   Has Jim paid
3   'm/am not going to take   9   's/is washing
4   did not/didn't play   10   've/have just turned
5   Do you want   11   has never travelled
6   's/is sleeping   12   don't we go
7   does

3
2   d   4   a   6   b   8   c   10   g
3   h   5   i   7   j   9   e

4
1   is   9   visited
2   'm/am having   10   showed
3   'm/am staying   11   haven't done
4   've/have been   12   haven't done
5   've/have already done   13   haven't been
6   saw   14   is
7   was   15   'll/will visit
8   've/have also visited   16   'm/am coming

5
1   Were   11   are
2   wasn't   12   is it
3   went   13   is
4   happened   14   was
5   fell   15   went
6   broke   16   did you go
7   Are you going   17   did you go
8   am   18   went
9   are you going   19   Did you have
10   will rain   20   was

Progress Tests Key

6
2 at → on
3 oldest → older
4 good → well
5 painted → paint
6 played → play
7 sugars → sugar
8 When → Where

7
1 'll/will open
2 came, found
3 are you working
4 Did you enjoy
5 lives

8
2 a	4 b	6 a	8 b	10 a
3 a	5 b	7 a	9 a	

PROGRESS TEST A – (Units 1-3)

1 B	6 B	11 B	16 C
2 C	7 B	12 C	17 A
3 A	8 C	13 A	18 B
4 B	9 A	14 C	19 A
5 C	10 A	15 B	20 C

PROGRESS TEST B – (Units 4-6)

1 A	6 C	11 A	16 C
2 B	7 B	12 C	17 A
3 C	8 C	13 B	18 B
4 B	9 B	14 A	19 A
5 B	10 B	15 C	20 C

PROGRESS TEST C – (Units 1-6)

1 C	6 C	11 C	16 A
2 B	7 A	12 C	17 C
3 A	8 A	13 B	18 A
4 B	9 B	14 C	19 A
5 C	10 B	15 A	20 C

PROGRESS TEST D – (Units 7-9)

1 A	6 A	11 C	16 A
2 C	7 A	12 B	17 B
3 B	8 B	13 B	18 B
4 C	9 A	14 B	19 A
5 B	10 C	15 B	20 B

PROGRESS TEST E – (Units 10-12)

1 C	6 C	11 B	16 A
2 C	7 B	12 A	17 B
3 A	8 B	13 A	18 B
4 B	9 B	14 B	19 C
5 A	10 C	15 A	20 B

PROGRESS TEST F – (Units 1-12)

1 C	6 B	11 C	16 B
2 B	7 A	12 C	17 B
3 C	8 A	13 C	18 C
4 A	9 B	14 C	19 C
5 B	10 A	15 A	20 A